To Jane & James

Happy and safe journeys

Allan Pendleton

NEVER SAY "IF ONLY"

JOURNEYS THROUGH LIFE

ALLAN PENDLETON

authorHOUSE®

AuthorHouse™ UK
1663 Liberty Drive
Bloomington, IN 47403 USA
www.authorhouse.co.uk
Phone: 0800.197.4150

© *2018 Allan Pendleton. All rights reserved.*

No part of this book may be reproduced, stored in a retrieval system, or transmitted by any means without the written permission of the author.

Published by AuthorHouse 08/28/2018

ISBN: 978-1-5462-9688-1 (sc)
ISBN: 978-1-5462-9687-4 (e)

Print information available on the last page.

Any people depicted in stock imagery provided by Getty Images are models, and such images are being used for illustrative purposes only. Certain stock imagery © Getty Images.

This book is printed on acid-free paper.

Because of the dynamic nature of the Internet, any web addresses or links contained in this book may have changed since publication and may no longer be valid. The views expressed in this work are solely those of the author and do not necessarily reflect the views of the publisher, and the publisher hereby disclaims any responsibility for them.

CONTENTS

Foreword vii
Preface ix

Chapter 1   A Royal Wedding 1
Chapter 2   The Beginning 4
Chapter 3   The Republic of Ireland 6
Chapter 4   Los Picos de Europa, Northern Spain 8
Chapter 5   Germany 11
Chapter 6   North America 13
Chapter 7   West Row 33
Chapter 8   Malaysia 39
Chapter 9   Pyrenees 45
Chapter 10   New Zealand 48
Chapter 11   Netherlands 63
Chapter 12   Romania 66
Chapter 13   Morocco and Mexico 68
Chapter 14   Andalucía, Spain 72
Chapter 15   Thailand 79
Chapter 16   The Teacher 83
Chapter 17   Bolivia and Peru 87
Chapter 18   Costa Rica 100
Chapter 19   U.S.A; Arizona to Alaska 106
Chapter 20   India 121
Chapter 21   France and Spain 127
Chapter 22   Australia 132
Chapter 23   Patagonia 145
Chapter 24   Slovenia 163
Chapter 25   Southeast Asia 167
Chapter 26   Yucatan, Mexico 180
Chapter 27   USA.; New Orleans to Washington DC 186
Chapter 28   Himalaya: Nepal & Tibet 196
Chapter 29   The Sky Falls In 206

Chapter 30	Thailand and Laos	208
Chapter 31	Ana	213
Chapter 32	Life Is Not Fair	220
Chapter 33	The Western Isles and Northwest Highlands, Scotland	224
Chapter 34	Quebec, Canada	229
Chapter 35	California, USA	232
Chapter 36	Sri Lanka	241
Chapter 37	Canada & USA	252
Chapter 38	Land's End to John o' Groats	262
Chapter 39	Costa Rica & Panamá	267
Chapter 40	Musgrave Hospital, Taunton	274
Chapter 41	India	279
Chapter 42	France	282
Chapter 43	Thailand	288
Chapter 44	Cuba	290
Chapter 45	Norway	297
Chapter 46	A Pain in the Arse	302
Chapter 47	Mark	304
Chapter 48	USA	306
Chapter 49	Rajasthan, India	309

Afterword 313
Acknowledgements 319

FOREWORD

Allan and Margaret Pendleton are very well known in Burnham-on-Sea for their sporting achievements. Former manager of the sports centre Allan, has always been a leading pillar of the sporting community since he introduced events such as triathlons that have retained their annual and national appeal. Maggie, also PE trained, a retired primary school teacher has cycled primarily on a tandem with Allan around thirty countries, covering thousands of miles over terrain from the steamy, tropical rainforest to the frigid, high Himalaya. Allan and Maggie are known for having a resilient and happy marriage that has helped propel them on their tandem: often on steep and hostile terrain that most folk would not consider for a holiday. The genesis of this book was intended to be a priceless reference to Allan and Maggie's daughters and grandchildren. However, the response to this story from the local community warrants this autobiography to be read by a wider audience who are either armchair adventurers, or who would be inspired to see the real world as intrepid travellers.

Michael Turner

Front cover: Julian Alps, Slovenia; photograph John Ashwell

PREFACE

When we began to cycle abroad Maggie's elderly parents insisted that we kept them well informed. This was before the days of e-mails, internet 'blogs' and digital cameras. Rather than lengthy letters we decided to keep a dairy. At regular intervals we would tear out the carbon copy and post it home with any rolls of film that needed developing.

Many years later, and to relieve the boredom while temporarily 'grounded' with prostate cancer, I thought that I would try to combine the dairies into one readable account of our journeys. This would also provide our daughters and grandchildren with a summary of some of the things their old folks had got up to.

My father was a landing craft coxswain during World War Two while Maggie's dad was a fire-fighter in London during the Blitz. They seldom spoke of their experiences and it wasn't until after they had died that we realised how little we knew of their lives. Now we have so many questions to ask, questions that, regrettably, must remain unanswered. Hopefully our children will not experience the same frustration.

Probably the attempt to relieve my boredom will result in boring the reader, but perhaps someone may find a touch of inspiration, someone who later in life can look back and not say "If only."

CHAPTER 1

A Royal Wedding

"I'm not afraid of death; I just don't want to be there when it happens."
Woody Allen

Friday 29 April, 2011

"Allan! Allan! Come quick!" Wes's voice echoed frantically across the swimming pool. Wes Harford, my friend of thirty years, gestured wildly from the side of the pool, encouraging me to hurry. "What's up?" I shouted back, thinking that one of the kids had fallen out of the tree-house or something similar. "It's Maggie" he answered as I, clad only in swimming trunks, grabbed my gear and ran to his car. "She has collapsed. But don't worry," he added as an afterthought, "The ambulance is there!" It was the royal wedding day of Prince William and Kate Middleton. The second in line to the throne was marrying his university sweetheart. The ceremony was being aired on TV across the nation to the fawning masses. My wife, Maggie, had invited some friends to watch the wedding. It was not my scene so I went for a bike ride, leaving just before our guests began to arrive.

I returned sometime after twelve and found that Wes had arrived. The wedding was still in full-swing. I decided to run down to Burnham Pool for a swim while Maggie prepared refreshments.

Apparently, Maggie, after serving the food, was sitting on the couch when, without warning, she slumped unconscious onto the floor. It soon became apparent that she was not breathing and I was sure that a certain amount of panic had set in. Thankfully, our friends kept their cool and rang 999. Wes went outside to meet the ambulance, which was just as well, as there was a street party going on and the medics were having difficulty locating our house. Then he drove to Burnham Pool to fetch me.

Allan Pendleton

When I arrived home my wife was lying flat on her back with a paramedic administering chest compressions, another was operating a ventilator with a tube down her throat. She also had a tube containing adrenaline inserted into her while a third medic placed defibrillator jump-leads onto her bare chest. Maggie's heart was not beating and her skin was the same blue colour as the Na'vi tribe in the film Avatar.

"Stand back!" Maggie convulsed as an electric charge shot through her body. This was the sixth electric shock she had been given and thankfully, this one was successful.

A stretcher was fetched from the ambulance while we moved the furniture to create a clear passage to the front door. Maggie was taken into the ambulance while a medic continually used the ventilator all the way to Musgrove Park Hospital in Taunton. I sat alongside the driver and the ride could have been, in other circumstances, quite exciting with siren sounding and lights flashing we weaved in and out of traffic at top speed along the M5.

Maggie was rushed into the cardiac unit where a team was already assembled and waiting. They had been receiving ECG readouts direct from the ambulance's computer. I had an agonising wait while doctors stabilised her and ran a series of tests; none of which showed a reason for the heart failure, her arteries were shown to be in remarkably good condition. Maggie was put onto a life-support machine and taken to the intensive therapy unit. She was heavily sedated and hooked up to an array of cables, tubes, probes and ventilators.

Meanwhile, my daughter Joanne and her husband Richard rushed to our nearest hospital, at Weston-super-Mare. There they had a horrific wait for the non-arrival of Maggie's ambulance. Fearing the worst, they were somewhat relieved to find that their mother had been taken to Taunton Musgrove Hospital. They raced down the M5 and arrived just as Maggie was being transferred to ITU.

A bank of monitors flashed and beeped and Maggie was festooned with bottles and bags of life-saving liquids that ran through tubes into her hands, arms, neck and groin. A ventilator continually pumped oxygen into her lungs.

The consultant cardiologist, Dr D McKenzie, informed us that Maggie had experienced a sudden cardiac death (failed), and an ECG had shown long QT syndrome. Further tests revealed low potassium levels which could have triggered the arrhythmia. Dr. McKenzie suggested cooling. We were told that recent tests had shown that by lowering the body's core temperature any permanent damage to the organs, particularly the brain, might be minimised, "should she survive!" Ice packs and crushed ice were applied to her arm pits and groin, while cold fluid was put into her body. Initially Maggie's temperature rose before dropping to 30° Centigrade. Her heart rate fell to thirty beats per minute.

These had been the most traumatic few hours of my life. My love, my life and my world had fallen apart. I could not believe that this was happening. It was unreal, a nightmare!

We were told that there was nothing we could do except wait. Not able to face seeing Maggie shiver and suffer, we decided to go home, I was still in shorts and sandals: but what if I were needed? What if she were to die while I was not there? I felt that my head was exploding. I had a beer, painkillers and a sleeping pill and miraculously managed to sleep for a couple of hours.

Saturday 30 April

I woke at 3am. The bed was empty beside me and it took a couple of moments before the horror of yesterday hit me like a sledgehammer. I was numb. My younger daughter, Julie, was also awake and we returned to the hospital. We sat beside Maggie, held her hands and tried not to cry. Surely my life, our lives, had been changed forever.

CHAPTER 2

The Beginning

"In the beginning God created the Heaven and the Earth. Later, man, not wanting to be outdone, invented the bicycle."
Anon

In 1989, to mark his retirement and closure of his decorating business, my dad gave Maggie and me £800. This was unexpected and a pleasant surprise but what should we spend it on or should we save it? As chance would have it, I had just seen a tandem for sale in our local bicycle shop, for the same amount as our gift. A few years earlier we had hired a tandem while on holiday and had a great time. Our daughters Jo and Julie were growing up and family commitments were diminishing. This was surely a sign that could not be ignored.

Our first ride on the new Dawes Galaxy Twin was across the Somerset Levels. After a couple of pints of Wadworth 6X at the Burtle Inn, we cycled home on a balmy evening and as starlight replaced sunlight bats were called off the bench to substitute for the swallows under a glorious harvest moon: we were hooked. For us a tandem was ideal. While we both cycled, Maggie mainly used her bike around town while I went for faster, longer rides having just completed an Ironman Triathlon in the European Championships in Germany and raced for England in the over 40s category. On the tandem we could ride together and chat easily. Maggie, as 'stoker' on the back of the tandem quickly became an adept spotter: like a tail gunner in a WWII Lancaster gun turret. "Buzzard 10 o'clock high" she would call and we enjoyed sights we would have missed if we both had to continually keep our eyes on the road.

We pedalled regularly on Saturday mornings with a cycling group from Weston-Super-Mare. Usually we were well off the pace at the back with the guys patiently waiting for us at the top of a hill or a junction. On one rare occasion however, we found ourselves at the front of the pack. Heads down and bums up we were working hard to stay at the front when suddenly a snake, yes, honestly a snake, slithered across the road in front of us. I automatically hit the brakes to avoid squashing it and immediately felt a thud from behind. A crash, bam, splat was accompanied by an avalanche of profanities. The whole peloton had crashed.

"What the hell do you think you are doing Allan?"

"There was a snake in the road."

"A snake? Pull the other one Al."

Anyway, apart from a touch of gravel rash, no-one was injured and, more importantly, no bikes were damaged. We were about to set off when a feeble cry could be heard, "Wait for me." Andy, dripping wet and bedraggled with weed, crawled through the hedge. Apparently he had crashed through the hedge and into a ditch while still attached to his bike. We hadn't even noticed that he was missing.

CHAPTER 3

The Republic of Ireland

"Travel is fatal to prejudice, bigotry and narrow-mindedness."
Mark Twain, "The Innocents Abroad"

<u>July- August 1991. 620 miles</u>

Regular Saturday morning rides and a few Audax bicycle events encouraged us to pedal further afield: Devon, the Yorkshire Dales and then our first trip abroad to the Irish Republic.

The 620-mile tour of South-West Ireland taught us a few things; the main lesson being not to take too much equipment. I learnt that if you might not need it, then do not take it! Apart from first aid and repair kits, which you hope will be superfluous, everything taken ought to be necessary. Many broken spokes and much wasted energy taught us the folly of being overloaded.

In a bar, on our first night in Cork, I ordered a Guinness. The barman partly filled the glass then placed it on the bar in front of me. This was at a time when Anglo-Irish relationships were not that healthy.

He knows I'm English I thought, *and this is probably as full a glass as I'm likely to get.* While debating with myself whether to demand a full pint or meekly accept the short measure, the barman returned and topped up the glass, which, I later learned, was the correct way to pull a pint of Guinness. In fact, an exact time should be allowed for the 'surge', although it felt a lot longer than the 1 minute 32.5 seconds officially recommended.

One day we were directed 'a mile' along a lane to a campsite. About four miles later we eventually found the campground. On returning the next day, we happened to meet the same elderly gentleman who had directed us the previous day. "Hey, that was a long mile down there!" I sarcastically exclaimed.

"Yes sir," he replied, "We do have long miles in Ireland but," he added with a grin, "They are extremely narrow."

CHAPTER 4

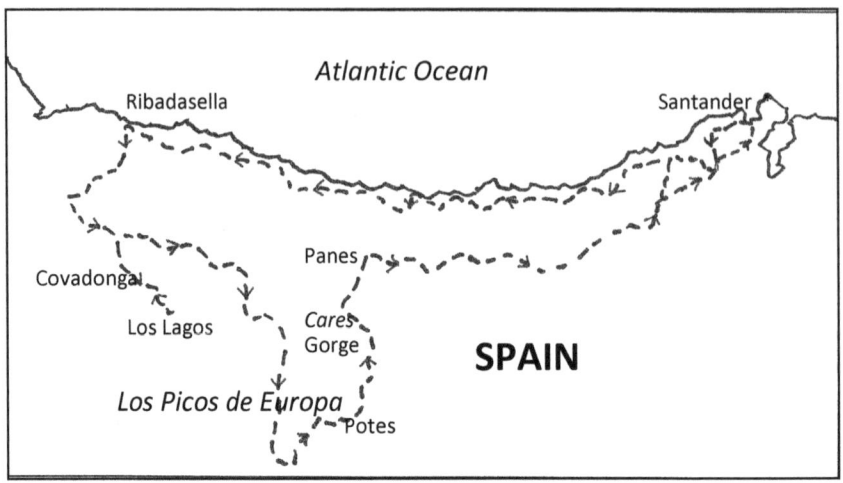

Los Picos de Europa, Northern Spain

*"Two things are infinite, the Universe and human stupidity;
and I'm not sure about the Universe."*
Albert Einstein

Aug, 1992. 330 miles

Although we had travelled to Ireland in August, we experienced wet and windy weather. So, the next year, searching for a spot of sun, we headed south to Spain. The ferry from Plymouth took us to Santander and once there, we were surprised to find that the local people appeared to get up in the morning and retire in the evenings much earlier than we had expected. Not until two weeks after landing in Santander did I realise that I had adjusted my watch in the wrong direction when allowing for the time difference between Spain and England and we had been two hours behind local time!

Being in the wrong time zone was the least of our worries once we rode inland from the coast at Ribadesella and into the mountains of Los Picos de Europa. We were heading for Los Lagos de Covadonga, recommended to us by a travelling friend. After passing the fantastic cathedral at Covadonga, which marked the birthplace of Christianity in Spain, the going got tough! The final ten kilometres climbed two thousand metres and took us two hours: much of it walking. Later we learned that this route was one of the epic mountain top finishes in La Vuelta de España, the classic three-week cycling race. On arriving at Lago Enol we erected our tiny tent among many others. Facilities were basic, actually there were none, but no way did we have the energy to venture further; not that there was anywhere else to go, except back down, which we did and much earlier than anticipated.

That night a wind of hurricane velocity hit Los Lagos. Our fly sheet was ripped apart and we quickly had to dismantle the inner tent to prevent it receiving a similar fate. All the tents that had been erected haphazardly around the lake were flattened. We huddled in the lee of a giant boulder and were able to watch the devastation by the light of almost continuous sheet lightning. By dawn the wind eased slightly, allowing us to escape back down the mountain to Cangas, where we bought thread in order to repair the tent.

Determined to reach Cares Gorge, recommended by the same friend who, we belatedly realised, never cycled but travelled on foot or by motorised transport, we set off uphill towards Posada, where we hoped to stay. At over 1,300 metres at el Pontón we were hit by thunder, lightning and torrential rain. Cold, wet and miserable we had yet another thousand feet of climbing before descending to the sanctuary of a *hostál* in Posada.

The next day, we pedalled down to Cain and from there visited Cares Gorge which offered one of the best walks in Spain. Twelve kilometres long, a precarious path had been carved into, and sometimes through, sheer limestone walls. Griffon vultures soared overhead waiting, one felt, for a missed step which could lead to a vertical drop of 200 metres into the wild Cares River – not one for vertigo sufferers.

We did not plunge into the abyss but the next day we found ourselves in a much smaller but equally dangerous gully. Free-wheeling at over sixty kilometres per hour down the awesomely beautiful La Hermida Gorge and admiring the sights rather than watching the road, I suddenly found our wheels in a deep but very narrow trench. We hurtled down, hearts in mouths and tried to avoid the smallest of wobbles when just the slightest touch on either side would result in a sudden, undignified dismount and a considerable amount of "gravel rash," if we were lucky! However, a few miles later, or more probably, a few hundred metres, we were ejected out of the mini-gorge – phew! The village of La Hermida, incidentally, is said to receive no winter sunshine because of the height and steepness of the valley walls.

Towards the end of our 500-kilometre odyssey in Spain as we headed for Santander and our ferry home, we found ourselves on a ridge overlooking a beautiful limestone ravine, reminding us of our own Cheddar Gorge in Somerset. We pulled over and decided to take a break. Clambering down a steep slope we stopped, out of view of the car traffic and settled down to relax and enjoy the view. The sun beamed down, conveying in its rays a celestial eroticism. I removed my shirt and Maggie did likewise. We embraced and things got heated. I looked up and saw a large coach full of camera wielding tourists roll into view. It stopped and parked immediately above us. We froze. Perhaps, if we kept still the audience would not notice us, or just think that we were German sunbathers. After a while, views digested and photos taken, the bus moved on. Our tryst broken and romantic aspirations literally deflated, we also moved on.

CHAPTER 5

Germany

"War does not determine who is right, only who is left."
Bertrand Russell

<u>July-August 1993. 950 miles</u>

In 1993 we cycled the length of Germany; Hamburg to Munich via Frankfurt. We pedalled nearly a thousand miles with, on average, a puncture every hundred miles. In Northern Germany we had rain, mud and gravel; while further south in Bavaria we found sunshine, *dunkel bier* and nudists.

From Hamburg we followed a so-called bicycle path along the River Elbe to Cuxhaven. I say "so-called" because for much of its length it was little more than a muddy cattle track along the raised river bank. There were many gates to cross, locked gates which we had to climb over: not an easy task with a loaded tandem. Occasionally, the gates were fitted with wooden ramps which allowed us to push the bike over, thus maintaining the pretence that it actually was a designated cycle path. We visited the Pied Piper town of Hamlyn and enjoyed the cobbled, narrow streets and overhanging half-timbered houses of Hann Munden, listed, by the great explorer Alexander von Humbold, as one of the most beautiful towns in the world. The castle of the medieval walled town of Rothenburg housed dungeons and torture chambers. During the Second World War, Rothenburg was spared

Allan Pendleton

devastation from allied bombing because an American general had, pre-war, visited and liked the town. Unfortunately, Hamburg was not as lucky and lost 42,000 civilians during a single night of allied bombardment. We happened to be in Hamburg on the 50th anniversary of this atrocity. A visit to the Nazi Concentration Camp at Dachau, however, showed us that war gives no man the moral high ground.

CHAPTER 6

North America

(Massachusetts, New Hampshire, Vermont, Washington, British Columbia, Alberta, Idaho, Oregon, California, Mexico)
"Every day is an adventure"
Anon

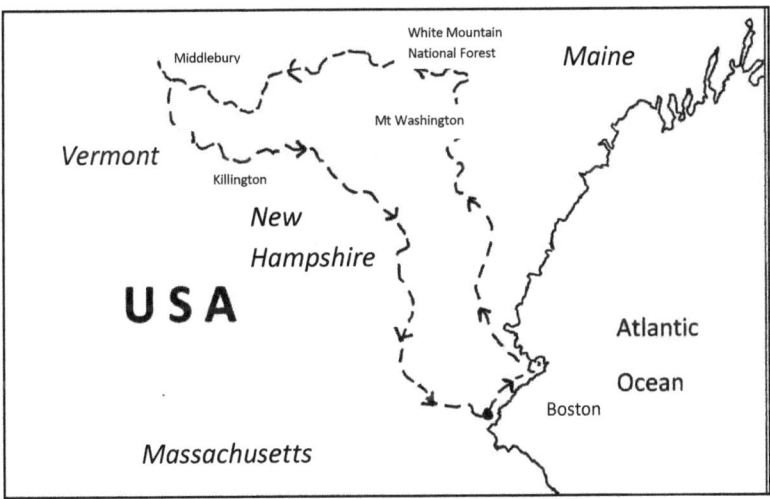

April-September 1994. 5,270 miles

While we were in Germany our daughter Julie was working for Camp America in the USA. She met a man there, fell in love and planned to return the next year. Maggie and I saw this as a great opportunity to visit the States ourselves on the pretext of 'vetting' her man. However, America is a big place for a bike ride and to do it justice, we would need more than just the two weeks of our normal annual summer holiday. Hence, we applied for extended leave. At the time I was managing a sports centre in Burnham-on-Sea in Somerset, while Maggie was teaching in a local primary school. Having earlier won the National Sports Council Award for Sports Centre Management, I was held in quite high esteem and managed to convince my management committee that my excellent deputy, Martin Rogers, would ably cope in my absence. Maggie was also well regarded at her school. Consequently, and luckily, we were both granted unpaid leave from April to September, 1994.

We booked our flights for Boston and prepared for a short trip in New England where Julie was working, before flying over to the west coast. However, Julie's romantic relationship was not working, so she decided to return to England to continue with her nurses' training. We almost passed each other mid-Atlantic!

We stuck to our plans and pedalled off into New Hampshire and Vermont in early April. This part of America had just suffered the coldest winter in living memory. We found snow, frozen lakes and closed campgrounds. In autumn the dense broadleaf trees must look beautiful but in early April the beeches, birches, maples and oaks were little more than skeletons.

On our first night in icy conditions we squeezed under the '*campground closed*' barrier in a State Park, cleared the snow away from a patch of ground near a picnic table and set up our little tent. There was a stream nearby where we could, after first breaking the ice, wash and get water for cooking. After our somewhat frugal meal, we donned all our spare dry clothes and snuggled into our sleeping bags as the temperature plummeted. I was awakened to the sound of chomping and chewing under the flysheet and only inches from our heads. Something was rummaging through our provisions – a bear? We had seen many bear warning signs but thought that it was just an American *macho* thing and had paid no notice. What should we do: ignore the 'bear' and hope that it would be content with our meagre provisions and not seek something more substantial inside the tent; or attempt to shoo it away? In a moment of reckless bravado, I chose the latter, ripped open the inner-tent zip and confronted the beast. In the beam of my headlight I was dazzled by the reflection from a pair of eyes. The creature was dark grey, with a long muzzle and black bands around its tail. Not a bear: but a raccoon. What a relief! I chased it away and returned to my sleeping bag. A few moments later the masked bandit was back enjoying the meal I had so rudely interrupted. The rest of the night was spent guarding our bags while the raccoon, treating us with disdain, sat a few yards away waiting for us to doze off again.

In icy rain we were breaking camp when a camp ranger drove by in his pick-up. At the time we were clearing up after the messy eater! We received a severe verbal reprimand for unauthorised camping.

Later that morning, pedalling through a small town; signed *'population 150, deer 584, moose 29, bear 6',* we saw a notice that warned residents of a recent outbreak of rabies transmitted by – raccoons! We took a break and sat on a bench with a flask and a sandwich. A passer-by bade us good morning and asked, "How is the weather in England today?" I was surprised because we had not said a word up to that point, "How do you know we are English?" "Ha," he laughed, "No one except the English would sit in the rain drinking tea and eating Marmite sandwiches."

We later stopped for American food. While getting stuck into an all-day breakfast wielding both knives *and* forks we became aware of the stares of a huge, unshaven man standing beside our table. He was wearing a baseball cap, cheque shirt, jeans with braces and cowboy boots.

"Doan you guys mind me" he drawled "but I just love to watch the way you guys eat!"

A few days later in freezing, driving rain, we resolved to seek indoor accommodation for the night. When a b&b, the 'Love Inn', appeared as an apparition out of the gloom we felt that someone was looking kindly down on us. We were not the only ones with that thought. Our hosts, Pam and Richard and their spooky son Christian, welcomed us with hugs and "Glory be, see who the Lord has sent by!" We were well fed and our wet clothes were tumble dried but we were subjected to a relentless bombardment of born-again Christian propaganda. For hours we faced a non-stop deluge of threats and prayers to persuade us to embrace the Life of Christ. For a committed atheist, this was torture indeed. As a guest I felt unable to argue my case, not wanting to antagonise my hosts and risk getting ejected into the stormy night. Eventually, near midnight, feeling rather shell-shocked, we were able to escape to bed. Alongside, on the bedside table, were four bibles and a book entitled "Heaven – how to get there." In the morning we departed after more prayers and religious cajolements. It would have been easier to face inclement weather and rabid raccoons!

We breakfasted at Wolfboro', the oldest tourist town in the USA and the setting for the film 'On Golden Pond.' Overlooking the frozen Lake Winnipesaukee, we continued the theistic theme and camped in a church graveyard. The next night we found a closed campground halfway up Kancamagus Pass at 2,860 feet in the White Mountain National Park. We wild camped, melted snow for washing and cooking and fed the chipmunks. After our bear-cum-raccoon scare, we began hanging our food bag on a high, overhanging branch well away from the tent. It was still raining as we summited the pass the following day in thick clouds with no chance of seeing the 6,288 feet high Mount Washington: the highest peak in North East America. Its erratic weather boasts nearly a hundred inches of precipitation each year and once held the world wind speed record with gusts of 231 mph.

More freezing, wet weather forced us, once more, to seek indoor accommodation. We found a motel in Woodstock and after warming and drying out, took a three-mile jaunt to "Franny's Place" for a drink and something to eat. There we met Nancy and Jack who claimed to be lumberjacks. They bought us a beer and instructed us in the noble art of tequila shooting. There were three stages. The first was to wet the hand between thumb and index finger and shake some salt onto the wet patch. Then you had to lick the salt off your hand and immediately 'shoot' the tequila down in one gulp and suck on a wedge of lime. I was not a natural 'shooter' therefore I needed more practice. Another round of drinks was ordered, then another and another – we ended up at Jack and Nancy's condo' for even more booze. How we pedalled back to our motel I will never know but I do know that I had one hell of a headache the next day.

Never Say "If Only"

We cycled into Vermont to encounter more hills, rain and snow. Our route took us to a mandatory cycle path that paralleled the US 93 Freeway on which no bicycling is allowed. However, at the entrance to the cycleway, we were met by a cross-country skier! The bike path was under two feet of snow! We had to use the freeway. Luckily, we saw no police patrol cars.

No trip in Vermont is complete without a visit to Ben & Jerry's ice-cream factory. Somehow, we managed to 'win' two tubs of 'Chunky Monkey' and not able to take it with us, we sat on the steps near the entrance, got stuck into the gallon buckets and did our best to empty them before leaving.

We experienced more mechanical problems. For example, in Middlebury, we spent over a $100 for a new chain, chain-wheels and free-wheel cassette but we could not afford to have the bothersome headset replaced.

We rode over Middlebury Gap at 2,150 feet onto Rochester and Pittsfield. We were inappropriately dressed for the continual climbing and descending in the freezing conditions. I had a Gore-Tex breathable jacket but Maggie had only a plastic-coated cagoule over her cotton tee-shirt and sweatshirt. We sweated profusely on the climbs but froze on the descents. By the time we reached Killington, Maggie was shivering like a jelly, so much so, that the whole bike was shaking. "We have t-t-to f-f-f-find somewhere t-t-t-o st-st-stay t-t-tonight." she stammered, "I'm t-too c-c-c-cold t-t-to c-c-c-camp."

We reached Turn of the River Ski Lodge. Two men were there but in response to our plea for a place to stay they told us, "Sorry but we are just shutting up for the season." Maggie then played her trump card. If all else fails, cry! Brandon and Dylan soon relented and found us a room. In the morning we were treated to muffins and jelly (toast and jam). Thanks guys!

On our way back to Boston we stopped at a State Forest in Massachusetts. There, Wesley, the head ranger, although the campground was still officially closed, not only found us a pitch for our tent but brought a load of logs and made sure that we had a roaring campfire. In spite of the rain, snow and freezing temperatures; the split lips and fingers and an ongoing series of mechanical problems with the tandem; I wrote in my log:

"We are so happy and so much in love. I sometimes wondered if the reality of our trip would live up to the dream. It is! We are savouring every moment, the freedom, the adventure, the whole experience. The only regret is that we are not sharing it with our family. Everyone is so hospitable and friendly. We only stop for a moment and are greeted with a 'How ya doin'?', 'Where ya goin'?' and 'Kinda cold for bicycling!' Few people pass without a friendly comment. The tandem, I suppose, makes us a bit of an oddity but so far so good. Here I sit beside the love of my life, in front of a blazing camp fire with a can of Budweiser – what more could a man want?" Mmm… a Wadworth's 6X?

At the end of April, after three weeks and 900 miles in New, we flew from Boston to Seattle. We spent the night on the floor in the airport lounge – one of many free airport 'hotels.' Saw the sights of Seattle; Aquarium, Omnidome, Seattle Centre, Monorail and the 530 feet tall Space Needle. Here, on the west coast, everything was so verdant: an array of shades of green. Back in New England, although buds and leaves were forming, the trees were almost bare.

From Port Angeles, on the Olympic Peninsula, we took a ferry to Vancouver Island in British Columbia. As we were disembarking in Victoria, a man pointed at us, turned to a small boy and said: "Son, they ain't tourists they're travellers." We took his comment as a compliment, for as the famous travel writer Paul Theroux penned, *Tourists don't know where they've been, travellers don't know where they're going.*"

We spent a lovely day "touristing" round Victoria. It was a beautiful city, with an impressive museum, clean streets, plush houses and fantastic views of the Olympic and Cascade mountain ranges. Then it was north through Duncan City, which, they claim, has more totem poles than any other city. We shared campsites with deer, watched bald eagles, heron and woodpeckers and were woken in the morning by the barking of seals and the honking of geese. Idyllic countryside, woods, meadows and intoxicating smells of pine, gorse, sawn wood and maple enhanced our sojourn.

After taking a ferry across to the Sunshine Coast on the mainland, we headed south towards Vancouver City. At one waterside camp, we were able to swop pedals for paddles and borrowed a Canadian canoe. While paddling we spotted an American bald eagle perched on a branch overhanging the water.

Suddenly it took off and like an arrow, with its wings flashing strobe-like in the setting sun, flew straight at us! It veered off at the very last moment to swoop and, missing us by inches, took a fish from the water and flew off, the fish jerking helplessly in its talons.

More mechanical problems! For quite a while, the rear cassette had been crunching and grinding. It finally gave up completely, leaving us with just one gear and no free-wheel. But hey, we were in Canada and the Mounties would surely come to the rescue: and they did! In a supermarket we enquired about a bike shop. There was none but we were advised to ask for the local Mountie, Tye Fraser, a cycling enthusiast. We found Officer Fraser in the Royal Canadian Mounted Police station, his steed was a mountain bike. We followed him to his home where he built us a new cassette. Three cheers for the Royal Canadian Mounted Police.

At Vancouver we took the 'Sea to Sky' highway Route 99 through the ski centre of Whistler and experienced some hard, yet exciting, cycling. Pine forests, white water rapids, waterfalls, snow-capped mountains and glaciers were our backdrop until, about twenty miles after Joffre, we enter a gigantic canyon with dark, foreboding walls. It was claustrophobic being entombed between sheer black, brown and grey cliffs. The road etched its way around the face of the cliff with vertical drops to the rapids below. We panted through Lilllooet, one of the original Gold Rush towns and now a Native Indian Reservation and into a semi-arid glacial valley. The mountains created a rain shadow for the valley and we found ourselves in acres of ginseng and heavily irrigated pasture and humming birds!

Passing through the 'Ghost of Wilhachin', a dry, sage bush valley, we learned that at one time it had been a fertile English settlement. In 1914 the men went off to fight in the Great War, only a few returned. A storm had ruined the irrigation canals – and Wilhachin was no more!

Some tough riding took us through the Monashee Mountains to Revelstoke by way of Eagle Pass. It was so named when, in 1865, Walter Moberly, a surveyor for the proposed Trans-Canada Railway, watched an eagle fly through a gap in the mountains. Subsequently it became the route for the 3,000-mile railway and the site of the 'last spike' which finally, in 1885, linked the east with the west. The Canadian Pacific Railway was built using many thousands of European immigrant navvies, but in British Columbia workers from China, known as 'coolies' were hired. These were little more than slave-labour and were made to perform many of the more perilous tasks such as working with explosives. Many were killed or received serious injuries. No compensation was paid to their relatives in China: nor were they even notified of the loss of their loved ones.

The railway brought prosperity to the West with land being made available to settlers. British Columbia is four times the size of Great Britain but has only five per cent of the UK's population and half of those live in the Vancouver city area.

We cycled through Revelstoke, Golden, into Alberta for Lake Louise and Banff, where Maggie worked as a waitress and chamber maid when travelling as a student in 1967; then onto one of the most highly acclaimed bike rides in the world, the Icefields Parkway to Jasper.

Paralleling the Continental Divide, the Icefields Parkway was built in the 1930s as a work creation scheme to help combat the Great Depression. No commercial vehicles were allowed onto the 230 Kilometre drive which offered some of the most spectacular views of the Canadian Rockies. We were in Wonderland watching for bears and elk, as thunder-like blasts echoed warnings of avalanches tumbling down the snow-clad slopes onto glaciers and the unbelievable blue of Peyto Lake.

At Jasper we made a U-turn and returned to Lake Louis which had not been seen by white men until 1882. It boasts a grand castle which hundreds of Japanese tourists use as a backdrop as they photograph each other.

Continuing south, between, and sometimes over, snow-clad mountains, we left Kootenay for the billboards, motels and gas stations that you will not find in the national parks. We had become accustomed to the tranquillity of the non-commercialised parks but now the fast-food outlets would not go amiss.

Leaving British Columbia for Idaho we said goodbye Canada, hello to the USA. We were dive-bombed by ospreys eager to protect their new offspring as we wound our way alongside the Pend Orielle River and passed through Kalispell Indian Reservation and the ubiquitous car cemeteries. Wild lupins lined the verges, with roses, buttercups and violets thriving in the damp climate. Gradually however, the green vegetation became less abundant, it stopped raining and as we climbed away from the Coulee Dam we entered an arid area of sage bush and cactus.

We rode into Wenatchee, *"The Apple Growing Capital of the World"* although the area only receives an annual seven inches of precipitation, mostly snow! Massive irrigation provides the needed thirty-six inches of water for the fruit. The cherries were yummy and scrumping was the order of the day as we rode through avenues of cherry trees and into Leavenworth before ascending the 4,100 feet Blewett Pass followed by the even higher White Pass.

Our adventure continued, from Idaho into Washington State and over the Cascades Mountain Range. Then our journey almost came to an abrupt end. Near the end of another long day and not thinking clearly, we approached a road tunnel. We could see light at the end of the tunnel and in spite of having no fixed lights on the bike, decided that we would not need, or rather could not be bothered, to stop and take out our head torches. We pressed on regardless. The tunnel was longer than we thought and when we were about halfway through and engulfed in darkness a convoy of vehicles approached from behind. In the light from the oncoming traffic, I attempted to pull over onto the dark hard shoulder, which, we quickly discovered, was nothing more than gravel and rocks – crash! To the angry blare of horns and the squeal of brakes, the cars somehow managed to avoid our sprawling bodies, leaving us bloodied but luckily not broken. We vowed never to be so stupid again!

Earlier, near the town of Colville, towards the end of another hard, cold and wet day and while mending our tenth puncture of the tour, a man asked if we would like somewhere to stay. Needless to say, we answered in the positive. A 'phone call and half an hour later, Charlie arrived in his pick-up truck and we were off up a dirt road to North Star Farm, set in the deep, dark woods of the Cabinet Mountains. Charlie, a forester and his wife Maureen offered accommodation to passing cyclists at their 13-acre homestead. No tariffs were posted for the cabins and bunkhouses but guests were simply requested to make a donation. A sign on the front door stated, *"Sorry no one is here to welcome you. Feel free to come in and relax, poke around and make yourselves completely at home. There are cold beverages in the fridge. We are happy to share our home.... and look forward to cooking up some great food and hearing about your adventures."* Fully refreshed, we departed the next day feeling positive and enriched by the friendship and hospitality shown to us from complete strangers.

I was also invited into another home a few days later. After Maggie and I had pitched our tent in Centralia City Park, I visited the public conveniences where there were coin-operated showers. I undressed in a little cubicle, inserted my 25-cent coin and stepped into the shower. Usually these showers would run hot for a number of minutes before running cold. I lathered up and just before I was about to rinse off, the water stopped, completely! Dripping wet and covered with soap and shampoo, I searched in vain for another quarter. The only thing to do was to exit my cubicle and rinse using one of the cold-water hand-wash sinks. This was not easy as the tap was a plunger-type which stopped the flow as soon as the pressure was released. Anyway, there I was standing stark-naked in front of a tiny basin trying desperately to rinse my whole body with one hand with the other pressing down on the plunger. I became aware of a well-dressed, middle-aged gentleman standing near the door watching me. I instantly felt embarrassed and apologised profusely explaining my predicament but he was unabashed and very generously offered me the use of the facilities in his condominium just across the road. I thanked him but said I was fine, washed off the last of the foam, dried and dressed. The gentleman once more offered his facilities should I need them in the future, smiled nicely and left. Back at our tent I told Maggie of my encounter. "But Allan" she told me rather pityingly, "If he has a condo' nearby, why is he using the public toilets?" Which, I recalled, he didn't!

Looking at our itinerary we realised that we would have a considerable detour to see Mount St Helens but this was one of our "must do's." So we hired a car and then debated if we felt an increase or decrease in status? On 18 May, 1980 Mount St Helens had erupted. The upper 1,300 feet of the once beautiful cone-shaped volcano was blown asunder leaving an ugly horse-shoe-shaped crater. Everything within an eight-mile radius was immediately wiped-out and the lateral blast flattened century-old trees, levelling the forests as would a gigantic steam-roller. Meanwhile, ash was blown twelve miles high and spread over 2,000 square miles. The devastation looked to be the result of a nuclear holocaust and affected over 200 square miles. Fifty-seven people died and 200 homes were destroyed. It was sobering to witness the result of this catastrophic act of nature but, fourteen years on, we could see the first signs of life reappearing with splashes of green emerging from this graveyard of ash.

At a cafe in Castle Rock near the Mount St Helen's Visitor Centre all the staff and indeed all the customers were crowded around a television watching aerial shots of a car chase. Cops were pursuing a white Ford Bronco SUV driven by the famous American footballer and film star, O J Simpson, who was being sought for the murder of his estranged wife, Nicole Brown and her man friend, Ronald Goldman. Our question: "Who is O J Simpson?" was met with absolute incredulity! The car chase had brought the whole nation to a standstill, as did the verdict of the ensuing trial a year later, when Simpson was acquitted. The verdict divided the country. A civil trial in 1997 found Simpson liable for the wrongful deaths of Brown and Goldman and he was ordered to pay $33,500,000 in damages. Several indictments followed and in 2005 Simpson was sentenced to 33 years in prison for a number of offences including armed robbery and kidnapping. A few days after our Castle Rock encounter, and back on the bike, we picked up a sharp steak knife by the side of the road. It is amazing what you can find when travelling! Since then, it was known to us as the 'O J Knife'!

From Washington we continued south into Oregon, the cycle-friendly state. At the entrance to tunnels, there were buttons which, when pressed, lit-up a sign reading *"Drivers beware, cyclists in tunnel."* They also have weigh-stations for heavy goods vehicles. These enable the authorities to collect the correct tax from commercial traffic. We rode onto one and weighed in at 420 pounds (lbs). Maggie clocked up 120 lbs and me 150 lbs, plus the bike with panniers weighing 150 lbs. So it was just as well the prevailing wind was from north and helping to push along our HGV.

We had discovered from our previous trips the importance of travelling light. We were amazed by the amount of gear some cyclists carried. For example, we saw tandems with four panniers like us but also towing a fully loaded trailer! Normally, we loaded our kit as follows: in one of the front bags we stowed the tent and cooking stove, in the other we put the billies, plastic cutlery and crockery plus food. The rear panniers held our clothes, books, first aid kit, tools and spare bike parts; the sleeping bags were stuffed into a dry bag which we bungeed onto the back rack. Not having expensive waterproof panniers, we always put our clothes inside plastic bin liners first. Our valuables were kept in the bar bag that was easily unclipped from the handlebars and accompanied us everywhere.

The early-morning sea fog tended to linger but at last we had no rain or snow. Inland there was a heat-wave but here on the coast with our following wind, the weather was perfect. We had slowed down, enjoying the beaches, although the sea was somewhat cold; then we ventured inland to visit some historical sights. Just south of Astoria was the settlement constructed by the explorers Lewis and Clark, who were the first American pioneers to cross the western portion of the United States in 1805. Fort Clatsop was named after a local native Indian tribe but just about everything else in this area was somehow connected to Lewis and Clark. An exception was the historical Indian village of the Yurack tribe. Not for them the characterised buffalo-skin tepee, instead they built low wooden lodges around a pit. Perhaps they found it easier to dig a hole than cut down a redwood? The men had separate lodges to the women and children; and come the summer, with the warmer weather, pregnancies occurred. The resulting spring births happened at a time when food was plentiful and the weather benign. To me, this sounds like sensible family planning, although for the young braves the winters must have dragged.

The wild life in these parts was abundant. Among many the many species we failed to identify, we saw grey whales, sea otters, pelicans, bald eagles, ospreys, vultures, wild turkeys, herons, kingfishers, robins that were twice the size of those in England, snakes, racoons, chipmunks, turtles, ground squirrels, elk, deer and back in British Columbia, moose and grizzly bears.

When we arrived at the Californian state line, it was like entering a foreign country. In a customs' shed, uniformed officials demanded that we relinquish all our fruit and vegetables in order to prevent the spread of disease into the Golden State. Instead we scoffed the lot!

One of the joys of bicycle touring in the USA was the camping. Every State Park campground pitch had a picnic table and often the views and surroundings were breath-taking. Many boasted *'hiker/biker'* sites which guaranteed a pitch, often, in 1994, for as little as $3 per person.

We were now in the Redwood National Forest, home to the tallest flora on earth. The tallest sequoia has reached 367 feet and the oldest has lived for

3,300 years. Cycling and camping in the redwoods was, as they say in these parts, "awesome." The downside was the morning and evening fog which enabled the redwoods to thrive. Some mornings the mist was quite thick, leaving us with a soaked tent and made cycling a tad risky, especially when a logging truck or RV materialised out of the gloom and roared past us. The resulting turbulence forced us to hang-on like a bronco-buster in a rodeo.

In Orick we went to a rodeo and witnessed the real thing. There was "bronco-bustin," "steer wrestling," "bareback riding," "cow-roping" and "bull-riding," although the latter never lasted for more than a few, often painful, seconds. This looked rather scary to me; I think that I would rather risk the Leicester Tigers rugby team's front row than sit on a 1,000-lb bull for even a few seconds. Several of the riders limped out of the arena holding bruised ribs or clutching their nether regions. The paramedics had a busy day.

In England we have touch-rugby as a safe introduction to the grown-up game. In a similar way the rodeo enthusiasts encourage their offspring in their chosen pursuit. For the really little ones, cowboys and girls of less than 3½ stones, their daipers are changed for denims, a cycle helmet is placed upon their cherubic curls and they are sat astride a sheep and told to stay on for a long as they can. Thus, we have 'mutton bustin'. Their older siblings advance to calf riding.

Relieved to be on a bike and not a bull, we returned to where we had set up camp: a parking lot with Portaloos on the outskirts of town. We had erected our little green tent on a grassy patch between two RVs (recreational vehicles or mobile homes.) On waking in the morning, we noticed a large 'something' pressing into the side of our tent. On emerging, we discovered it was the back wheel of a coach-sized RV. During the night the driver had reversed into the gap between the vans without noticing our miniature abode, or waking us. I roused our new neighbours and politely asked if they would mind moving their home off ours. Luckily our tent had a fibre-glass ridge pole which had bent under the pressure but did not break. Apart from the tyre-tread marks on the flysheet we escaped unscathed.

An elderly gentleman shuffled across from his smaller RV and asked if we were alright. He was short, stout and on top of his open-necked shirt, wore an ornate necklace embedded with, according to him, mountain lion teeth and elk horns.

He introduced himself as Grey Cloud, the 85-year-old chief of the Piaute tribe. He had no sons and was the last Piaute chief. He displayed his bracelets, telling us that one was 230 years old, dating back to before the white man came to this area: before even Lewis and Clark. Another bracelet was made by the grandson of Geronimo, the famous Apache warrior. During this interesting encounter he made no attempt to sell us trinkets or to plead poverty; just the opposite, he appeared to be a very proud man. We were introduced to his wife and felt that we were witnessing the end of an era. This was rather sad, but encounters like these are what cycle travel is all about. Somehow being on a bike exposes you to all sorts of experiences.

We continued through the Redwood Forest to the '40-mile Avenue of Giants'. These trees were so imposing, almost overpowering, being 300 feet tall. The 'Immortal Tree', a mere youngster of 1,000 years, had withstood fire, floods, lightning strikes and even the axe. Further on was the 'Eternal Tree' which had a 20-foot living room built into its trunk and it still lived! We found a hiker/biker site in the Redwood Grove as a branch crashed down from 200 feet to land too near for comfort. We hoped that we would be safe here. It would be extremely bad luck for a 2,000-year-old tree to decide to expire on the one day that we were camped underneath. It is remarkable that the roots of these giants go no deeper than about six feet. Apparently, they spread out laterally and connect with their neighbours, a bit like we did with the recreational vehicle last night. The sad thing is that only about four per cent of the original redwood forests remain; but as each tree could be worth $80,000 and provide enough wood to build forty houses, it was hardly surprising.

We rang Joanne last night to congratulate her on her 21st birthday. "Sorry we can't be with you Jo but have a good time." It was not until we returned home that we were told that Jo had spent most of her birthday in accident and emergency at Weston Hospital with Julie who had injured her neck on a trampoline. What awful parents we are!

Our bike was falling to pieces. Richard, our camp host at Hendy Wood State Park, very kindly took us on a sixty-mile round trip to Ukiah to source new rear bearings. What a nice man!

Allan Pendleton

Bath time (bio-degradable soap of course)

Between 1811 and 1841 the Russians had an outpost here. They owned Alaska at that time and used Fort Ross as a supply depot for grain and to supplement the sea otter trapping trade. Sea otter pelts were very valuable and a thousand otters might be caught in a single month. Needless to say, the sea otters were nearly hunted to extinction.

Much of the coast road clings to the hillside overlooking the Pacific Ocean but, judging by the amount of re-routing and shoring-up works in progress, it was not clinging very successfully. Maggie and I followed the San Andreas Fault into San Francisco. All of California west of the Fault is slipping into the Pacific Ocean at a rate of two inches a year and a major earthquake, like the one that ruined San Francisco in 1906, is a distinct possibility.

The Golden Gate Bridge into San Francisco is 1½ miles long, 220 feet high and was the longest single span bridge in the world, until the suspension bridge over the River Humber in England. Regrettably that record has gone with the longest now being in Japan with a span of nearly 200 metres. The Golden Gate has had over 700 suicides. We heard a tale of one such depressed person who, after hours of negotiation, was persuaded to step down from the brink. Safe and secure inside the ramparts, he reached into his pocket for a cigarette and was promptly shot dead by a cop who thought that he was reaching for a gun. Where else but in the US of A?

In San Francisco we were accommodated by a guy named Jonathon, who we had met at a campground in Oregon. His flat was in Haight Ashbury where Maggie, with flowers in her hair, had visited as a student in the 1960s. Like all cities, San Francisco has its share of down and outs. On our first visit downtown, after I had rejected an appeal to subsidise a junkey's next 'fix', I was threatened with, "Give me some cash man, or I'll shoot you dead!" Luckily for me he didn't. Thankfully the good guys far outweigh the bad and we had a ball cycling up and down the hills, cruising around the Bay area and Fisherman's Wharf and exploring Golden Gate Park, which was an island of green within the City.

We moved onto the Globe Hostel and arranged a trip to Yosemite. In a minibus full of students we were soon referred to as mum and dad. Our 200-mile journey took us through another forest, this one not of redwoods but of wind turbines which stretched as far as the eye could see. In Yosemite the sheer 3,000 feet granite walls of Half Dome and El Capitan were a climber's paradise but not for the faint hearted as it took days, not hours, to ascend them. The climbers slept overnight in hammocks hanging perilously from bolts secured in the vertical rock face. It was not until January 2015 that climbers managed to scale El Capitan 'free', that is, without using previously attached anchors. Such was the difficulty; this little escapade took them nineteen days.

In the High Sierra Nevada, we saw giant sequoias trees, a type of redwood not as tall as its coastal neighbours but fatter; in fact, the biggest living things on earth.

Back in 'cisco we shared our hostel room with an African, a German, a Swiss and a Canadian Inuit called Steve. The latter complained of being victimised by police in Texas and Los Angeles because he looked Mexican but, ironically, being a Native American, he had the right to go anywhere in North America unimpeded.

We reclaimed the tandem from the roof of the hostel and headed south once more passing Half Moon Bay, Santa Cruz, Monterey and Steinbeck's Cannery Row, from where sardines were nearly fished to extinction in the 1930s and '40s. From the redwood forests into a vegetable jungle, mile upon mile of cabbages, artichokes, peas, leaks, beans, sprouts and lettuces. We passed an army of Mexicans harvesting hundreds of acres of strawberries. From Big Sur we continued hugging the coast with vertical drops to the Pacific Ocean below. The highway was narrow and winding, as if were etched by a shaky hand.

Hearst Castle beckoned. W.R. Hearst, a media and publishing tycoon, the son of a rich industrialist and grandfather of the infamous Patty, built his castle at San Simeon. His family owned 250,000 acres of the countryside, including fourteen miles of coastline. Hearst Castle was quite large, it had fifty-six bedrooms, sixty-one bathrooms, nineteen sitting rooms, 127 acres of garden, indoor and outdoor pools, tennis courts, a movie theatre and even its own airfield. The Neptune Pool featured an original ancient Roman temple facade. Indeed, much of the furniture and fittings were plundered from Europe, as were many of the volumes that filled the shelves in the library. Meanwhile, on the beach below the castle, a hundred elephant seals basked and trumpeted their disapproval of such extravagance.

Maggie was suffering from a severe rash of poison ivy, probably received during one of our roadside natural breaks.

On 1 August, our 24th wedding anniversary, we were cruising sedately along when suddenly overtaken with a whoosh and a, "Hi guys" by another tandem. After a few hundred yards they slowed down and allowed us to catch up. Ed Rodriguez and Joe Sevilla talked us into following them to their homes in Santa Barbara and insisted that we stayed with them for a couple of days. Santa Barbara was a city unknown to us but we felt a spiritual connection as this was the home town of Barbara and Larry Savage who completed an around the world bicycle venture in 1980. Their wonderful book *"Miles From Nowhere"* inspired us to embark our own big bike ride.

We enjoyed relaxing and being pampered but all too soon it was time to move on. We bade Ed and Joe a sad farewell not knowing that we were to share more cycling adventures with Ed in the future.

Our route to and through Los Angeles was either manic or idyllic. There was heavy traffic on 4-lane highways or quiet cycle paths along sun-bleached beaches. After Ventura we rode through a never-ending expanse of fruit and banana plantations, peach trees, lemon and orange groves. These blessings of nature were so cheap that we could not afford to *not* buy some. Loaded with oranges, grapes, plums, cherries, nectarines, cantaloupe melons, peaches, strawberries, courgettes and an onion, we struggled to the nearest camp to enjoy a very healthy meal.

From Malibu the paved cycle path stretched for fifteen silky-smooth miles along Baywatch Beach, Santa Monica, Venice Beach with its famous outdoor gym and Redondo Beach. We shared the path with teems of walkers, roller-bladders, joggers and other cyclists while attempting, with difficulty, to keep my eyes on the path rather than the bikini-clad nymphs playing volleyball alongside. After eighty-eight tiring miles we arrived at a private campground at Newport Beach, only to be told, "No room, we are full!" Although there were acres of space between the luxury recreation vehicles, we and our little green tent, were not welcome. We were told, "There is a State Park just thirty minutes down the road." Great but that 30 minutes was by car! The eighteen miles took us almost two hours because a front pannier broke that required first aid in the form of a tent peg and duct tape. It was very dark when we eventually rolled up at Doheny State Park. A uniformed ranger greeted us at the entrance kiosk. He gave a long and grave look at our weary demeanour before shaking his head sorrowfully saying, "Sorry guys but we are full!"

Oh shit! What were we to do? We were so tired and it was too dark to venture further. The ranger shook his head sadly as he absorbed our crestfallen features. Then moments later he clutched his sides and burst into laughter with, "Oh man, I'm so sorry but I couldn't help it. You should have seen your faces! Of course we have room. Here let me help you get set up your camp!" All's well that ends well and at least we notched up our third 'century' of the tour.

The next day we rode through San Diego and over the border for a day trip into Mexico at Tijuana, from absolute affluence to extreme poverty. We were overwhelmed by hawkers and beggars, many of whom were mere children. At the customs post on our return into California we were stripped of the fruit we had earlier bought at a local market.

We had more mechanical problems in San Diego but luckily in a city with an abundance of bike shops we were able to buy and fit new chain rings and spokes. 'America's Finest City' also boasted several Denny's diners that offered great all-day breakfast deals: three eggs, three bacon rashers, three sausages, three pancakes, three hash browns and coffees, all for only $3.

Time was running out and our five-month, 5,000-mile odyssey was coming to an end. We returned to Los Angeles to stay at the Inter Club Hostel at Venice Beach, from where we arranged a day trip to Disneyland and another to Hollywood, the Sunset Strip and Beverly Hills: what a contrast to Tijuana!

After a 'free' night's accommodation at LAX we flew to Boston to be met by our daughter Julie, who had returned to New Hampshire to complete her Camp America contract. We left for home on an earlier flight than Julie but somehow, she managed to arrive back in England before us, again passing in mid-Atlantic but this time both in the same direction!

CHAPTER 7

West Row

"He who is not courageous enough to take risks will accomplish nothing in life."
Mohammad Ali

1946-1964

I was born at my mother's home in Inverness, Scotland in 1946. My mum and dad had met two years earlier during the Second World War. Dad was in the Royal Navy and mum was a Wren. Dad had been orphaned at a very early age and sent to live in West Row, a small Suffolk agricultural village, with a relative, uncle Jack Butcher, and his auntie, the district nurse. At 11 years of age my father was sent as a boarder to Kingham Hill public school in Oxfordshire. One year after the start of the Second World War, when he was just 17 years old, he dismissed himself from school and enlisted in the Royal Navy.

He volunteered for 'combined operations' which involved air, land and naval forces acting together. Consequently, as a pilot of an LCT (landing craft – tank), he was involved in the D-Day Landings, the greatest armada ever assembled; this led to Allied Forces gaining a foothold in France and subsequent victory in the war.

After the war my parents moved to the village in Suffolk where my dad had been brought up. I think that mum found the transition quite hard; the villagers of West Row probably viewed any stranger with suspicion. Mum was once reported as saying in response to some hostility, "You might think that I am a barbarian but at least we have flush toilets in Scotland." In West Row we did not. I was about eight years old before I first enjoyed a good 'flush.'

In the winter of 1942 at the height of the Second World War, the brother of dad's uncle Jack was ploughing in West Row when he made an incredible discovery. Gordon Butcher unearthed a priceless cache of Roman treasure. It was not until

1946 that the discovery of the silver pieces came to the attention of the authorities. It was promptly declared a treasure trove and is now on display in the British Museum, and is known as the Mildenhall Treasure, although the 'West Row Treasure' would be more accurate.

Roald Dahl, the famous writer of children's fiction, was a fighter pilot in the Royal Air Force and visited RAF Mildenhall, an airfield adjacent to the field where the treasure was unearthed. Dahl read about the remarkable event in a local newspaper and conducted his own investigation; he then wrote, *"The Mildenhall Treasure,"* a non-fiction story and one of Dahl's first efforts as a writer. As a boy, I often wandered across that field but never made a single discovery, unlike my brother Colin who was always digging up arrow heads, scrappers and other stone-age implements. Colin followed his passion and became one of the country's leading archaeologists.

My childhood was idyllic. West Row was situated on the edge of the Fens and I spent every free moment playing outside. There was little traffic, no barriers, I had absolute freedom to play as and where I liked. One of my hobbies was bird nesting; this entailed collecting birds' eggs, which, to my knowledge, was not illegal at that time. I had accrued a sizeable collection. One species I did not have, although they were quite common, was a rook's egg. Rooks built their nests in the uppermost branches of very tall trees, branches that were unlikely to take the weight of even a small boy. However, needs must and one day my friend Rusty and I were determined to add a rook's egg to our collection. Rusty, being braver than me, ascended the tree, spreading his weight carefully between the ever-slender branches. He got within touching distance of a nest, reached up and shouted down, "This one's got three eggs in but they are cold." So, Rusty claimed all three eggs, placing one in each side pocket and one in his mouth; the accepted safe place for an egg when climbing trees. Crack! A branch gave way and down he plummeted, coming to an abrupt and undignified halt astride a more substantial branch. Rusty squealed, gagged and spat. The egg in his mouth had broken and was rotten, as were the eggs in his pockets; hence, we never did get a rook's egg and phew, did he stink!

We spent a lot of time in or on the River Lark, which flowed by the village. One beautiful sunny day we decided to go for a swim. As it was February, I was unlikely to get permission from mum, so I smuggled out my swimming trunks and cycled to the river with Rusty and my other mate Meady. The latter was blessed with a somewhat corpulent physique, he waded into the river, shivering but persevering. Trying to outdo him I dived in headfirst. 'Oh, thee of little brain!' Cold, cold, cold, the pain in my temples was indescribable. I barely managed to crawl out, and lay on the river bank expecting my head to implode. Rusty also lay on the grass but he was curled up with laughter. He had more sense than to swim in February but, after all, he was a grammar school boy!

Whilst on the subject of schools, I have very few recollections of my time at West Row Primary School apart from getting the cane from the headmaster for spilling an ink pot over his desk by kicking a football. Even worse, I was banned from the forthcoming football session.

I failed the 11 plus and was sent to Mildenhall Secondary Modern, which was ideal for football but, regrettably, little else. No, I take that back. It was good if you wanted to be a horticulturalist or a handyman. Boys spent a whole day, every week, every term, in every year, on gardening and woodwork. Languages, literature, chemistry, physics and Latin for example, were not in the curriculum. But we had a good football team, often winning the County Championship. I was a reasonable player and consequently enjoyed a raised status.

The headmaster, Mr Star, nicknamed 'Twinkle', patrolled the playground at playtimes with a ramrod straight right arm. The reason for this was that his sleeve was a scabbard for his cane which, at a flick of the wrist, would appear in his grasp to be wielded in a manner befitting a cavalier.

One rainy day we were being shown slides in the gardening shed about "double digging" or something equally important. Our gardening teacher, Mr. "Bogey" Ward, so-named because of an ever-present dewdrop on the end of his nose, dimmed the lights and as he started projecting, a voice came out of the darkness,

"I thought I saw a bogeyman a creeping up on me, I did I saw....."?

The ditty was stopped mid-chant as the master roared, "Who said that?"

"Me Sir" owned up Robbo immediately. Peter Robinson was a Fen Tiger, he lived deep in the Fens and was as hard as nails. He was probably one of the kids that got sewn into his liberty bodice in autumn and not cut out of it until the spring.

"Hold out your hand!" thundered the Bogeyman, grabbing his cane: whack!

"Bugger me!" exclaimed Robbo, sucking his fingers to ease the pain.

"What did you say? Hold that hand out again boy!" Whack!

"Bugger me!"

"Again Robinson!" Whack! "Bugger me!" Whack! "Bugger me!" This game went on and on until eventually Mr Ward, exhausted and taunted by the cheers and laughter from the rest of the class, had to relent and sent Robinson to face the headmaster.

One benefit from my time at Mildenhall Secondary Modern was that I learned how to box. During my fourth, and final, year at school we had an ex-army physical education teacher, Sergeant Lawrence. He introduced us to the noble art and I took to it like a fish takes to water.

During my last term at school, Mr Lawrence took up employment at a private school in Bedford. Shortly after, he invited me to take part in a boxing demonstration at his new school's summer fair. A boxing ring had been erected amidst marquees and stalls in the sports field. When it was my turn to box, I climbed up into the raised platform and glanced across at my opponent. He looked back at me with a grin through his gum-shield and shrugged off a bright red dressing gown to reveal a school singlet and shiny blue silk boxing shorts. He shadow-boxed in his corner, Ali-shuffling in black calf-length boxing boots while I quaked, wondering what I had let myself in for. My gear consisted of a white vest, football shorts and plimsolls. Anyway, I could not have done too badly for at the end of the bout Mr Lawrence, rather generously, declared a draw. Suitably encouraged by my first fight, I joined Ely Amateur Boxing Club, the nearest club to West Row but fifteen miles away.

Although this was my last year at school, I had no idea what I would do when I left, I had not really thought about it. I started to panic when farmer Ford, for whom I worked during the Easter holidays 'singling' sugar beet, offered me a job as a farm labourer. A job? I did not want a job! I wanted to continue playing football, cricket, going fishing, that sort of stuff. However, I was leaving school next term so what to do? The answer, of course, was to stay at school. But my school did not even have a fifth year, year eleven in today's language, never mind a sixth form. Thanks to the dogged determination of my dad, I wangled a place at Cambridge Technical College in the next county. It meant a fifty-mile round trip by bike, bus, train and foot: but at least I did not have to work for a living.

I signed forms for Cambridge United Football Club but after half a season only playing the occasional game in the reserves, I chucked it in. The senior professionals in the club treated us juniors with contempt; they swore like troopers, smoked, spat and offered a regime of which I just did not want to be part. On the other hand, the environment provided by my boxing club in Ely was respectful, caring, encouraging and friendly. I was doing quite well and that helped. Unbeaten as a junior, I then lost my first two senior bouts but went on to win a London divisional title and the Eastern Area Championships three years in a row at three different weights.

The trips to and from Ely for training during the winter of '63 tested my resolve. 1963 was the year of the "Big Freeze," the coldest winter in the 20th-century. We had sub-zero temperatures for months in a row and not until March did Britain record a day without frost. I had a fifteen mile journey each way and travelled on my Lambretta Scooter. I wore a thick US Air Force flying jacket but even so, needed a brisk rub-down with a coarse towel in front of a hot stove when I arrived at the club. The twice weekly trip across the Fens became more bruising than the boxing. I regularly hit icy patches and fell off the scooter. On one occasion, the accelerator twist grip was broken leaving the metal interior exposed to the elements. Then, if I did not continually rev the engine, the throttle would freeze and I would be unable to slow down. This happened frequently and in order to stop, I had to steer into one of the snow drifts that flanked the sides of the road. Sometimes I was lucky and received a 'soft' landing: sometimes not.

Another memorable boxing experience occurred in Jersey. I was representing the Eastern Counties in a contest against the Channel Islands and was matched with a Commonwealth Games representative and the local hero. Our bout was an ugly affair. My opponent was shorter than me and dangerous when he got in close; I tried to keep the fight at long range. Whenever my adversary did get past my jabs and hooks, I clinched and held on. The referee had a busy time having to continuously break the clinches but, at the final bell I received the decision. For the first and only time in nearly a hundred fights did my opponent refuse to shake hands, I shrugged and thought "poor loser". After the tournament, as I was leaving the auditorium with my team mates, a bulky youth stepped forwards and head- butted me in the face. I was still on an adrenaline high so automatically swung a right hook that connected flush on my antagonist's jaw sending him sprawling to the ground. This was not an act of bravery, just a reflex action. As the thug staggered to his feet, I saw the glint of a blade in his hand: so much for heroics, I just turned and ran. I did not stop running until I was waved down by a police car. When reliving the event later in the hotel, the rest of the team admitted to taking a similar course of action, namely 'legging it.' However, on our return to the mainland a local newspaper, the *Bury Free Press*, reported how one of our team, middleweight George Bayliss, had held back our aggressors by wrapping his coat round an arm as a shield against the knife attack, thus enabling his team to escape. George was a good boxer and also modest, for he never once mentioned this act of bravery to us at the hotel.

While studying at Cambridge Technical College, I went out with a lovely blonde girl called Christine. We were together for over a year and I was very much in love but living twenty-five miles away and studying for A- levels made regular intimacy a rare thing. In your teens absence does not make the heart grow fonder and Christine dumped me for a work colleague who had more time on his hands than a boring youth who spent most of his time studying or boxing.

West Row 1963

CHAPTER 8

Malaysia

*"I asked God for a new bike but God doesn't work that way.
So, I stole one and prayed for forgiveness."*
Emo Phillips

Feb-March 1996. 950 miles

After our American experience it was back to work revitalised. Well, no! Although we both enjoyed our professions, it was hard to return to the sameness of the normal working day. During our North America trip every day had been an adventure. There were so many unknowns, for example what would we see today? Who would we meet? Where would we stay? Would we be safe? Each day had been exciting, almost intoxicating. We were 'hooked' and wanted more: we craved for our next 'fix'. We bought a new tandem. Tired of the never-ending mechanical problems with the Dawes, we upgraded to a Thorne Discovery.

To fuel our addiction, we pedalled Audax long distance cycle events and took a few domestic rides including a 190-mile pedal in Norfolk with our daughter Julie. We also rode 200 hilly miles in Devon and Dorset and 550 coast-to-coast and back miles either side of the English-Scottish border.

Allan Pendleton

In February 1996, we arranged to go to Malaysia with our friends Pat and John Ashwell. They were old acquaintances from our running days, and we had completed the London Marathon together. They, like us, had caught the cycling bug and had already pedalled in such far-flung places as Alaska, Kenya and Tibet. We had a three-week time slot and used our annual leave, while Maggie managed to scrounge two weeks unpaid absence from school added to the half term holiday.

Heavy snow was forecast for the day of our departure to Malaysia, so we travelled to London Heathrow a day earlier. Pat and John stayed in an airport hotel while we cheapskates bunked down in the arrivals lounge surrounded by bikes and panniers. Just after midnight, the fire alarm sounded but 'no panic', only testing. An hour later we were woken again, this time by cleaners vacuuming the carpets. Later still a noisy electric floor polisher disturbed our sleep. Well, "you get what you pays for."

We flew Malaysian Airlines, with the most beautiful, slim stewardesses, to Kuala Lumpar and then transferred to Penang. After the snow and ice of England the steamy sauna-like heat on Penang Island was almost overpowering. On assembling our bikes and leaving the airport, our senses were put on override trying to ingest the myriad of smells, sights and the blare of a thousand honks and beeps as cars, motor bikes, scooters and mopeds frantically whizzed by. We were very hesitant as we left the airport about venturing into the melee, but soon we relaxed a little and grew to enjoy the experience of sharing the road with so many other two-wheelers. Cycling with the flow towards George Town we became lost several times but eventually found the Cathay Hotel, our base for a couple of days. From George Town we explored Penang Island, visiting China Town, the huge State Mosque, a Korean Temple, a giant reclining Buddha a Jewish synagogue and Christian church. A real ethnic mix but one that today, I'm sad to report, is said to be reeling from the prejudices and ignorance of religious bigotry. This was for Maggie and me our first experience of life outside the European and American first world culture, and we had eyes on stalks.

Perhaps climbing Penang Hill on the bikes was not a good idea on our first day in the immense heat and humidity, for, on reaching the top of the 2,500-feet hill, Maggie climbed off the tandem, removed her helmet and promptly keeled over. Her head hit the road with a clonk, like a coconut falling onto concrete. Luckily, she recovered after a few moments and apart from an egg-sized lump, escaped unscathed.

We ate at roadside stalls, which was to become the norm for this trip. Our staple diet was often a selection from mee or nasi goreng, bean sprouts, noodles, mixed vegetables and fried rice: all cooked in a flaming wok before our eyes.

We shared the ferry to Butterworth with masses of scooters and motorbikes; after which we were swept along with the tide of traffic towards Taiping. We left Butterworth's new housing constructions and developments, and soon the traditional kampongs of shanty houses and wooden structures, all on stilts and capped with tin or thatched roofs, lined our route.

Ubadiah Mosque

Outside Taiping to Kuala Kangsar, there was less traffic; which made a lovely ride through the plantations of rubber, bananas, durians, coconuts and rice paddies. We admired the Ubadiah Mosque from the outside. We, being infidels, were not allowed in. It was the third largest mosque in the world and had spectacular copper minarets.

We then peddled north and up through the tropical rainforest, avoiding elephant droppings. We struggled in the heat and humidity to 3,500 feet on our way to Kota Bharu. The dwellings in these forest kampongs are mainly built of bamboo with thatched roof; again, on stilts to help stay dry during the monsoon floods. Many of the villagers rushed to the roadside when they saw us pass and shouted, "Hello! What your name? Where you from?"

In spite of there being an abundance of roadside eateries, we were hard pushed to find one open because it was Ramadan, when Muslims are forbidden to eat or drink between sunrise and sunset. We had to carry all we needed or find a Chinese stall. In a few days' time it would also be the Chinese New Year, then all shops would be closed.

We cycled into the Provence of Kelantan, where the Muslim faith was very strong and a large proportion of the population were pressing for partition from the rest of Malaysia to form their own independent Muslim State. We stocked-up during the evenings but often received hostile stares whenever we stopped in daylight hours for a drink or a banana. After dusk, however, it was a different story, the city came to life! We went to the night market in Kota Bharu where there were hundreds of stalls offering a variety of oriental dishes. We had roti, fish, prawns, squid, fried rice: the works! For us this was worth fasting for.

The Beach of Passionate Love, ten kilometres north of the city, promised to be an interesting excursion. Lovely beach, but all the females were fully clothed, and some! Full burkas and hijabs were the order of the day: even when bathing in the sea.

When we came to leave Kota Bharu the traffic was chaotic. Vehicles were parked willy-nilly forcing pedestrians onto the streets. Bedlam ensued as cars, trucks, buses and motorbikes fought to find gaps through which they might pass, fingers glued to the horn. The scooters often carried four, sometimes more, as some families had little ones on board. Two-wheeled vehicles carried an array of cargo such as chicken coops, barrels, a pig, literally 'hog-tied'. We saw a monkey sitting on the handlebars of one old man's bicycle and a bed being transported on a motorbike! The downside of this motorised madness was that well over 5,000 people were killed each year on Malaysia's roads, making it one of the world's most dangerous road networks per head of population.

Never Say "If Only"

When travelling south beside the South China Sea, we were accosted by a man in the fishing town of Kuala Besut. "Quick!" he implored us, "The boat is about to leave for the Perhentian Islands, we can take you if you are quick." We had a hasty discussion and having heard favourable reports about these tropical islands we threw caution to the wind, unloaded the bikes, locked them in the harbour compound and jumped aboard the ferry. Two hours later, after getting stuck on a sandbank, a coral island hove into view. However, the promised accommodation on Moonlight Beach was full. The ferry then beach-hopped looking for certain hoisted flags that signified vacant chalets; we had left our tents in the booking office. On Paulau Perhentian Besar we were lucky. Abdul had rooms at his complex. Utopia! The best rooms and best food we had found in Malaysia, and all on a white sand beach with crystal-clear sea, coral reefs and copious sea-life.....shoals of exotic fish of assorted sizes and colours, crabs, anemones, star fish and sponges.

I wondered how long we could stay and still leave enough time to cycle the 500 miles to Singapore for our flight home. That decision was nearly taken out of our hands. On the third day on the island as we prepared to leave, we received a message that the ferry was unable to sail due to rough seas. Sure enough, the wind had picked up and the sea was quite rough with abundant white-caps Our beach was leeward of the storm and quite sheltered, but when we strolled over to the other side of the island the surf was thunderous, the undertow treacherous and we could understand why there was no ferry and the fishing flotilla had taken refuge. The next day there was still a big sea and it was too rough for the ferry. I wondered if I could send a message home to say, "Sorry but unable to return to work, marooned on a desert island!" I was sure that that would be greeted with not a small amount of scepticism.

For tourists willing to risk it or with flights to catch, a fishing boat was commissioned to take passengers to the mainland in lieu of the ferry... A small dinghy shuttled the willing and possibly foolhardy passengers to the fishing boat. Several tourists had a change of mind as we approached the much-weathered wooden hulk and were ferried back to the island. We stuck with the replacement and obviously illegal so-called ferry and enjoyed a rather bumpy cruise back to the mainland. There we were taken up a river to a makeshift dock, where we disembarked by scrambling over several other fishing boats. We then had to hire a taxi to take us the 10 Kilometres back to our bikes in Koala Besut.

Ramadan was over but the people were celebrating Hari Raya to mark the ending of the thirty days of fasting. Looking for somewhere to stay we felt a bit intrusive, like strangers gate crashing at Christmas. Finding food remained difficult because this was the first time in thirty-five years that the Chinese New Year had clashed with Hari Raya.

When continuing south alongside the China Sea, we sometimes found chalets, usually huts on stilts; and occasionally we camped wild. Toilets were similar in either case but one had to exercise caution when squatting in the jungle, as one was never sure of what may crawl, creep or jump out of the undergrowth. Our jungle camps revealed gymnastic monkeys, platoons of soldier ants, a flying fox and water buffaloes.

We took a ferry over to Singapore and camped in the only campground in the city. Mr Wong checked us in insisting that we signed a form stating that we had hired 'nothing.' Before we left two days later, we had to sign another form declaring that we had returned the 'nothing' that we had hired: all in good condition!

Our final bike ride was to Singapore Changi Airport and the only road that we could find to reach the airport was an eight-lane 'expressway' where bicycles were forbidden. We lifted our bicycles over a barrier and pedalled on the hard shoulder. As we approached Changi we were dismayed to see that the outside two lanes veered off to the airport, while the inner two lanes and the hard shoulder, continued straight on. We had no alternative but to wait for a break in the speeding traffic, cross the inner two lanes as fast as we could and join the airport flow. A gap appeared and, to the blaring of horns, we went for it, barely making it across. Phew! This was not an experience we would wish to repeat.

CHAPTER 9

Pyrenees

"There is more to life than making money."
Mutated from Mahatma Gandhi

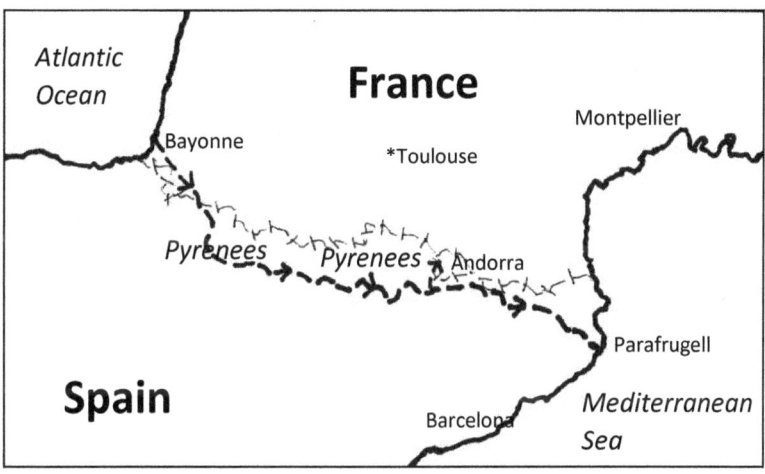

August 1997. 575 miles

Later in 1996, we cycled 200 miles in Wales from Ryader to Cardiff on the Taff Trail, then 300 miles struggling over some of Mount Snowdon's highest road passes.

Meanwhile, back at work at the Burnham-on-Sea Sports Centre, I was adding more activities than usually found at a dual-use, school and general public, sports centre. We introduced running events including a half-marathon, the Brent Knoll Fell Race, cross-country races, including the South West Championships, a duathlon, a gruelling run-bike-run, and staged the National Championships. We then added a triathlon that comprised a swim, bike ride and a run. Many of these races have become popular annual events in Burnham.

Allan Pendleton

Although I was kept busy, my ears pricked up when I heard rumours of Sedgemoor District Council having to make cost-cutting exercises including redundancies. The national government were also putting pressure on county councils to cut their expenses and as a result, older and therefore higher-waged teachers were being offered early retirement. This was an opportunity for Maggie no doubt and perhaps, I could benefit as well.

We were barely into our fifties and retiring at this early age would mean a huge reduction in our income. We sat down and struggled with the figures. There was a small mortgage to pay off, plus utility bills, food, clothing, transport and other expenses to consider. We worked out that we would not have enough to live on. On the other hand, we had saved a slice of Maggie's teaching salary and perhaps, when we were not travelling we could find part-time work, Maggie as a supply teacher and me as a sports coach. However, it was a gamble. We were very unsure of what to do until our youngest daughter Julie, told us, "Mum, Dad, go for it, life is not a rehearsal!" Thus, prompted, we decided that we would rather 'do things' than 'buy things', and we applied for early retirement. Both our daughters were by now adults and Jo had a very steady boyfriend. Our parents, although elderly, were still in good health; but we knew that this situation would not last forever.

New Zealand was top of our 'places to go' list but first we would need to do some serious training. On TV in July, we watched Tour de France cyclists, including our own gold-medal Olympian Chris Boardman, climbing Pyrenean cols and thought, 'That looks fun!' In August, whilst taking our final work vacation, we boarded the Bike Express, a coach with a special trailer for bicycles. The twenty-two hours hour journey took us to Bayonne, in the south-west of France. From there we pedalled from the Atlantic Ocean along the Pyrenees to Parafrugell on the Mediterranean Sea to take the 'bike bus' home.

The Pyrenees offered dramatic scenery and tough climbing over mountains and through gorges. Some of the climbs were on the actual 1997 Tour de France route, where the roads were graffitied with the names of favourite riders: Ullrich, Virenque, Pantani, Cipollini, Boardman, Pendleton – well, perhaps not the latter, but as we came close to the top of one such col, in my mind's eye, I could see us being hemmed in by hordes of spectators waving Union flags and shouting, "Allez, allez, allez!" and "Go tandem, go!" Thus, encouraged, we sprinted for the mountain top finish and triumphantly reached the summit with arms aloft before collapsing, exhausted, onto the roadside. As the excitement waned, the cheers from the crowds metamorphosed into polite clapping from an elderly French couple who, in their car, had passed us halfway up the hill, took pity on us and then waited to make sure that we arrived safely.

In hindsight, the Pyrenees were not the ideal destination for us at that time. Winding-up our careers was tiring, both mentally and physically. I had a bad neck and what we really needed was some rest and recuperation: not cycling up never-ending mountains on a loaded tandem. Because we were not in the right frame of mind, we didn't derive as much from the journey as the magical landscape offered. I remember countless cols, hairpin bends, cobbled pueblos, games of *pelota and* nightly thunder and lightning. We visited Andorra and had a number of blowouts caused by over-heated rims as we attempted to slow our descent down a mountain that we had just spent hours climbing! Once, when we treated ourselves to restaurant in France, we chewed endlessly and tastelessly on a locally recommended delicacy, which turned out to be pigs' ears!

CHAPTER 10

New Zealand

"Even if you are ahead in the rat race, you are still a rat."
A sign in Auckland Airport, 1997

Nov-March 1997-98. 5,540 miles

On Maggie's 51st birthday we flew to New Zealand via Los Angeles. It was a very long birthday. Twelve hours after leaving Heathrow at 4pm, it was only 7pm when we landed in LA. However, following Maggie's long birthday, we lost an entire day when we crossed the International Dateline.

We reclaimed the tandem at Auckland only to find the back wheel buckled beyond repair. Qantas Airlines accepted responsibility and arranged for a taxi to take us to a bike shop, but they had no compatible wheel. We had to make do with a mountain bike wheel, without a hub brake. This was an inauspicious start but when we eventually reached the campground we found it to exceed our expectations. There was a fully equipped kitchen complete with oven, hob, grill, fridge, microwave and a hot water dispenser. We soon realised that this was normal for New Zealand's campgrounds, known as motor camps and only when we camped wild did we need to use our own stove and billies.

We spent a couple of days in Auckland which, as far as area was concerned, was one of the largest cities in the world but only ranked 352nd regarding size of population. There were only a few high-rise buildings or terraced housing; most houses were detached and single story: Auckland has spread out rather than risen up!

Heading north from Auckland we found the cycling hard, very windy and hilly. That year, New Zealand was suffering from the *El Nino* effect and we were buffeted by gale-force winds, evidenced by the number of overturned trucks that we passed.

We reached the most northerly part of New Zealand, Cape Reinga and returned along Ninety Mile Beach, which was actually only fifty-six miles long. The scenery was fantastic, very green with beautiful beaches and sub-tropical rain forests dense with creepers and ferns. Here the giant kauri trees grow, the second largest tree in the world after the redwoods. They were extremely rare having been extensively harvested. Their tall straight trunks made ideal masts for the many ships that bought settlers here from the Britain.

As Maggie and I were riding along the east coast near Mangawhai Head we saw a house out at sea! At first, we thought this was an optical illusion or perhaps it was on an island but no, it was a real, large wooden, 1920s, three-storied house being transported on a massive barge towed by a tug. Moving house New Zealand style! Whilst we were pedalling later that day, we saw a pod of orcas, killer whales: all swimming parallel to the shore at the same speed as we were pedalling. They were diving and jumping as if giving us a private display.

After riding 700 miles and climbing over 12,000 metres, mostly, it felt, into a howling head wind, we cycled back and through Auckland. According to a local radio station, this was the windiest November in the history of New Zealand. Undeterred, we pedalled around the Coromandel Peninsular enjoying better weather and spectacular scenery.

We rode round the Bay of Plenty, with views of White Island and the steam from its active volcano. Then at Te Araroa we visited the most-easterly cinema in the world, complete with settees and armchairs. There are many native settlements in the East Cape area and at Tokmanu we were entertained by a Maori sports day, complete with chain-saw relays and log-cutting competitions, sustained by delicious pavlovas.

Sleeping in alpine-style lodges, we spent three days tramping the forty-six-kilometre perimeter of Lake Waikaremoana, one of New Zealand's *Great Walks*. It was a really fabulous hike, much of it forested but offering outstanding views from the highest points and refreshing swims from the lowest points!

Bath time (no soap)

It was back on the bike to continue through Gisborne, '*First City of the Sun*'and onto Napier. Napier was completely destroyed by a volcano and fire in 1931. It was rebuilt in Art-Deco style, becoming the newest city in the world and having the most concentrated collection of buildings of this style.

From Napier and with gales forecast, we boarded the train to Wellington, followed by a ferry through the Cook Strait to Picton on South Island. Here we took a boat to Ship Cove, where another of the great walks started. Paralleling the Queen Charlotte Sound we walked the 67 km back to Picton.

Back on the bike on Christmas Eve there was hardly a fairy light to be seen as we pedalled along the east coast of South Island looking for a place to camp. At Blenheim we stopped at a store to stock up with food and drink for Christmas Day. There were just two people in front of us at the checkout, each clutching meagre rations. The woman at the till, however, was hot and bothered. "Oh, I'm so sorry to keep you waiting," she panted, "But we are so busy at this time of year!" Busy? She should try our local Tesco at any time of the year! We were over-loaded with two bottles of Aussie Red, vegetables, pasta, porridge and enough supplies for the next few days. We pressed on through the Marlborough district which was suffering from a severe drought. This famous wine producing area consisted of parched, yellow, dusty hills with a very serious threat of fire. The drought, which was causing serious bush fires in Australia, was thought to be caused by the *El Nino* effect. It was associated with a band of warm ocean water that was accompanied by high air pressure in the western Pacific Ocean and low air pressure in the east. While this caused hot, dry weather in countries west of the International Date Line, it can bring rain and floods to those who live in the eastern side of the ocean; especially the west coast of South America.

Congestion New Zealand style

Allan Pendleton

The hot, dry wind blew us south. Thirty-five miles after Blenheim we saw a sign for "Pedaller's Rest." Mm, this could have possibilities, so we followed the sign along a rough gravel road to a sheep and cattle farm. The farmer Jim and his wife Denise made us most welcome. They gave us cold beers and suggested that we might prefer indoor accommodation rather than our tent. They had a bunkhouse for sheep shearers but since it was not in use we were welcome to it. At that festive time of the year, the bunkhouse was second best to a stable so we said "Yes please." It was fully contained with a cooker, fridge, crockery, cutlery, radio, settee, even a little Christmas tree. This was an ideal place to spend Christmas Day. We bought some lamb and beer from Denise, she gave us some Christmas cake. We were all set-up for a quiet and romantic Christmas when one of the three wise men rolled in. This particular magi's steed was a mountain bike not a camel. He was also called Jim and he hailed from Ontario, Canada and although not bearing frankincense or myrrh, he was a really nice guy.

On Christmas morning we cycled 10 kilometres along a dusty track, through a brown landscape that offered little sustenance to sheep and none for cattle. Jim and Denise were having to sell their cattle as they had no food or water for them. We rode to Blue Mountain Farm, where we left the tandem. Then we walked to the Waima River and waded knee-deep, sometimes waist-deep. Enormous limestone cliffs appeared as a solid wall ahead of us as we proceeded upstream. A narrow crack materialised in the sheer rock-face out of which the river flowed. This chasm was no more than three metres wide but the imposing walls reared up, perhaps fifty or more metres, revealing a ribbon of blue sky at the crest. We tentatively entered the appropriately named Sawcut Gorge, a shady ravine sculptured by aeons of rushing water as if giant hands had welded a colossal chainsaw. We spent a long-time swimming and jumping in the pools of this geological marvel before returning to the sunshine and back to our bike. At the farm we were each given a beer by the farmer, the first person we had met since leaving some five hours earlier.

On the way back along the gravel road we gave way to an oncoming car. It stopped and we were pressed with a load of cold "stubbies" which we took back to the sheep shearers' shack to share with Jim from Ontario. We had lamb stir-fry for Christmas dinner washed down by a bottle or two of red wine. Farmer Jim loaned us his phone and we rang home to wish our daughters a merry

Christmas, and to hear the news that Jo's boyfriend, Rich, had proposed to her. This was a great Christmas!

On Boxing Day, we continued south along the east coast to the whale watching centre of Kaikoura. Then we pedalled to Hammer Springs, a thermal spa town surrounded on three sides by mountains with the Canterbury Plains opening to the south. From there we climbed to 3,000 feet at Lewis Pass where the weather changed dramatically. From the hot, dry, dusty and parched landscape of Blenheim and Kaikoura where they were experiencing the worst drought of the 20th-century, it was rain as usual in the west! It was not just rain but it was cold, cold, cold! From the dry and sunny 30^0 Celsius it was wet and windy eight degrees today. The scenery made up for the chill, however, for as we free-wheeled down from Lewis Pass there was a rushing, white-water river on one side and lush, green beech woods cleaved at regular intervals by waterfalls on the other. This area used to be gold and coal-mining country, with extensive logging; but now many of the old settlements had become ghost towns. On the way to Reefton, we passed an old coal mine that caught fire in 1951; the Garvey Creek Mine was still burning when we were there at the end of 1997. Reefton, in 1888, was the first town in the world to have electric street lights, the water of Inangahua River powered a generator.

New Year's Eve was spent camping beside Lake Brunner near Greymouth and we greeted the New Year, 1998, under a beautiful starlit night. On 1 January we left the Tasman Sea and returned over the backbone of South Island via Arthur's Pass at 920 metres. We climbed slowly alongside the Tranz Alpine Railway, which could have taken us much more easily over the mountains to Christchurch. The sides of the valley closed in on us and through the beech-clad slopes we could see the snow-capped mountains beyond. Waterfalls rushed down the mountain side into the ice-blue water of the river as we laboured up 500 metres in just four kilometres into Otira Gorge. The road followed the river as it cut through the mountain and wound its way up a series of hairpin bends to the top. But no, it was a false summit! We plunged down before climbing again to eventually reach Arthur's Pass.

We decided to camp in Arthur's Village where we bumped into Jim from Ontario again. In the Visitors' Centre we watched a video about how the native fauna and flora was being decimated by introduced species such as rats, mice, stoats, weasels, ferrets, deer, rabbits and especially opossums. There were now 70 million opossums in New Zealand and they did untold damage. However, when we returned to our tent, one of the endangered species, a kea, a type of Alpine parrot, had taken revenge on one particular pair of interlopers – us! It had pecked its way into our tent and wreaked havoc with our provisions.

I woke to a rustling beside my ear and opened the inner tent door in time to see a loaf of bread disappearing under the fly sheet. Naked, I gave chase and managed to retrieve our bread but the pair of thieving possums had the last laugh. The tandem was leaning against a post and the possums sat one on each saddle, sniggering at my antics. They had a good nibble of Maggie's handlebar tape before emptying their bowels onto the seats and scampering off.

The next day we walked up Avalanche Peak, climbing a thousand metres for tremendous views of the surrounding ranges and valleys. The suggested time for tramping was six to eight hours but we did it in five since we had some cycling to do. After a hilly twenty miles we saw tents at Lake Pearson. Maggie pleaded to stop but Allan's ego said, 'Go on' and go on we did, only to encounter a very steep climb at Broken Hill. This was aptly named as it nearly broke us! We were hot and tired. I promised Maggie that we would stop at the first available camping spot, and Cave Stream Nature Reserve, just a little further along the road, should do nicely. We arrived to be confronted with a sign, *No camping*. There were a few people around wearing swimming costumes and carrying towels, so we thought that if we lingered until people left we could then put up our tent undetected.

Talking to the bathers, we discovered that Cave Stream was just that, a stream that ran through a cave! Taking just our head torches and handlebar bag, we entered the river and waded waist-deep, upstream into the cave. It was fantastic! A fast-flowing torrent of cold, crystal-clear water swept through the tunnel, which was not more than two or three metres wide and had silky smooth white limestone walls and roof. It was a tough battle to make headway against the rushing water, often having to hold our bar bag high above our heads as the water surged; at times neck deep. There were small waterfalls that we had to clamber up against the swirling current and all to the pinpricks of illumination offered by our totally inadequate headlights. It was like trying to climb up a waterpark's flume in the dark. We were engulfed by a blackness that felt solid and were overwhelmed by the deafening and frightening roar of the water echoing through the cavern. It was scary but also exciting. Over an hour after entering the cave we emerged upstream to a metal ladder that took us out of the gorge. By this time, it was twilight and we were all alone, hence we were able to dry-off, erect our tent and cook and drink with the water from Cave Stream.

Ski fields lined the route over Porter's Pass on our way to Christchurch. In the city we camped near the international airport and were immediately presented with food from fellow travellers who were leaving that day. We felt tired and decided to stay in Christchurch for a couple of days' rest and recuperation. The provisions left by departing tourists were an added incentive. Christchurch was a lovely city with a great botanical garden, which, when we were there, had demonstrations from morris dancers. Morris dancing is a traditional hobby from the English west country. We travelled halfway round the world, just about as far as one can be from our home county of Somerset, and found morris dancers, minus, regrettably, the scrumpy.

From Christchurch our route took us through the Canterbury Plains into a spitefully strong and cold headwind blowing up from the Antarctic, to Mount Cook, the highest mountain in New Zealand at 3,754 metres. Here we met Hudson, an Aussie chef who was cycling our way and travelled with us for a few days. After an enjoyable hike to the Hooker Glacier with unforgettable views of the mountain, we trundled south through Cromwell and into Arrowtown, an old gold mining settlement that promised untold riches in the 1860s but often delivered no more than toil and hardship; especially for the many Chinese who were shipped here as navies but in reality, were little more than slave labour.

We took a trip in a four-wheel drive vehicle to Skippers Canyon and the Pipeline Bridge the location of New Zealand's highest bungee jump. Our driver, a local farmer, explained how Skippers Canyon divided two sheep stations: one of 100,000 and the other of 85,000 acres, and that each sheep required five acres and every cow needed thirty-six acres on which to graze. We did not hear what else he had to tell us, because one of the passengers, an American bungee jumper in his mid-twenties, was too busy regaling us with his many exploits – "I've already done the highest bungee jump in the world in South Africa" he boasted and I've done this and I've done that, I've been here and I've been there. He ranted on and on, oblivious of the blank, bored looks from the rest of us. One of the other passengers, equally unimpressed, introduced himself as one of the jump-masters, "I'll take you for your jump," he volunteered to the American. On the bridge our jump-master secured the bungee cord to the American's ankles, who balanced precariously on the edge – some 300 feet above the Shotover River. "Ready" the jump-master said, "Okay, one, two," and just as the Yank passed the point of no return, the jumpmaster held up an unattached end of a rope and yelled, "No! No! Stop! You're on the wrong rope!" The American screamed all the way down and was still sobbing when he was released from the bungee cord into the boat that collected the dangling jumpers. On the way back to Arrowtown, our subdued friend never uttered a word.

Then we cycled through Queenstown, the adrenalin capital of New Zealand, alongside a range of mountains known as The Remarkables, to Te Anau. From there we took a bus and boat ride to the Milford Sound. We were not able to walk the famous track, it needed to be booked months in advance, but instead did another of New Zealand's 'great walks' the Kepler Track, a sixty-seven-kilometre three-day hike. This was a magical walk; much of it along ridges high above a mattress of cloud, as a fly might clamber round the edge of a glass of Guinness. Nearby, in the Murdock Mountains, a sanctuary had been created for the *takeha,* the world's rarest and only flightless parrot, probably the reason for it being so rare. Rather than share the fate of the dodo, it enjoyed the safety of thousands of acres into which the public were not admitted.

We forged south, then west, always into the wind, to Invercargill. One hundred and seventy years ago, Invercargill's founding fathers were very far-sighted, for the city boasted wide avenues planned on a grid system and forty acres of parkland with gardens, a golf course, sports pitches, animal pens, playgrounds, a pond and statues, all in the middle of the city. However, in recent years the population has declined. Perhaps the breezy weather of the world's most southerly city, discounting smaller Patagonian towns, was losing its appeal to local youngsters?

Mount Luxmore on the Kepler Track

Bluff, New Zealand's equivalent of John o' Groats, is South Island's most southerly point and like John o' Groats, it had a big signpost. On this one London was 18,958 km distant.

Continuing along the Southern Ocean the wind was still unfairly aggressive. The prevailing wind came from the west, as evidenced by the trees that all lean in an easterly direction, battered by months and years of westerlies. However, today pedalling east we encounter vicious easterlies: oh, I hate the wind! It was cruel, vindictive, noisy, tiring and took all the fun out of cycling; regardless we soldiered on.

We camped at Curio Bay overlooking the Southern Ocean and one of the world's finest fossil forests. We scrambled down the steep cliffs to the petrified wood, which, in the Jurassic era 180 million years ago, was covered with volcanic ash. Although the wood was now stone, it looked much as it must have done all that time ago when it was probably flattened by an eruption. The stumps were still as they grew with large fossilised branches spread around on the ground.

We then went to Porpoise Bay where a school of hector dolphins were playing in the surf. Maggie and I swam with them but could not match their skill and dexterity. Despite the cold, it was such a thrill and so exciting to be swimming in the waves with these wonderful creatures. Often, we thought a collision was inevitable as the dolphins surfed around us but with a flick of their tails they always avoided us. We were chilled to the bone but ecstatic.

The New Zealand Masters' Games, an Olympics for old folk, were being held in Dunedin when we arrived. There were a host of activities including track and field, cycling, indoor rowing, swimming, logging and many more. It was inspiring to see people of our age and older competing for medals.

We hung around for four days before dragging ourselves away and headed west into the now warm westerly wind. We pedalled through dry, tussock-clad and barren hillsides to Wanaka then up and over the Haast Pass, where there was a sign greeting us to the West Coast. Someone had appropriately erased the 'S' in West and, as if prompted, it started to rain. The rain didn't dampen our spirits as we descended through thick bush and ferns, down the magnificent gorge carved out by the Haast River and fed by dozens of waterfalls cascading down through the birch forests.

Camping wild in the rain we had a cold skinny dip in the river before enjoying a camp meal of soup, followed by tuna served on a bed of pasta *al dente*, with lightly steamed courgettes and onions with cream cheese, garlic and tomato dressing, topped with a liberal garnish of sandflies. Dessert was a medley of freshly cut slices of orange and kiwi fruit with sandflies accompanied by a gallon of freshly brewed Tetley Tea '98, with one or two teaspoons of sandflies. Maggie cooked all this on a single MSR multifuel stove: is it any wonder that I love her?

As you may have noticed, we had visitors to our meal, as we had on many occasions. The blackfly, known in New Zealand as a sandfly, is probably one of New Zealand's best kept secrets, never mentioned by the Tourist Board. This irritant is equal to the Canadian mosquito and far worse than Scotland's midges. In 1773, Captain James Cook wrote:

"The most mischievous animal here is the small black sandfly which is exceedingly numerous....wherever they light they cause a swelling and such intolerable itching that it is not possible to refrain from scratching and at last ends in ulcers like the small Pox." [*The Journal of Captain James Cook and his Voyages of Discovery*, vol. 2, ed. J.C. Beaglehole.1961]

It rained all night and was still pouring down when we broke camp in the morning. The low cloud gave the forests the eerie impression of being on fire. It continued to rain all day. The streams were overflowing and the rivers we crossed were wild, foaming maelstroms of brown, turgid water, rushing impatiently to the Tasman Sea. The road on which we cycled was a river in its own right, with water covering the surface from shoulder to shoulder. Some of the many bridges we crossed were interesting; we called them "pick-a-plank" because the surface of these bridges consisted of long wooden planks laid lengthways along the road. Often there were sizeable gaps between the planks, wide enough to swallow a bicycle wheel. Thus, when we approached such a bridge, we had to pick a plank to ride on and, hopefully, stay on: any divergence could lead to a nasty spill and buckled wheel. On one scary occasion as we were aquaplaning down a steep slope leading onto a pick-a-plank bridge, I looked up to see a huge logging truck that completely filled the width of the single-track bridge approaching us. There was no passing room, even for a bike. I applied the brakes – no response! I squeezed harder, but still nothing! Panic! If anything, we were gathering speed. "Oh shit!" I yelled. I sat astride the crossbar and pushed my heels hard onto the ground trying to find some traction but to no avail. It was going to be headfirst into the truck or into the river. I chose the softer option and steered off the road towards the surging water. A small lake had formed on the river bank and it was this that saved us. We hit the pool with a massive splash, collapsed sideways and stopped inches short of the river and being swept into the Tasman Sea. It was a close call!

That night, our hundredth day in New Zealand, we booked a cabin in a motor camp so we could try to dry many of our possessions. Every item was soaked. Soon our cabin was festooned with clothes, sleeping bags, paper money, guide books, passports and flight tickets. There was a small electric fire and soon our room steamed like a sauna.

We spent two days in the cabin drying our stuff and pedalled out to look at Fox Glacier which is one of the few advancing glaciers in the world. At times we were able to view the peaks of Mount Tasman and Mount Cook over the glacier as small windows opened up in the cloud, like patches rubbed off on a scratch card.

Allan Pendleton

Camping had become a tad trying with the constant rain, thieving opossums and swarms of blackflies. We cycled parallel with the coast, where a school of dolphins playing in the surf raised our spirits. We travelled straight through Greymouth, the largest town on the west coast with 10,000 inhabitants and was, as stated on the label, "grey." It appeared a bit down on its heels and reminded me of a Welsh Valley town.

Twelve days after cresting Haarst Pass we went from the green, damp and wet fern and forest over the Divide to brown fields, tussocks, pasture and planted pines and, we hoped, less cloud and rain. At the Abel Tasman National Park, we were able to hire a sea kayak and paddle up the coast with the single and simple warning that if it was rough enough to prevent us from seeing the coast over the top of the waves then we should think about heading for the shore. After three days with me at the back for a change and not one cry of "He is not paddling in the back," we were able to leave the kayak and make the two-day walk along The Abel Tasman Track back to our bike.

From Nelson we took the ferry back to North Island where, in Wellington, we had to call in at the Qantas Airlines office to get replacements for our flight home tickets which had disintegrated due to their regular dousing. From Wellington we took a train to Whakapapa in the Tongariro National Park, where we coined a new word *'Tongariroed!'* Like many in a close relationship, we often used words or phrases that, while meaning nothing to strangers, would have a secret meaning to those involved, such as a mispronounced word from one of your children. Maggie and I, as shortly will be explained, invented *'Tongariroed!'*

We camped at the winter ski resort of Whakapapa and there bought a permit to walk the Tongariro Northern Circuit, one on New Zealand's Great Walks. It was a thrilling walk through a stunning volcanic landscape. Emerald Lakes, black lava fields, active volcanoes, and steam from thermal springs gave the impression of the earth being alight. Plant life was limited due to the hostile conditions but there was an abundance of colours in the rock formations and lava flows. The walking was tough over loose scoria and pumice, a volcanic scree, with the constant whiff of sulphur fumes, an aroma like bad eggs. We summited the volcanic cones of Mounts Tongariro and Ngauruhoe. Ngauruhoe usually erupted about every nine years and when we were there in 1998 it had lain dormant since 1977! Tongariro was last active in 1926 but Mount Ruapehu, the highest point on North Island at 2,797 metres, had blown its top just two years earlier. Luckily there were no eruptions while we were there but it did erupt again in 2007. At the end of the second day we crawled back to our tent at Whakapapa. We were absolutely knackered, footsore and bone-weary, fatigued, zombied, glycogen deficient or, what we came to call this feeling of total exhaustion, *'Tongariroed!'*

Over the next couple of days, we pedalled to Lake Taupo, the biggest lake in New Zealand, formed after an enormous eruption in the first century AD. En route we had to run a gauntlet of honey bees. Edmund Hillary, the first man to conquer Mount Everest, owned a large apiary nearby; but his hives were on one side of the road while much pollen-rich heather was on the other. We had to cycle through a wall of bees as they crossed back and forth in search of nectar, bouncing off our faces and bodies as we pedalled along. Some got trapped in our helmets and clothes, and buzzed madly seeking release. We made sure to keep our mouths closed and luckily only received a couple of stings.

Feeling "Tongariroed" we took it easy and enjoyed the geothermal stuff of the Rotorua area: thermal pools, silica terraces, steam vents, geysers, bubbling springs, fumaroles and craters. Then, feeling so weary, we opted to pedal to Hamilton to watch a Super 12 rugby match rather than hiring a kayak to paddle down the rapids of the Wanganui River, which was our one regret of the trip. After Hamilton we travelled to Auckland to watch the New Zealand Ironman Triathlon.

We found New Zealand so accessible for adventure touring because there were always buses, boats, accommodation and information that made independent travelling a joy, plus like-minded, helpful people. Mind you, this was pre-Hobbit days and New Zealand was relatively quiet and not commercialised

We arrived at LAX airport in Los Angeles six hours *before* we left Auckland and after an eleven-hour flight. We had gained a day when we crossed the International Date Line. The traffic in LA was horrendous, especially the 8-lane Lincoln Boulevard. At Venice Beach we took the biker/roller blade track along the beach to Santa Monica, then the Pacific Coast Highway. Alongside pelicans skimmed above the breaking waves, and we were escorted by a pod of somersaulting dolphins and a grey whale on its annual journey north to Alaska.

Allan Pendleton

Although we had only met Ed and Pat Rodriguez for a few days nearly four years earlier, they had no hesitation in inviting us to stay at their home in Santa Barbara. They even left their house and car keys with us when they had to go to Los Angeles for Ed's dad's 80th birthday celebrations. Rather than stay at "home" we went for a bike ride to Solvang, a pseudo Danish settlement, then onto Lake Cachuma where we shared a campground with herons, ospreys, woodpeckers, bluebirds, turkey vultures, humming birds and a dead skunk!

The weather, however, was not at all Californian, it was a mere six degrees Fahrenheit with rain and our intended route to Figueroa Mountain was covered in snow! We were pleased to learn that State Highway 154 had been repaired and reopened after landslips had washed much of the road into the Ocean, but, after last night's torrential rain, who knows if it will still be open when we get there? The Californian Coast had been devastated by storms brought on by the influence of *El Nino*. Now, after 150 days on the road, we were feeling jaded and less resilient. It was time to go to our own home.

CHAPTER 11

Netherlands

"Bizarre travel plans are dancing lessons from God"
Kurt Vonnegut

<u>July 1998. 700 miles</u>

While in New Zealand we had done a fair bit of uphill riding: 197,000 feet to be precise. Consequently, Maggie thought that it might be pleasant to pedal on flat terrain for a change; Holland being the obvious choice!

West Row, my childhood village in Suffolk was just a day's ride from Harwich and would provide an ideal starting and finishing point. Plus Mum and Dad would look after Mac, our border collie, just as they had on our previous trips, bless 'em! Actually Mac was our daughter Julie's dog. When Julie was small she had pestered us endlessly to buy her a dog. For years we had resisted, pointing out the commitment needed. But, like water wearing away stone, we finally relented and Julie got Mac. She had solemnly promised us that she would be fully responsible for her pet, and she was, until she went to college! Actually, Mac was a cool dog. Maggie and I were both marathon runners and Mac would accompany us on our training runs and being a border collie was more intelligent than normal dogs and extremely well-behaved. But, he was not so good on the bike, which is where Mum and Dad came in.

In Holland we followed the North Sea Coast Path and saw many other cyclists. We would wave and say, "Hello" but rarely received a reply. We soon realised that greeting every passing cyclist was like acknowledging every shopper on a busy high street. Cyclists in Britain in the nineties were still quite a rare breed, but not so in Holland! With no one to wave to, we pressed on through the windy and rainy, albeit flat, terrain. There were cycle paths everywhere, many of concrete, bricks or cobbles but some of fine gravel which were not a lot of fun in wet weather. Sometimes this preponderance of cycle-ways made navigating through a large town somewhat difficult. Often bicycles were prohibited on roads, running directly through a metropolis and strangers, such as us, could be confused and spoiled for choice by the maze of bike routes.

In Arnhem we crossed a "Bridge Too Far," now known as John Frost Bridge in memory of the commander of the paratroopers who so heroically attempted to defend the bridge against Nazi incursion in September 1944. It was so sad to see the hundreds and hundreds of young men's graves in the military cemetery where the dead of the British 1st Airborne Division were laid. The inscriptions on some of the graves brought tears to my eyes, such as, "Daddy, you never said 'Goodbye.'"

We headed for Nijmegen where Julie, was representing the Territorial Army. She was taking part in the International Four Day Marches or *Vierdaagse*. These walks consisted of four days, each of forty kilometres, that is hiking a hundred miles in just four days. Some participants were walking four times fifty Kilometres! They must have been crazy! In fact, over 40,000 crazy people from all over the globe were taking part in this annual event which has been held in the oldest Dutch city since 1016. The military were well represented and our daughter, Private 1028034 Pendleton of C Squadron, 243(twx) Field Hospital (V), Territorial Army, was doing her bit for Queen and Country. The whole City was consumed by a fantastic carnival atmosphere. Nijmegen was a heaving mass of humanity, cafe tables spread across the streets, platforms on every corner where live bands were performing, fireworks and a huge pop concert in the town square – quite an experience!

After two days of boozing with the military, we threaded our way through the walking wounded; so many shuffling, hobbling and limping, ignoring the pain in order to complete the infamous Nijmegen Walks. We rode to Utrecht, a beautiful city with old period houses lining cobbled streets and the obligatory canals; then onto Delft and the Hook of Holland for our ferry home.

Never Say "If Only"

Julie & Maggie at Nijmegen

CHAPTER 12

Romania

If at first you don't succeed, sky-diving is not for you.
Anon

<u>Sept-Nov. 1998</u>

We had been retired from full-time work for a year and Maggie felt the need to do something useful. Julie, a children's nurse, had volunteered to work in a Romanian hospice for a charity called Children in Distress and my wife thought it would be a good idea to join her. Julie had volunteered for a six-month shift but Maggie, aware of my domestic incompetence and in fear of leaving me too long to my own devices, opted for a three-month term, September to November.

St. Laurence's Children's Hospice in Cernavoda, two hours from Bucharest, had forty HIV-positive children. When Caecescu was in power, he decreed that all women should have at least four children, so he banned contraception. However, the families were poor and many children were abandoned in orphanages. Conditions were abysmal and malnutrition was rife, hence, many children became very weak. The authorities then made the callous decision to inject the youngsters with blood, supposedly to make them stronger. This practice had been discredited in the West for a long time. A lot of contaminated blood was taken from sailors based in the Black Sea ports. Consequently, many of the children contracted AIDS and were locked away in conditions of unimaginable brutality and squalor. Children in Distress sought to rescue these poor, lost children and make their lives more tolerable with volunteers, such as my wife and daughter, acting as nurses and surrogate mothers. The mission statement of the CID was to help these abandoned children "live with love and die with dignity."

When Julie had completed her 6 months' contract she returned home jobless and penniless. While wondering whether to return to National Health Service

Never Say "If Only"

nursing or seek employment in a children's hospice, she saw an advertisement that looked interesting and somewhat unusual. Utterly Butterly Barnstormers were looking for a new recruit. There were a thousand applicants for the wing-walking roll but not everyone had what it took. Applicants needed to be small, agile, graceful and above all, extremely brave. Juliette, a former teenage gymnastics champion, ticked all the boxes and to her great surprise and delight, became only the tenth British professional wing-walker. She spent the summer perched precariously on the top wing of a vintage 1940s Boeing Stearman biplane dressed in a spandex suit performing adrenalin-pumping loops, rolls and stalls, while travelling at speeds of up to 150 mph. As a member of Europe's only professional wing-walking team, Julie performed in front of millions of spectators climaxing in a stunt known as the mirror manoeuvre. This spectacular and dangerous piece of aerial acrobatics consisted of Julie's aircraft flying upside down over another biplane, close enough for the two wing-walkers to touch hands. It was captured for the first time on film and featured in national newspapers.

Not content with standing on top of aeroplanes collecting flies in her teeth, Julie decided that it would also be fun to jump out of them. As a member of the air cadets, she enrolled onto a sky-diving course and quickly became an adept sky-diver. At this time Julie met and fell in love with Staff Seargent Dean Morgan, her husband to be. That summer she was in all ways flying high!

CHAPTER 13

Morocco and Mexico

"True love is like ghosts, which everyone talks about and few have seen."
Francois de la Rochefoucauld

Oct-Nov, 1998. 500 miles

"No probs'" I thought when Maggie announced her plans to accompany Julie to Romania. But sleeping alone and returning each day to an empty house for the first time in nearly thirty years was not easy. I had not realised that I would miss her so much. To fill the void, I went on a mountain biking expedition to Morocco with a company called Discover Adventure. We flew into Casablanca and on to Marrakech before heading towards the High Atlas Mountains by four-wheeled drive trucks. Apart from our time in Marrakech, we camped wild, often in the middle of nowhere, and miles from the nearest village. However remote we thought we were, children would miraculously appear. Sometimes these ragged youngsters were accompanied by Berber tribesmen dressed in haiks, toga-like home-spun robes, with cloth turbans. They all appeared pitifully poor but were friendly enough and seemed content to just watch us. Privacy outside our tents was impossible; and while washing in a muddy pool with spectators was bad enough, alfresco toilets!

On one occasion, just after we had set up camp, a small group of worried-looking Berber adults turned up with a sickly child. The poor little boy had fallen and fractured his skull and his family had no means of getting him to a hospital, or paying for any treatment. Luckily a member of our group was a doctor who stitched him up and gave antibiotics. Our doctor, through our interpreter, advised the family on how they should continue to treat the child. We had a collection that would enable them to reach a hospital. As they set off we crossed our fingers.

En route between the Sahara Desert and Marrakech, we passed the fortified village of Ait Benhaddou. This has become the Hollywood of Morocco since more than twenty major films have been shot there, including: *Gladiator, The Mummy* and several other "Jesus" movies. We followed the ancient Telouet route that was used to transport slaves and gold from Timbuktu over the Atlas Mountains. Past Ouarzazate, where *Lawrence of Arabia, Last Temptation of Christ, Salmon Fishing in the Yemen* and others were filmed, to the edge of the Sahara Desert and sand, camels, storks and more sand.

We cycled from Jebel Sarhro to the beautiful Dades Gorge in the Atlas Mountains with some serious climbing and white-knuckle descents. It was dry and barren but it had amazing rock formations of mesas, monoliths and needles. This was an enjoyable trip but many of our group suffered from upset tummies, only to be expected under the cooking and camping conditions. We ate couscous for breakfast, lunch and dinner. I won't be sorry if I never see another bowl of couscous in my life!

Upon returning home, I missed Maggie terribly. The mountain biking had been good but without my soul mate to share the sights and experiences it somehow felt a bit hollow. While we were apart we communicated by occasional phone calls but mainly post.....this was before e-mail was common. While mine were passionate love letters, Maggie's were more platonic. In the conditions in which she was working, surrounded by desperately ill children, this is hardly surprising; but in my self-pitying mode I couldn't shake off the sense of abandonment. Perhaps, I wondered, our love was not as all encompassing as I had believed. After one particularly sad telephone conversation, I slammed down the 'phone, went out and got hopelessly drunk. A few days later, and feeling that perhaps it was not particularly healthy to be totally emotionally dependent on another person; 'If you don't love as much you won't get so hurt', I left for Mexico for stage two of my *'Discover Adventure'* mountain bike experience.

This time we were treated to hotel accommodation and on our first night in Mexico City a few of us went "out on the town." Our first bar was a strip club which featured young girls who looked bored and were as erotic as a cold shower. We quickly moved on to another drinking hole which was showing live Grand Prix action on a big screen. This was more to the liking of my friends but I soon became bored and decided to return to our hotel. I strode out confidently in what I thought was the right direction but quickly realised that I did not have a clue and was totally lost. I could not even find my way back to the bar to rejoin my colleagues. After an hour or so of wandering blindly around and finding myself in some quarters not prudent to visit after dark, I hailed a taxi, a well scratched and dented Volkswagon Beetle. But I did not know the name of our hotel. I thought that it began with a letter P but was not even sure about that. The taxi driver reeled off a few names that sounded vaguely familiar and we set off on a search. Eventually and many hotels later, we came to a building that I recognised – *Hotel Colina*. It did not even begin with a P! I gratefully paid the patient taxi driver. It was so late that everyone had gone to bed and the hotel had been locked up for the night. I had to bang on the door to wake the porter. I hadn't even been missed!

The cycling was demanding with formidable climbs and heart-stopping descents to a back-drop of cacti rather than the camels of Morocco. On Saturday, 31 October we were in a small hostl in the mountain village of Ixtlan. It was Halloween, or as they called it in Mexico, *Noche del Muerte* – Night of the Dead. This was an important time of the year in Latin America, a time to remember the departed and celebrate their lives. All shops, bars and cafes were adorned with cobwebs, skeletons, witches and ghouls of every description. For *All Hallows Eve* children made altars to invite the *angelitos*, spirits of dead children, to come back for a visit. In the churchyard graves were decorated with flowers, candles and food. Our small hotel was situated next to the church and just as we went to bed the church bells rang and continued tolling all night long! Sleep was impossible as all the town's inhabitants partied in the graveyard.

A trip to Mexico would not be complete without visiting a pyramid or ancient city of the Mayan or Aztec empires. We rode up to the Zapotec pyramid of Monte Alban in the Oaxaca region and also to the imposing Temples of the Sun and Moon at Teotihuacan near Mexico City, some of the largest pyramids in the world. These temples, known as *teocalli,* or God's Houses were renowned as places where the Aztec priests made offerings, often human sacrifices, to their gods. It was claimed that thousands of people were sacrificed each year, often by the removal of their hearts. These were held up to the sun god, while the bodies were discarded and thrown down the temple steps. Captured enemies were often used for these offerings but so were the empire's own citizens. In the end, this incredible loss of human life weakened the once powerful Aztec nation.

Maggie's homecoming was at times a bit fraught. I doubted the sincerity of her love, while she accused me of being an egotist. In hindsight, it was wonderful and courageous work that Maggie performed in Romania. Clouds of doubt and self-pity had blanketed my view of the world – a world that would be such a better place if only more people were as altruistic as my wife.

CHAPTER 14

Andalucía, Spain

"The world is a book and those who do not travel only read one page."
St. Augustine

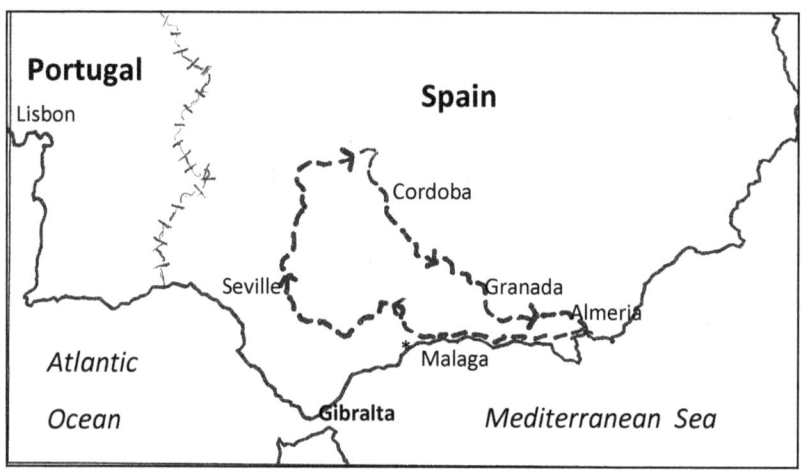

April 1999. 970 miles

It was a beautiful two-day ride over the Severn Bridge to Chepstow, Ross-on-Wye and the Malvern Hills, through country villages with lots of posh houses, to Birmingham International Airport, before flying to Malaga in Spain. In Malaga we experienced the usual difficulty in cycling out of the airport, being serviced by motorways and dual-carriageways with little provision for cyclists. The advertised campground at Alhaurin de la Torre was closed and apparently had been for three years, but the friendly owner of a nearby tavern allowed us to camp in his back yard. And so began a hot, hilly and hard four weeks in Andalucia.

Our first cycling day led us north through lemon and orange groves, alongside the Rio Guadalhorce passing the old Moorish mosque perched high on the hill at Alora, to Garganta del Chorro, a spectacular limestone gorge. It was a popular attraction for climbers with disintegrating walkways contouring the perpendicular walls, impassable, except for the intrepid. We followed a railway line through several tunnels to view the Gorge from different angles, pausing to watch climbers clinging to and hanging from the vertical rock face like four-limbed spiders.

Although we cycled parallel to the river it was hilly. The next day was even harder, continually up and down with twenty-five kilometres on dirt tracks, past cork oaks harvested for their bark and through scrubby, mountainous landscape. Unsurprisingly, we met very few vehicles but many tree-climbing goats. One of the few cars we met was a right-hand drive that hurtled towards us over a narrow bridge. We moved as far as we could to the right but it continued on our side of the road aiming directly at us. At the very last moment the driver slammed on his brakes, showering us with dust and stones and sliding to a stop just inches in front of us. The driver and I looked angrily at each other before the dawn of realisation struck him. He lowered his window, stuck out his head and said in a plum English accent, "Whoops, dreadfully sorry!"

A winding road led to the top of Puerto del Viento, Gate of the Wind, with magnificent views of the countryside and the ancient city of Ronda. Ronda sits astride the Rio Guadalevin which divides the city by way of a hundred metre canyon, El Tajo, spanned by three bridges towering nearly four hundred feet above the valley floor. The city dates back to the Neolithic Age and has been ruled by Phoenicians, Romans, Goths and Arabs before succumbing to the Catholics in 1485. The Spanish Inquisition insisted that Muslims and Jews had to convert to Christianity or depart, leaving all their possessions behind. Today we are able to witness much evidence of the eight-hundred year Islamic presence. Not just the architectural wonders in Seville, Cordoba, and Grenada but the excellent irrigation system of aqueducts and canals, still obvious and functional. Much later Ronda was renowned for its bullfighting and has the oldest bullfighting ring in Spain.

About a hundred kilometres from Ronda we reached Dos Hermanas on the outskirts of Seville. Everywhere was in a festive Easter mood. There were processions of floats with life-like wooden sculptures, scenes depicting the crucifixion and images of a grieving Mary. Seville cathedral was the largest cathedral in the world and the burial site of Christopher Columbus. The equally beautiful royal palace, the Alcazar, was also originally developed by the Moors. We enjoyed visiting both of these World Heritage Sites.

Continuing north, we rode into the Sierra Morano on a badly pot-holed gravely road into a strong wind on an extremely hot day. Just as we were hoping that the imminent thousand foot climb was as big a problem as we were likely to face that day, bang! A back-wheel blow out. The puncture caused a huge split along the tyre wall. Not having a replacement we repaired it as best we could by using a rag to pad out the rent. We limped carefully back to San Nicholas, the last place we had passed, but, unfortunately, no help could be found there. We continued another eight tentative kilometres to Alanis, but again no luck. We were directed to Guadelcanal, another twelve kilometres where there might be a bike shop. But we found the road to Guadelcanal under repair and covered with loose chippings. There was absolutely no way we could make it on our mortally wounded back tyre. So we returned to Alanis to find a bar where Maggie could stay while I hitch-hiked to Guadelcanal. Our predicament caused some interest and amusement in the village and, just as I was about to set off on my hike, I was beckoned by an elderly man in the street who was sizing up the tandem wheels. He mumbled something about mountains and *"Un momento"*, before wandering off. He returned with two old mountain bike tyres. Luckily our tandem had 26" wheels and while one of the gentleman's tyres was fat enough to fit a tractor, the other, albeit very knobbly, looked promising. I had to take off the rear mudguard and release the back brake, but eventually got the freshly-shod wheel back onto the bike. Split tyre in a bin, a thousand pesetas (£4.20) to our saviour and we were on the road again.

The next section was rough, no way could our old tyre have survived. It was also exceedingly hot and hilly. After forty kilometres we called it a day and found an idyllic spot beside the Rio Bembezar and camped wild. We had our own sandy beach with a pool deep enough for bathing. We skinny-dipped then sat, listening to hunters and the hunted scuttling about in the undergrowth and watched as the bats and stars emerged. With no light pollution we were treated to a wondrous night sky.

Avoiding the main roads, we cycled the minor byways which were inevitably much lumpier but led us to a glorious thousand-foot descent into Cordoba.

Never Say "If Only"

We found *el camping municipal* without much bother but the shop was closed, as was the restaurant, while the swimming pool had no water! We were allocated a tiny dirt patch for our tent. Other campers arrived including more cyclists, a Dutch couple and a family from Oregon riding two tandems. Leon and Tina Skiles, with their son Jessie (15) and daughter Michaela (10) were on the first leg of a sixteen-month round the world adventure. We sat, drank and swopped tales all evening. We maintained e-mail contact with them and were pleased to hear that they completed their amazing journey.

During the 10th-century Cordoba was the most populous city in the world and under Islamic rule became a centre for education with medical schools, universities and numerous libraries. The Great Mosque, *Mezquita de Cordoba*, now a catholic cathedral, was an incredible and imposing building featuring 856 columns in the main hall alone. We were overwhelmed by its size and grandeur.

Leaving Cordoba, we made quite good time except for climbing the hills on which every town and village was perched. A big effort was required to reach each of these hilltop *pueblos blancos,* which then demanded a bar stop for a cold beer in order to slake the thirst acquired in getting there!

Earlier on this tour we had passed through orange and lemon groves, cactus causeways, cork oak orchards and even goats up trees. The Cordoba region supported mile upon mile of olive groves. Consequently, every *cerveza* stop included a complimentary plate of olives. As we journeyed on, it became progressively hotter and the steepness of the hills increased until we eventually crawled into Priego de Cordoba. Whilst savouring a compulsory beer and olives, we asked for the whereabouts of the campground.

"No, camping aquí" we were told but that there *was* one at Carcabuey, just seven kilometres down the road. This was not too far and one of the locals insisted on showing us the way. He would lead us there on his motor scooter. He jumped onto his vehicle and set off while we, already exhausted and slightly inebriated, attempted to follow. The "down the road" was inevitably up, but from somewhere we found hidden resources and chased after the scooter as fast as we could.

Our intrepid leader cruised through Carcabuey, onwards and upwards. We thought that we had literally "been taken for a ride," but finally arrived at Los Villares camping site. No one else was there but a small *posada* across the road accepted our booking and had supplies of beer, which our guide insisted on buying. He downed a couple of *fino,* local dry sherry, then jumped onto his scooter and shot off down the seventeen kilometres back to Priego. We were at a lovely campsite, surrounded by mountains, all to ourselves and decided to have a rest day tomorrow. Just as well because the following day was another "hard day at the office," in fact one of the toughest sixty kilometres that we have ridden. It was a chilly start in the shadow of the 1,500 metre high mountains but we enjoyed a panorama of the endless olive groves. By the time we had reached the first of our two 1,000 feet climbs, the sun was high in the sky and had targeted us hapless cyclists struggling up the hill. We sweated up the incredibly hard climb to the hilltop town on Monte Frío averaging only eight kilometres per hour. Rather than continue another fifty kilometres to Granada as planned, we decided to call it a day and took a room next to a bar.

In the morning we found the bike with a rear wheel puncture. While replacing the tyre I punctured the new tube. At least we should have a downhill ride out of Monte Frío; but no, we continued to climb out of this hilltop town which obviously was not! The first ten kilometres took us an hour. We crested the ridge at 1,300 metres and could see the snow-capped peaks of the Sierra Nevada ahead. Then it was downhill all the way to Grenada where we would visit the magnificent Alhambra Palace.

From Grenada we rode into the Sierra Nevada Mountains and camped at Pitres. We used Pitres as a base from where we managed some fine walking in the Alpujurras, a region of mountain villages, deep sheltered valleys and gorges that ran down to the Mediterranean. We also took a long circular route on the tandem to the highest village in Spain, Travelez, at nearly 1,500 metres.

With just a few days remaining we beach-bummed our way back to Malaga along the Costa del Sol, making time to visit the Cuerva del Nerja caves which boast the biggest stalactite yet known. The caverns were so enormous that musical concerts were held there.

Andalucia was a challenging ride and extremely rewarding, often very hot although it was only April.

Also in 1999 we took a ride that was on many British cyclists' bucket list, the 'End-to-End', Land's End to John o' Groats. We went with friends from our bicycle group from Weston-Super-Mare celebrating Gordon's 70th birthday. The 930 miles took us twelve uneventful days, with the first two, in Cornwall and Devon, being the toughest.

A month later in August, Joanne and Richard were married. It was a sweltering hot day with the wedding being held in the leaning church of St Andrew in Burnham. After the ceremony Reverend Mark Bond, with whom I shared an interest in real ales if not in faith, shed his cassock to reveal an attire of sandals, tee shirt and flamboyant Bermuda shorts. "Anyone can be uncomfortable" he explained.

We first met Richard, our new son-in-law, shortly before Joanne went to Plymouth University. "What a shame" we thought as we had taken a shine to Jo's new boyfriend and thought it highly unlikely that the romance could survive four years apart. At the beginning of her first term we took out tearful daughter to her new student flat. Inside we found the ceiling of the front hall festooned with condoms. It was my turn to be tearful as we returned home without her.

However, Richard regularly made the 150-mile round trip and their relationship thrived. After two years he joined her in Plymouth. Richard worked in the engineers' department for Bristol City Council and somehow managed to persuade them to sponsor him for a two-year University course in diving! His argument was that an engineer might be required to investigate something under the water in Bristol Docks.

While Jo and Rich honeymooned on some exotic island we walked across the country, coast-to-coast, from St. Bees Head on the Irish Sea to Robin Hood's Bay on the North Sea. This was 200 miles of fun and blisters that took us ten days to complete. Walking was harder than cycling, especially when you are carrying camping gear. Pubs often offered camping and we crashed out on a few pub lawns. In Keld we stopped at a farm where the enterprising farmer offered a pitch for the tent, a bucket of hot water in lieu of showers and a small increase in the camping fee if a complimentary bottle of wine was required, as he was not licensed to sell alcohol. The following day we met a fascinating gentleman from Kent. Arthur was also hiking the coast to coast, so we spent the day walking together. We were so intrigued by Arthur's stories that we became hopelessly lost. It was an extremely hot day as we puffed and panted up and down hills and gullies and wandered aimlessly around old mine workings. Eventually, after several extra miles, we found our way to Reeth. During a pint and a meal together in the pub Arthur revealed that he was just recovering from a hip replacement, and four years earlier had suffered a heart attack and that he was 74 years-old. Some people just do not know when to quit – good for him!

Unfortunately, earlier in the year, Maggie's dad, aged 89, active until the end, had died after a short illness. We were thankful we were home and able to support mum as much as possible.

CHAPTER 15

Thailand

"It is better to see something once than to hear about it a hundred times."
Russian Proverb

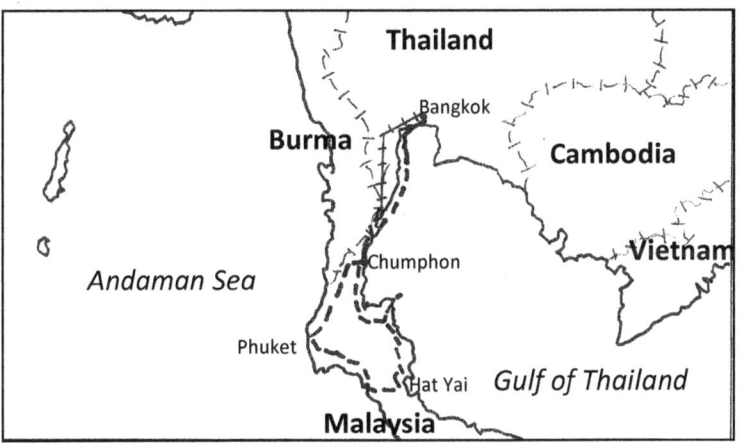

Nov-Dec, 1999. 1,200 miles

South East Asia beckoned, sand sea and sunshine. We flew to Kuala Lumpur in a new Boeing 747 with individual video screens for each passenger. Mine did not work! Although it was still early morning, we were given lunch immediately on departing from London Heathrow. Then the lights were dimmed and we were encouraged to sleep. My seat wouldn't recline but the one belonging to the passenger in front of mine did: excessively! Thus, I spent much of the flight unable to sleep with a stranger's snoring head on my lap and no screen to watch, although the balding pate made an acceptable book-rest.

The new Kuala Lumpur Airport was suave, clean and shiny. There was an automatic monorail between terminals and glass lifts between floors. Everything was cool and air-conditioned, only the tropical plants giving a clue as to the actual location. Having five hours to wait for our connection to Phuket, we thought we might grab a little shut-eye. We went soundly asleep only to be woken, which felt like, just moments later by a pretty Thai Airlines hostess urging us to hurry as they were closing the gate for our onward flight. I had set the alarm on my watch but had not realised that Thai time was one hour behind Malay time.

Heat and humidity hit us as we left the 'plane in Phuket and were surrounded by a large crowd as we put on the pedals, replaced the chains, removed the protective pipe-lagging and pumped up the tyres of the tandem. Several onlookers inquired about our ages; we were fifty-three but obviously looked much older! Our age was a constant fascination for the Thais. Maggie was told that she should be home looking after her grandchildren!

We pedalled out of the airport and shortly arrived at a T-junction. The road signs were in Thai script, which was one of the most elaborate alphabets in the world using eighty symbols. We did not know which way to go: "eenie meenie…," we went to mo! This was a good choice, for we found accommodation near a beautiful beach for only 700 bahts, just £12. Complete with fan, shower, towels, soap and a double bed this turned out to be one of our more expensive stops. We took a plunge into the surf before a dinner of chicken and stir-fry vegetables in oyster sauce for me, with sweet and sour vegetables and chicken-fried rice for Maggie; plus, cold beers. Already we were in love with Thailand!

Our odyssey of pristine beaches, delicious food, friendly people, hot weather and cold beers continued. We paused to watch a game of takraw taking place on a beach. Takraw was a cross between volleyball and head-tennis. The players only used their feet and heads, they were very talented playing three-touch and setting up for a scissor-kick spike. Regrettably, this type of beach volleyball only had blokes playing, no bikinis.

Primarily we found accommodation on or near a beach usually in bungalows, which were little more than huts constructed of bamboo with tin roofs or banana- leafed thatch, often on stilts, and some sported balconies and hammocks. At one beach-side bungalow there were frogs in the privie and an enormous spider on the ceiling over the bed. The spider was so large that we needed a waste paper basket to catch it. It was even too big for the resident gecko to challenge. The sea, at this particular spot of heaven, came alight with fluorescence as we swam at dawn or dusk, caused, I think, by algae or plankton, with a firework-like display radiating out from our arms and legs as we swam. It was really magical! As a sad postscript, I must report that we believe that the tsunami of 26 December 2004 destroyed this idyllic setting and we can only hope that the charming family who provided for us so excellently, survived.

Each morning we encountered the Thai version of the school run. Typically mums with three or four youngsters always immaculately dressed astride a small moped. Mopeds and small motor-cycles were the main mode of transport but pick-up trucks were becoming more common. Tuk-tuks, three-wheeled rickshaws, were everywhere, either motorised or pedal-powered. They were an essential form of cheap transport. Another vehicle which was ubiquitous was the songthaew, a small truck with sideways facing seats for passengers. One day, as we passed a school at 8am, the national anthem was played and everything came to a halt. The children in the playground stood to attention and we felt obliged to stop and do likewise.

We followed the Andaman Sea to Ranong and looked over to Myanmar, formerly Burma. We then crossed the Isthmus of Kra to Chumphon through rubber and banana plantations, palms, jungle and the occasional rice paddy, occasionally negotiating a road covered with drying coffee beans. Often, we were forced to find shelter from sudden downpours, when, within minutes, the roads turned to rivers. But it was never long before the sun was shining again, the roads steaming and we were able to continue in sauna-like humidity.

From Chumphon we took a train to Bangkok, leaving the bike behind. Two tickets for Bangkok cost only 180 bahts (£3) for the 400-mile trip. We loved Bangkok, organised chaos, frenetic but fun. Vibrant, all-inclusive markets, a long-tailed boat river cruise, Grand Palace, Wat Phra Kaew, Lumphini Stadium for Thai kick boxing, tuk-tuk rides in manic traffic as adrenaline-pumping as a bungee-jump, the Golden Buddha sixteen feet tall and fifty tons of solid gold. We saw the Bangkok Marathon which was dominated by Kenyans as are marathons world-wide. We missed the red-light district of Patpong, perhaps next time?

Thai script has something like eighty-five letters and thirty vowels; words can have up to five inflections, changes of tone, to denote completely different things. Off the beaten track with little English being spoken, we found it difficult to comprehend but became very proficient at sign-language which, when accompanied by a smile, always seemed to be understood.

The island of Ko Pha-Ngan offered us sea, sand, sun, super snorkelling and all-night beach parties; but being twice the average age, Maggie and I tended to give the parties a miss. Back on the mainland we cycled around the Thai peninsular before island-hopping along the Indian Ocean back to Phuket and home.

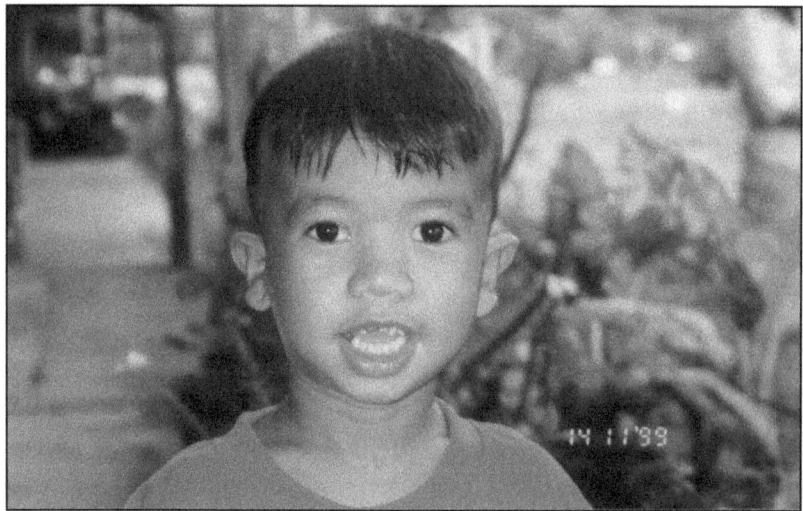

Yung Thai

CHAPTER 16

The Teacher

"Nobody sets the rules but you. You can design you own life."
Carrie-Ann Moss

<u>1965-1974</u>

I attended Keswick Hall College of Education in Norwich, specialising in physical education. During my first year I went out with a third-year student called Franki. When she left to start teaching, our romance continued but in a fragmented manner as we did not see that much of each other. At the Christmas ball one of her friends informed her that, in her absence, I had not always been sleeping on my own: dumped again! Still, life was good, I was captain of the College football team, boxed at the Norwich Lads Club and was generally having a pretty cool time. Also, I had found myself another steady girlfriend, Sue.

All too soon it was time to look for a proper job, something I had avoided since I was fifteen. My flatmate Dave and I applied for teaching jobs in Bedfordshire; as it was roughly halfway between his girlfriend, who lived in Northampton, and my girl Sue in Barnet. This seemed like a good idea; but Sue, after her year of journeys to and from Norwich and who was now expected to make regular excursions to Bedford, decided that a beau nearer to home would be preferable; I was dumped yet again!

During my transition from student to teacher, I was asked by a boxing promoter if I would like to become a professional fighter. I thought long and hard about it but decided that I had a profession as a teacher and, to be quite honest, I do not think that I would have been good enough. I would have been no more than a journeyman, fodder for potential contenders.

My first two years as a physical education teacher were spent at Robert Bloomfield Secondary Modern School in Shefford. There, in addition to my teaching role I had to be the groundsman and mark out the pitches and running track. We had no gymnasium but used the school hall for indoor lessons. This meant truncated classes before lunch as the hall had to be prepared for dinner. One day I caught a lad from class 4C in the showers having a wank in front of his friends. He grinned and gave me a challenging look that said, "What are you going to do about it?" I decided that my next lesson with 4C would be boxing. I volunteered the 'wanker' as my sparring partner. He was a big lad and full of bravado but two or three rounds later, while not being humiliated, he had learned who was the 'boss'. The gamble paid off and from that day I received no more insolence, back chat or bad behaviour.

My flatmates in Bedford all played rugby and it was not long before I was persuaded to switch allegiance to the oval ball. I soon grew to love the game and was especially fond of the post-match experience. Not so much for the shared bath, playing for Bedford Queens Extra Thirds my team were usually last for the communal soak, meaning that at least thirty sweaty, muddy bodies had already used the tub. I progressed to the 2nd XV and played scrum half but at 5' 7" tall and just 10 ½ stones, I was never likely to make an impact. I buzzed around the rucks and mauls like a wasp at a picnic, an irritant but unlikely to spoil the party.

I moved to Robert Bruce School in Kempston. It had better facilities and a groundsman. The River Ouse ran by the school field and was ideal for canoeing. On Saturday, 21 June 1969, I attended a canoeing course for potential instructors. An attractive young lady, with short, curly hair, was also there. During a capsize drill this pretty girl emerged from the depths in a wet tee-shirt; wow, she was not just pretty, she was beautiful! It was love at first sight. Margaret Marsden taught at a primary school in Dunstable. I saw her as often as possible in the few weeks before she went to Austria on a pre-arranged holiday.

While we were apart I went camping in Wales with my flatmate and teaching colleague Dai Morgan. At Rhossili Bay in the Gower I went for a swim and struck out alongside the Worms Head Peninsular. After about fifteen minutes I stopped and realised that I was much further out than expected. I was over a mile out at sea, almost at the end of the headland. "Wow, I am swimming well" I thought to myself and started swimming back to the shore. After a few minutes, I realised that I was not making much progress, in fact I might actually have been going further out to sea. I felt a surge of panic and swam as if my life depended on it: it did! In what felt like an age later and with my

Never Say "If Only"

energy almost depleted, I managed to reach the surf line, was swept in by a large wave and deposited unceremoniously onto the beach in an exhausted, gasping heap. Dai wandered over to my prostrate form, looked down and asked, "Have a nice swim boyo?"

The longest weeks of my life crawled by before I saw Maggie again. I could not live without her and just six weeks after our first meeting, I proposed. A year later we were married. Three years on, with a two-month-old baby girl, Joanne, we moved to Knaresborough in Yorkshire. I had enrolled on a degree course at Leeds University. As we knew that we would only be in Yorkshire for a year, we spent every available moment exploring the area. Most weekends would find us somewhere in the Dales with Joanne in a papoose on my back. For some obscure reason, we were particularly fascinated by a forty-mile hike across the North York Moors, the Lyke Wake Walk, which should be completed in less than twenty-four hours. It seemed a good idea at the time. I contacted my old canoeing pal from Bedford, Keith 'Bluey' Topham. He could only get time off at Christmas, so, on one of the shortest days of the year, we set off for Scarf Moor near Osmotherly, leaving Maggie literally holding the baby. Not only was it dark for most of the walk, it was also very wet and extremely foggy. The trail, if there was one, was glutinously muddy and under water. We were forced to battle through thigh-high heather, bracken and gorse. By half-way, I was already in considerable discomfort with a nagging ache in my groin. The pain increased as we walked and by the time we reached Ravenscar on the east coast, twenty-three hours after we started, I was hobbling along like a hundred-year-old arthritic cripple, which was exactly how I felt.

Bluey drove us home, we tried singing rugby songs in an attempt to stay awake but I was so, so tired, zzzzzzz. Suddenly: biff, blam, bing, bam, bang! My eyes shot open as yellow missiles hurled themselves at the car, bouncing off the bonnet and windscreen and ricocheting left, right and over. We were like a ball in a skittles alley. Bluey, now also wide awake, steered away from the roadworks and back onto the highway. "A strike, Bluey," I yelled, "There's not a traffic cone left standing!"

Following our year in Yorkshire I decided on a career change, from teaching to coaching. I began working at Lodge Park Leisure Centre in Corby in Northamptonshire. After another two years we were on the move again, this time with our second daughter, Juliette. I was to be the manager of the King

Alfred Sports Centre in Burnham-on-Sea in Somerset. It was a career move, to work my way up the leisure industry ladder. That was 1977and today we are still in Burnham. I applied for a couple of jobs but tears from Joanne and a long list of the friends and things she would miss if we moved from Somerset, persuaded me that there was more to life than money or power. Instead, we committed ourselves to Burnham-on-Sea and the Sports Centre. I use the royal we, because Maggie helped and supported in a way that was far above and beyond the call of duty. In addition to the normal sports centre activities, we organised many regional and national events and won the National Sports Council Award for Sports Centre Management; this all helped when it came to requiring favours; like early retirement!

1970   1990

CHAPTER 17

Bolivia and Peru

"Travelling broadens the mind but opens the bowels."
Anon

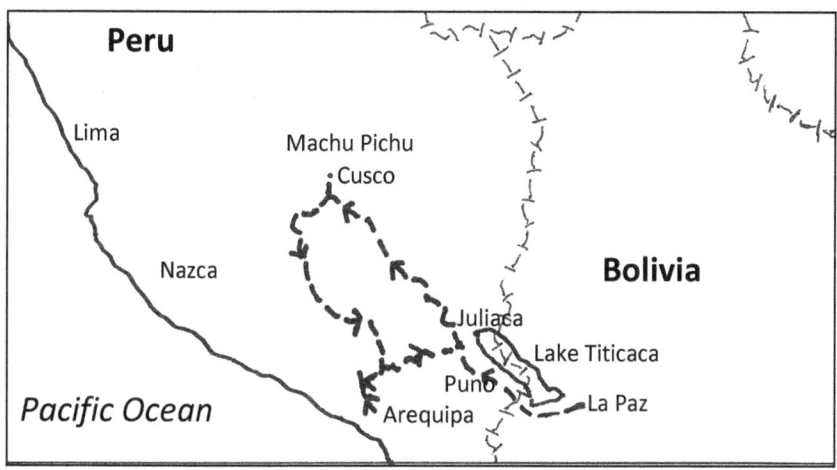

April- May 2000. Bikeless

Mike Truman, a friend of ours, had spent much time hitch-hiking in South America. On his recommendation we thought that a trip into the Andes could be fun. We decided it might be prudent to leave the tandem behind and instead travel by local transport. We started to learn Spanish before flying into the highest international Airport in the world at *El Alto,* situated above the Bolivian capital of La Paz, where we secured basic accommodation.

Suffering from jet lag and altitude sickness, our woes were aggravated on our first venture into the city streets of La Paz by the loss of our camera to a pickpocket. This was compounded by our poor command of the Spanish language and utter turmoil caused by protesting *campesinos*. These country peasants were campaigning against the government who had put a new tax on water and were controlling newspapers, or so we thought. Armed police and soldiers patrolled the streets and blockades had halted all traffic into and out of the city. It looked as if our tour of Bolivia might progress no further than La Paz itself! We found a taxi driver willing to attempt to run the blockade for $100. We haggled him down to $70 but he would take no less, so we declined his offer.

In retrospect, it probably was not an excessive price considering the risks he would be taking because lives had already been lost in the dispute. Instead and being ever positive, we walked to a *salida de autobuses*. At this bus stop we were told that we might find a bus still leaving the city. However, everyone we asked gave different and conflicting directions and suggestions. While patiently and fruitlessly waiting, I was struck on the shoulder by a rock! I turned, seeking out the culprit, when a man ran up to us shouting and pointing. I then realised that one of our bags was missing; obviously stolen while our attention was momentarily diverted. We lost our new fleece jackets and camera, a radio, binoculars, sunglasses, torch, compass, maps and guide books. Feeling really pissed-off we returned to the *Hostál Sacre* and reclaimed the room we had earlier vacated.

A city bus took us across town, threading through a multitude of police and protesters to the office of the tourist police where, for insurance purposes, we were able to report our loss. We were seated on one side of an old wooden desk across from a gum-chewing Hollywood stereotype of a South American cop, complete with baseball cap and sunglasses. He listened to our tale of woe then, taking his cowboy-booted feet off the desk, commenced to one-finger tap his report on an ancient type-writer, complete with carbon paper. He needed copies of our passports so we were sent to find a photocopier. Eventually, with most of the day long-gone, we emerged from the *Policía Turistico* with our insurance claim document.

Perhaps it was just as well that we had failed in our attempt to leave La Paz, for Maggie was sick during the night and was in no condition to travel. Unable to go far from the toilet we spent most of the next day in our room with Maggie in bed sleeping fitfully. Meanwhile we heard that downtown a policeman had been shot dead.

Never Say "If Only"

Two days later and determined to make good our escape from the beggars, thieves, police, military and protesters that, in our eyes, constituted La Paz, we went to the almost redundant main city bus station and took the only bus leaving the city destined for Perú. Five more people were killed overnight but luckily our bus, full of young backpackers, was allowed through the cordon and with a sigh of relief we left La Paz. The coach climbed out of the city basin to the shanty town of El Alto, then continued along the Alto Plano with a backdrop of the snow-capped Andean Cordillera Real. This extensive region of high plateau averaged an altitude of 3,750 metres; it was sparsely populated with llamas and the occasional mud-bricked, thatched dwellings, home to a hardy race who somehow eked out an existence on this barren, remote land. Our bus drove alongside the sparkling blue waters of Lake Titicaca and passed the docks containing the entire Bolivian Navy. Bolivia had been landlocked since it lost the War of the Pacific but had maintained a naval force of some 5,000 personnel to patrol lakes and rivers to prevent smuggling and drug trafficking. It also had hopes that one day it may be able to reclaim the coastline ceded to Chile in 1879. We continued into Perú and disembarked in Puno, from where we took a tour of Lake Titicaca's floating reed Uros Islands. On our return to Puno, we were again faced with soldiers in riot gear. This time they were trying to contain demonstrators complaining about the previous Sunday's (rigged?) general election result.

Onwards we rolled by tourist bus through Juliaca, over a mountain pass of 4,335 metres down to a beautiful valley of grazing alpacas and an abundance of small, cultivated terraced fields. Depending on the altitude, the main crops were coca leaves, maize and potatoes. Over two thousand species of potatoes are grown in the Andes. Markets were dominated by women wearing bowler hats, a remnant from the 1920s when the British railway workers brought them to the region. The hats were edged with different colours to indicate the area they represented. We passed through small villages known as *pueblos*. The adobe buildings, many of which were derelict, were daubed with electoral graffiti. The streets were unpaved, the *campesinos* over-dressed and unwashed: especially the children.

In Cusco we found a room and booked to go on the Inca Trail to Machu Picchu. The Plaza de Armas at the city centre was spectacular, as was the huge floodlit cathedral. Many churches were built by the early Spanish colonists, often on the foundations of ancient Inca buildings. Cusco was voted the 'Best City' by readers of the travel magazine Wanderlust but it had more than its fair share of pickpockets and streetwise kids.

A guided tour took us to the Sacred Inca Valley of Pisac to Urubamba and Ollantaytambo where the finest examples of Inca stone-laying were found. In colonial times a protective wall had been built across the whole valley. Within the village huge terraces led up to a religious temple. The stonework was remarkable! Massive blocks of granite had been extracted then transported across the valley, cut, then fitted together like an enormous jigsaw; no easy feat with blocks weighing up to sixty tons. This was in the 15th-century when the Incas had not invented the wheel, nor had beasts of burden. Instead they relied on the muscle power of hundreds, probably thousands, of men and women, using only logs to transport the mighty rocks.

Our Inca Trail group consisted of eighteen men and women from ten different countries, all at least a generation younger than Maggie and I. Our guide, Raphael, a small, stocky Quechuan, was unable to hide his disappointment when he realised that us two geriatrics, standing self-consciously to one side, were part of his team. However, we were received with much more enthusiasm by several local youngsters selling home-made walking sticks. They clambered around us convinced that they were certain to make a sale while completely ignoring the younger members of our group. Regrettably, this was not a lucky day for the young entrepreneurs, we all strode off stick-less.

The four-day Inca Trail to Machu Picchu was rated by many to be one of the top five treks in the world. It had beautiful mountain scenery, lush cloud-forest and Alpine tundra, much of it following the ancient paved Inca trail. Settlements, tunnels and Inca ruins were located along the trail which terminated at the Gateway to the Sun and the famous iconic view of Machu Picchu. The Incas built Machu Picchu around 1450 but abandoned it about a century later at the time of the Spanish Conquest. It then remained unknown to the outside world until an American historian, Hiram Bingham, discovered it in 1911. It is now a UNESCO Heritage Site and in 2007 was voted one of the New Seven Wonders of the World. Built with polished dry-stone walls, it

Never Say "If Only"

was perched on a high mountain spur with astounding drops on three sides: it was simply incredible!

Also wonderful were the porters. Each day, after providing a breakfast of quinoa porridge and coffee, they would wash and clear up, dismantle the camp and stow all the gear into massive backpacks. Shod only in sandals, they would then catch us up, storm past and have the camp ready for our arrival at the end of the day's trek. Although we were no match for the Quechuan porters, Maggie and I set the pace for our group and were not the liability that Raphael had feared. In fact, at the end of the Trail he approached my wife and said "Maggie, you very strong woman!" Praise indeed.

Maggie at the Gateway of the Sun, Machu Pichu

After a tour of the Machu Picchu site, we descended to the small town of Aguas Calientas, and went for a dip in the hot springs that inspired the *pueblo's* name, 'hot waters'. Aguas Calientas is situated in a deep gorge and cut off from all vehicular roads. The valley is enclosed by steep mountains and contains the turbulent Rio Urubamba, the only access to *Machu Picchu Pueblo,* as the town is also called, is by rail, *la Ferrocarril Santa Ana,* The railway line has become the 'Main Street', with shops, stalls and cafes on either side of the line.

We purchased tickets for Cusco and boarded the train, sharing wooden seats with itinerant locals high on *chicha*, the local maize-based brew. The train left on time at 5:45pm but after a few minutes of unhealthy-sounding crunches, bangs and clanks, it ground to a halt. The engine was uncoupled and departed, leaving the carriages behind. Surely, we were not being abandoned? But we received no information to the contrary, in fact, we received no information at all! One of the Peruvian passengers tried to lift our spirits by playing his panpipes and some others half-heartedly sang along. It was getting darker by the minute, and with no lights in the carriage it was difficult to keep an eye on our belongings. After two hours the train engine returned and we set off again, rattling and clanking alongside the raging torrent of the *Ríos* Urumbamba and *Willkamayu,* scarily illuminated by a full-moon. The carriages were not connected to each other for access between them, the ticket collector had to climb out of one compartment and swing across the void to reach the next. An ugly scene ensued in our carriage on the unexpected arrival of the gallant ticket agent as he unearthed several ticketless passengers before receiving their levies.

An hour or so later, with two more mechanical grindings enough to put our teeth on edge, we screeched to what sounded like a terminal halt. The lights were again extinguished, leaving only the light of the moon shining through dirty windows. Rumours spread along the coaches that another train was being dispatched to tow us in; another report was that relief buses were being sent, but no-one really knew what was going on. It was dark and becoming even colder.

Meanwhile, resourceful local *campesinos,* hearing of our plight, had driven a cattle-truck on a dirt trail alongside the railway line to where we were stranded and were offering a lift to Cusco for seven *soles* (£1.50). Together with two dozen or so 'escapees' we climbed aboard and set off over the mountains to Cusco. It was freezing in the open truck! We were buffeted by an icy wind and all huddled together trying, unsuccessfully, to keep warm. We felt like refugees fleeing a war zone. Much later, in the early hours of the morning, we arrived at the outskirts of Cusco. Our driver did not, with his illicit cargo, dare to drive into the city. With frozen limbs we awkwardly disembarked and piled into taxis miraculously waiting our arrival. Seven of us squeezed into one taxi which took us to our *hostál*. In our room, Maggie and I shared a single bed fully clothed as we were so cold! However, we were probably not as cold as those that chose to stay on the train, for they were not rescued until the following day when buses were arranged.

Arequipa was our next destination but first Cusco bus station tested our resolve. We had to run the gauntlet of pickpockets, beggars and touts camped outside the terminal, get our bags labelled and find the right bus, all in a confined space where the bus drivers left their engines running, creating obnoxious and sickening fumes. However, our *hostál* host had negotiated a very reasonable price on a tourist coach on our behalf: tourist coach be buggered! The bus for which we had been given tickets was an old, bald-tired, rattle rust- bucket crammed full with *campesinos* and a menagerie of livestock. Many of the women on board wore the national costume of brightly-coloured dresses worn over multi-layered petticoats. We were the only *gringos* on board! At least we had seats, many did not. It was a twelve-hour overnight journey, perhaps we might at least get some sleep.

Just after the town of Juliaca, with another seven hours to go, I could no longer ignore an increasingly urgent bowel problem! I struggled in the dark to reach the front of the bus, stepping over and on many of the bodies sitting and sleeping in the aisle. The driver was locked in his driving compartment and I had to rap repeatedly and with increasing urgency on the window to attract his attention and attempt to convey my predicament with sign language. He eventually got the message and pulled over to the side of the road. I rushed out and relieved myself with not a second to spare! A journey I would like to forget.

Volcanoes dominated the Arequipa skyline and the city had a history of earthquakes, such as the one with a magnitude 8.4 on the Richter Scale in June 2001 that caused much damage. The Central Plaza and Cathedrals are a UNESCO World Heritage Site and quite outstanding, albeit with an ever-pervading aroma of urine. The area was thronged with, it seemed, all of the city's million inhabitants celebrating *Semana Santa* (Easter). Processions paraded through a tunnel of vendors and stalls offering a paraphernalia of religious goodies, candles, incense, crucifixes, statues of a pained JC.

A five-hour, one hundred-mile journey by mini-bus on a rough, dirt, sand, gravel and pot-holed road took us up to the crater of an extinct volcano. We then climbed even higher through wild, dry and desolate landscape inhabited by llama and alpaca to a pass at 4,800 metres. We saw the endangered vicuna (a type of llama) and a zorro (fox) in driving snow on the way down to a fertile valley and the town of Chivay. There were no passable roads between Arequipa and Chivay until the 1940s, when roads were built to serve the region's silver and copper mines. Chivay was the gateway to our destination, the Colca Canyon.

Maggie had descended and ascended the Grand Canyon in the USA as a student and not wanting to be outdone, I suggested that a walk into the Colca Canyon which, at 10,725 feet was twice as deep, would be a good idea. Well, it seemed a good idea at the time, but as we stood on the edge of the abyss, rucksacks laden with camping gear, and were unable to even see the valley floor deep below us, our enthusiasm waned somewhat. Soaring in the Canyon were several Andean Condors, huge, majestic birds but vultures nevertheless. Apparently they frequently fly to the coast where they feast on dead seals. Let's hope our little venture doesn't save them a trip to the sea-side.

Down, down, down we scrambled, sliding and stumbling on the almost vertical canyon wall, zigzagging on a dusty and rocky path to the *Río Colca* where we found a flat, green area suitable for camping. Figs, avocados, almonds and even palm trees grew here in the aptly named Oasis. The next morning, we trekked up the far side of the Canyon to *pueblos* inhabited by traditionally dressed Andean peasants who still cultivated the pre-Inca stepped terraces to produce an abundance of fruit, including oranges. The climate was so different from that at the top of the Canyon some 1,000 metres higher. The evenings were mild and it was really hot during the day. Snakes, lizards, butterflies, dragonflies and giant hummingbirds were common. However, many of the adobe buildings had been abandoned, although the *campesinos* that had not fled to the cities appeared to be happy and contented. Notwithstanding, life must be a struggle with no electricity, plumbing or vehicular access. Only steep, stony footpaths linked the villages with the outside world. Being so hilly the wheel was redundant, donkeys were the main mode of transport.

An invitation into someone's backyard yielded a coke; it is amazing that however remote an area one can always find Coca-Cola. We were given directions to our destination for the night, San Juan Chucco.

"Solamente trienta minutos," only thirty minutes we were told but over an hour later we were still wandering around hopelessly lost. We turned back, wondering if we had missed a path. Night was drawing-in; it was too late to

retrace our footsteps to the Oasis. We reached a ramshackle building that showed signs of habitation and several loud *"holas"* brought forth a wizened crone, 80 or 90 years old with just one upper front tooth.

"Cómo se va a San Juan Chucco, por favour?" we enquired. Which way to San Juan Chucco, was greeted with much cackling and gesticulations pointing back the way we had come but then off to the left. We had passed a side junction presuming it was just a water gully. This took us to a deep gulch containing a fast-flowing tributary of the *Río Colca*. We explored but there seemed no way down into this mini-canyon, or up the other side. Another ancient lady working her land pointed into the gulch and sure enough, we discovered a tiny disused path leading down to the river. We crossed the river with our loaded rucksacks which was no easy matter but we made it with skinned shins and wet feet. We then found a trail that required the use of all fours to ascend.

By this time it was getting dark, so we scouted around and found a flat patch on which to pitch our tent. Nearby was a house inhabited by a young girl and even younger brother. We tried to explain that we wanted to camp nearby and went to set up our tent. There was not much twilight in the tropics and by the time I had returned to our flattish patch it was already dark. Three men and a donkey materialised out of the gloom. *"Permitimos acampar aqui?"* This request solicited this positive reply: *"Si, si, no problema"*. So, with running water from the nearby stream and toilets being a rocky corner of our field, we cooked pasta and chilli under a starlit sky.

The next morning heralded another beautiful day. We breakfasted then went to the nearby house to give our friendly landlord ten *soles* This was only £2 to us but a small fortune to him. We found our way, at last, to San Juan Chucco. There we bought three litres of water to add to our litre of treated stream water in preparation for the long, hot climb out. It was hot, it was hard. Nearly 1,200 metres straight up. Looking at the Canyon wall from the valley floor there seemed to be no way we could reach the top. But a dusty, rocky trail etched its way, switch-backing, up the arduous climb. 3,900 ft. higher, 5 hours later and 4 litres of water lighter we reached the top and, as if rewarding our effort, were treated to a flypast of condors.

Colca Canyon

From Cabanaconde a local bus, *una colectivo,* took us along the edge of the Canyon back to Chivay. The bus was packed; ladies in national costume sat crunched forward because of huge blanketed bundles on their backs. *Los hombres* were more sombrely dressed than the women, most sporting baseball or cowboy hats. The bus shook, rattled and rolled along the edge of the canyon with deep, vertical drops into the abyss. We did not dare to think of how many buses may not to have made it round the hairpins. At one such bend, our driver had to make a three-point turn to get round the tight corner. A hush descended on the passengers as the driver reversed towards the edge. Maggie and I were seated near the back, and I swear that at one point we had nothing but a thousand foot drop below us. In my mind's eye I visualised the bottom of the Canyon full of the rusting carcasses of buses that had previously attempted our current manoeuvre. When the driver eventually crunched into a forward gear and we inched away from the Canyon edge, there was a collective sigh of relief and spontaneous applause.

Cactus lined the route as we climbed towards snow-clad peaks. Cactus and snow do not seem compatible. We ground on through one *adobe pueblo* after another; all the buildings were tin-roofed or thatched; the thatch more often than not, yielded growth, including water melons. Many of the houses had fallen into disrepair. One of the villages, Maca, suffered an earthquake in 1991 and many of the survivors still lived in the tents provided at the time, although a bunch of small prefabricated dwellings appeared to be nearing completion. We drove through a tunnel so filled with dust that it was impossible for our headlights to penetrate more than a few yards. At Achoma, we picked up more people and packages. Like sardines we were squeezed into the bus. I estimated that there must have been as many people crammed into the aisle as the forty-five seated. It took three and a half hours to rattle along the thirty-five miles from Cabanaconde. Then we had a two and a half hour wait in Chivay for our connection to Arequipa. The market in Chivay was interesting with vendors spreading out their wares in the street and just squatting down to wait patiently for a sale. Two *hombres* dressed in native Indian gear were selling liniment that would, they claimed, cure all ailments and even put Viagra into the shade, which they were demonstrating with two mating iguanas! Another stall had a tank crammed full of frogs.

The hundred miles to Arequipa took over four hours with no stops. From Chivay we climbed to an altitude of 4,800 metres to the edge of an extinct volcano. The countryside was dry, barren and boring. The only escape from the lunar landscape monotony were small herds of vicuna, the snow-capped volcanoes and politically-inspired graffiti daubed, somewhat professionally, on every suitable wall, fence, rock and building. We had even seen left-wing slogans painted in the Colca Canyon – miles from anywhere.

The next day we booked a bus to Puno for only twenty-six soles (five pounds sterling) for a twelve-hour journey, 6pm to 6am. Once more we had to face the fume-filled, chaotic environment of a major bus station. It was a more acceptable coach this time but still packed with livestock, furniture, food, boxes, crates and people. We departed more or less on time but had a breakdown in the early hours which took about an hour to fix. The 200-mile journey took fourteen hours.

An army of touts greeted us in Puno, offering buses, tours, hotels, postcards, shoe-shines. An English speaker persuaded us that the only bus going straight to and through, the Peruvian border with Bolivia was leaving *now!* So, it was off one bus onto another, although the driver was kind enough to stop outside a hotel to allow Maggie a pit-stop. Two miles further on, there was another breakdown that required application of a sledge-hammer on the front wheel.

Finally, after twenty non-stop hours on a bus, we arrived in Copacabana on the shore of Lake Titicaca and found a hotel with a double bed: bliss at last!

We took a ferry to *Isla del Sol* then hiked and became hopelessly disoriented before finding an ideal spot for wild camping with fantastic views of the snow-covered Andes and Lake Titicaca, the highest navigable lake in the world at 3,820 metres. I helped an old *campesino* load his donkey with sacks of *papas* and asked if we could camp here. "Si, si no problema" he answered and offered us some of his potatoes.

Back in Copacabana on 3 May, *La Fiesta de Santa Cruz del Tercero de Mayo* was in full swing. There were dozens of bands, mostly featuring brass instruments with big drums and cymbals. The bands had different uniforms ranging from brown suits, gangster-type black coats, hats and sunglasses to more ethnic costumes; each band was followed by elaborately dressed dancers. There were women in national dress, others in very short skirts and knee-high boots, plus those wearing outlandish outfits and masks. The parade marched past the basilica where raised seating had been provided for the dignitaries. Each troupe took a long while to dance past as the choreography appeared to consist simply of repetitive steps: two steps forward then one to the left, one to the right, followed by one and a half steps backwards! Each group continued on through the streets of the city.

Much later as we retired to bed, the bands were still playing. By 'playing' I meant repetitive use of the same few bars, over and over again dominated by the drums and cymbals: music it was not, loud it definitely was. We settled down about 11 pm thinking that by midnight they would have run out of puff. No chance, they played *all* night and were still going strong when we sleepily emerged in the morning. Some looked a bit fragile and most had been on the booze, but when they started doing a march-past in the plaza again we quickly decided that it was time for us to find somewhere quieter. We went for a walk by the water's edge and took a swim in the two-and-a-half-mile high lake. Back in Copacabana weariness and drink had taken its toll and just a few of the bands were still making token efforts.

The following day, 4 May, there was a wedding and a few bands revived themselves enough to lead the happy couple through the town accompanied by firecrackers. We regarded this as an apt send-off for ourselves and fled back to La Paz and our flight home but not before having a farewell meal in a Copacabana restaurant where we had previously enjoyed trout caught locally in the lake. For some obscure reason I decided to have a meat dish instead of the tried and tested *trucha*.

An El Alto Niña

La Paz airport was situated near the depressing shanty town of El Alto: a metropolis of a million people, many of whom had fled from poverty in the countryside to a ghetto of low-rise, unfinished, adobe buildings: a huge landfill site of humanity. Before catching our plane, we shared the night in the darkened departure lounge with security guards and cleaners. Luckily the toilets were nearby as last night's meat dish was proving to be less fresh than the trout. The flight home via Santa Cruz and Miami proved to be a test of endurance that was spent equally between sleeping and visiting the lavatory. Back home in Burnham, I slept for another fifteen hours and found that I had lost twenty pounds in weight!

Reflecting on this trip, we agreed that although we had a fantastic time we missed the freedom and tranquillity of having the tandem. We had missed stopping in all the remote villages and decided that buses and towns were not for us. Next time it would be back on the bike.

CHAPTER 18

Costa Rica

"Travel is the only thing you can buy that makes you richer."
Anon

November-December, 2000. 935 miles

"Brace! Brace!" I yelled, as a wall of water towered above us like a hungry mouth about to consume a tasty morsel. Our two-man kayak was sideways on to the massive wave and seconds short of being engulfed and sent tumbling in the surf. Our only chance was to lean with our paddles into the oncoming wave. I raised my paddle above my head as the mini-tsunami hit with unbelievable power. I felt a burning pain in my shoulder as if a red-hot poker had been applied. The edge of the cockpit slammed into my ribs as we were swept unceremoniously onto the beach. At least we had not capsized. Maggie was angry, "I told you that we couldn't surf this thing, you idiot! You were just showing off!" She was right, the two-person sea kayak that we had hired handled very differently to the light slalom canoes I used to paddle. It was my fault but I was hurting. I could not take deep breaths and my right shoulder was at an odd angle. I walked back into the surf thinking that the cool water might lessen the pain. As a wave tumbled in, I automatically lifted my arms above the crest and was rewarded with a "clunk" and an excruciating jab of agony. However, my shoulder bone no longer protruded the way it had I think I may have accidentally popped it back into place.

We were in the third week of our traverse of Costa Rica. The first week had been spent in the small town of Orosi where we took a Spanish language course; after which we had crossed the country, 'against the grain', so as to speak, across a country under which tectonic plates are battling each other for supremacy creating active volcanoes and earthquakes. In 1991 an earthquake claimed 48 lives, destroyed roads and bridges, houses and hotels. The landslips and deep crevices we passed were evidence of the disaster, known as the 'Limon Earthquake' because the epicentre was near to Puerto Limon where we were heading.

It had been a hard ride to the Caribbean coast, very hilly and steamingly hot between daily downpours. We passed through plantations of sugar cane, coffee and bananas. As we headed east we noticed a change in the common ethnicity as well as the increasing humidity. In the west the people were mainly of Hispanic origin, while further east Afro-Caribbeans prevailed. In Puerto Limon, after riding alongside miles of banana groves we stopped for breakfast, Maggie asked for a banana to go with her tortillas. "Hey baby, we ain't got no bananas!" replied the giant West Indian waiter. We continued on, past endless fields of bananas.

We had no bananas but did witness an astonishing abundance of wild life, it was like cycling through an open-air zoo. We saw hummingbirds, iguanas, lizards, white-nosed coatis, macaws, sloths, tapirs, toucans and butterflies the size of dinner plates. Each morning, at first light, we were woken by the raucous cries of howler monkeys In the jungle by the Caribbean coast we found it difficult to find a patch on which to set up the tent which wasn't an 'ant freeway'; everywhere we looked there was a Spaghetti Junction of leaf-cutter ants. The jaws of these tiny creatures vibrate 1,000 times a second to cut off leaves. They then have to carry the leaves, which may weigh up to twenty times their body weight, to their nest to be composted into an edible fungus to feed their larvae.

After a few days on the east coast we set off back to the west but broke up the journey with a tough 20 km dirt road climb to the rim of the active *Volcan Rincon* that emitted sulphurous steam like a giant kettle on the boil. We also swam in mountain pools, went white-water rafting, took alfresco showers under waterfalls, visited bubbling mud pools and steaming ponds, and saw dart frogs, tiny but deadly!

At one point a friendly black mongrel approached us as we were taking a roadside break. We made a fuss of him then got back on the bike and rode off. The dog followed. We stopped and encouraged him to go home, wherever that was? But still he followed. We rode as hard as we could but still he followed. We would gain some ground on the descents but as soon as the next hill came along there was *'Sigo'* panting along beside us. We called him *Sigo* because it means 'I follow' in Spanish. We met a man feeding melons to white-nosed coatis, also known as *pizotes*, racoon-like creatures, and asked him to keep hold of *Sigo* while we made good our escape. All to no avail, for minutes later there he was running beside us again. Eventually, miles later, exhaustion got to the poor mutt and he began to drop behind, and after one long descent we saw him no more. We felt terribly guilty.

By this time we had posted our tent back to Orosi, camping wasn't easy with so many creepy crawly, biting and stinging creatures about, and there appeared to be plenty of available accommodation. Not all were first class I might add, for in one cabin I received 112 volts in my elbow and was thrown naked from the shower cubicle after touching an exposed live wire. This was the day we had abandoned *Sigo*, perhaps it was divine doggy justice!

As we pushed west the climate changed subtlety, from humid and hot to warm but dryer air. The plantations transmuted into cattle country and palm oil *fincas*, small farms. At San Miguel, our poor command of the Spanish language led to an embarrassing moment for Maggie. Outside a bank, where I was changing some traveller's cheques stood a guard toting a pump-action shotgun. Maggie, ever friendly, tried to engage him in conversation with a smile and, *"Buenos días senor, estoy caliente!"* The young man responded with raised eyebrows and a querying look before Maggie realised her mistake. What she had meant to say was, "Good day, I am hot!" due to the weather: not meaning I am a hot woman.

In Canas we noticed a sign for a rodeo but our Spanish was again not up to the challenge. After an hour of investigation, the *"no"s* outnumbered the *"si"s* so we shrugged, gave the rodeo a miss and peddled westwards. At the Pacific Ocean we found a beautiful beach, aptly named *Playa Hermosa,* where we enjoyed a sundowner. The setting sun, here in the Tropics, took only three minutes to be totally extinguished after first touching the edge of the Ocean. The two metre wingspan of frigate birds, alias scissor-tails, was silhouetted pterodactyl-like in front of the submerging blood-red orb while a peloton of pelicans swooped low over the surf. This was indeed *Hermosa!* The next day we hired a kayak!

After our canoeing misadventure we limped back to our cabin past a spinney of dead trees, on which eerily perched dozens of black vultures. We were forced to rest for a couple of days with pain killers and alcohol aiding my recovery Then we pressed on to *Parque National Marino las Baulas* in order to witness one of nature's marvels. We watched endangered Pacific leatherback turtles laying their eggs in the sand. These magnificent but primitive creatures, weighing up to 400 kilograms but with brains a tad over a quarter of an ounce, dug holes in the sand to lay about eighty eggs before emerging from a trance-like state to return to the ocean. It could take up to forty or fifty years before a sea turtle was ready to mate and reproduce; then, amazingly, they returned to lay their eggs on the same beach where they hatched so many years before.

We spent the next few days following dirt tracks and fording rivers. Maggie was magnificent as I was able to contribute very little. I had constant pain in my shoulder and ribs and as Maggie so subtly put it: I pedalled like a slug!

However, our coastal route afforded us many splendid resting spots. We spent hours snoozing on the sand. On one such occasion, I was abruptly woken from my slumbers by a coati which had its head deep inside one of our panniers and was devouring our provisions. I batted the racoon-like animal away but had to grab the bag as the thieving creature tried to escape with it clamped between its jaws. During this fraught encounter a gaggle of giggling onlookers were clicking away with their cameras and mobile phones. Not one of them uttered one word of warning or tried to help: thanks folks!

One beautiful moonlit night with the Milky Way presenting a magical backdrop to shooting stars and a satellite, we wandered down to Ostional Beach, hoping to enjoy another magical turtle moment. Ridley Turtles had laid their eggs on this beach about sixty days earlier, so now, with the incubation period coming to an end, we were in for a treat. As we strolled along the darkened beach, with our eyes becoming accustomed to gloom, we saw activity taking place around our bare feet. The beach was alive! Hundreds, no, thousands of baby turtles, barely three centimetres long, were emerging from the sand and scurrying towards the ocean. It was a short journey but not without risk. Crabs were digging deep holes: traps into which some turtles fell. Also, lights from nearby human settlements beckoned them in the wrong direction, away from the sea's natural fluorescence. Then, at dawn, with the rising sun came the scavengers: vultures, feral dogs, frigate birds, gulls and crabs looking for easy pickings. But wait, here came the cavalry! Onto the beach marched dozens of local people armed with buckets, bowls and plastic bags into which they scooped the small Ridley turtles. We helped to release them into the relative safety of the sea; only relative safety however, for less than one in a thousand hatchlings would reach adulthood and make it back to *Playa Ostional* to start their next generation.

We continued south through Samara and Nicoya to the seedy town of Puntarenas and onto Tarcoles and Quepos. Here we spent a couple of days bussing it to the *Manuel Antonio Nacional Parque* which resembled an open zoo. We observed coati, agouti, giant iguanas, 'jumping' crabs, acrobatic squirrel monkeys, armadillos and sloths. White-faced monkeys swung from branch to branch above our heads, babies clung precariously to their backs; their faces, including the babies, resembled those of wizened old men. Maggie had laughed at my earlier encounter with the thieving coati but on my return from a swim, I found her engaged in a tug o' war battle with a masked racoon that was trying to steal our lunch. I believed that the racoon would have won but for the intervention of two armed policemen on mountain bikes.

Eventually it was time to leave the Pacific Ocean. It was only thirty-five kilometres to our destination of *San Isidro de el General*. I was recovering my fitness and we were slightly complacent. However, what a ride it turned out to be! It was continuously upwards in searing heat. We had to take regular rest stops and, I hate to admit, we dismounted and pushed our tandem. We climbed over a thousand metres in just twenty kilometres. From San Isidro our route continued through the mountains over *Cerro de Muerte* (Hill of Death), twice as high as today's journey at nearly 11,000 ft. We decided to take the bus!

While waiting for the bus the following day in the busy and rather hectic bus terminal, we had a pannier stolen. While loading the bus with the tandem, four panniers and a bar bag, one of the bags went missing. I rushed around searching and asking, but to no avail. Lose the bag or miss the bus? We left the bag, hoping that its new owner would enjoy my wash-bag, set of billies and camping stove. The road to Cartago was narrow, twisty and busy with trucks and buses. It was carved into the mountain side with enormous sheer drops into the valley far below. The *Cerro de Muerte* was well named and has been featured in a TV series 'The World's Most Dangerous Roads'. It was a good road <u>not</u> to pedal. We are learning!

We cycled to Montana Linda in Orosi, home of the language school from where we had started nearly six weeks earlier. There we spent a couple of days relaxing with other foreign students including a group from Israel who were taking a year-out before their compulsory national service. "Don't you mind having to forfeit time to the military?" we asked.

"Not at all" they replied, "Someone has to fight the 'fanatics'!" Perchance a case of the pot calling the kettle black?

Our flight from San Jose to Amsterdam was delayed causing us to miss our connection for Birmingham. We took a later flight but the whereabouts of the tandem was unknown. A lift home to Somerset was required. Julie kindly obliged: but that's what daughters are for. The bike arrived four days later on Christmas Eve.

CHAPTER 19

U.S.A; Arizona to Alaska

(Arizona, Nevada, Utah, New Mexico, Colorado,
Wyoming, Montana, Idaho, Washington, Alaska)
"Alcohol maybe man's worst enemy but the Bible says love your enemy."
Frank Sinatra

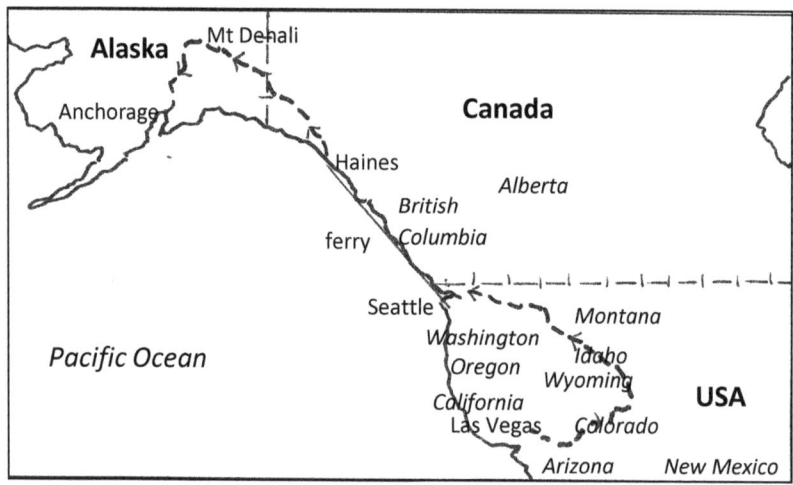

May-Aug. 2001. 4,390 miles

In 2001 we bought a new bike. Airlines were becoming somewhat finicky about carrying bicycles; many now required them to be boxed. Finding a box large enough for a tandem was difficult to obtain and handle. Consequently, we purchased a new Thorne tandem with S&S couplings which enabled the bike to be split into two. We were then able to transport it in two individual bike boxes.

At the same time our daughter, Julie, was planning her marriage to Dean Morgan, an army staff sergeant she had met when sky diving with the

Territorial Army. Las Vegas was to be the wedding venue followed by a tour of California for their honeymoon. Great, we thought, a good excuse for us to see more of the US. So Maggie and I flew into Phoenix then onto the Grand Canyon where we met Julie and Dean with their hired Pontiac Sports Coupe. We found somewhere to leave the tandem, then, after a couple of days of wonder and awe in the Grand Canyon, left for Las Vegas via Bryce Canyon and Zion National Park.

After the sadness and stress of the previous few months when Maggie's mother died, it was good to be able to wake up each morning looking forward to the day. We relished each moment, the incredible sights and breath-taking scenery. We giggled like children over silly things, such as Maggie's comment that one would need a camera with a powerful flash-gun to take a good picture of the starlit sky, and Japanese tourists taking endless photographs of each other. We knew that mum would not have begrudged us our fun, but it was sad that we would no longer be able to relive our experiences with her when we returned home. She would have been very happy to see her granddaughter so contented. Julie and Dean were so much in love and spent much of their time laughing and leg-pulling. We hoped that the future would treat them kindly.

In Las Vegas we booked rooms in the Luxor Hotel with its huge pyramid. Our rooms were on the 21st floor and were only half-way up! The interior was entirely decked out with Egyptian paraphernalia. Other hotels also followed themes…. the adjacent Excalibur was medieval, Caesar's Palace not surprisingly exhibited a Roman slant, the Tropicana had live lions. The wedding was enjoyable and uncomplicated. We celebrated with a ride on the world's highest roller-coaster on top of the 1,000-feet high 'Stratosphere.' I had not expected to enjoy Las Vegas but was very impressed.

We cruised back to the Grand Canyon in the Pontiac to reclaim our tandem and to wish our daughter and new son-in-law bon voyage and a happy honeymoon. Then we set off on our own adventure. My fifty-fifth birthday present was a tough hundred and five-mile cycle, much of it uphill into a raging gale through featureless desert, apart from the occasional butte or crag. We were excited if we saw a bend in the road! The scenery became more interesting as we struggled closer to Monument Valley but we were too tired to appreciate the breath-taking country. Huge sandstone monoliths reared vertically for hundreds of feet, the result of millions of years of erosion. The final few miles took us uphill to the Navajo campground in Monument Valley. The sun was setting as we arrived, highlighting the buttes and mesas in gold, reds and yellows. This was just reward for a hard, hard day.

A vivid, flawless blue sky greeted us as we woke after ten hours undisturbed sleep but it was still very windy. Sand was everywhere; in the tent, in our sleeping bags, in food, our eyes and crunched between our teeth. It was so windy that we had difficulty pouring tea into cups and when I dropped the camera case it was blown across Arizona! We had arrived in the Navajo Nation where nearly everyone, apart from tourists, were Indians. They maintained many traditions, much of their culture and spoke their own language which, interestingly, was used by the American Army in their battle against Japan during World War II: its secret code was never broken.

A friendly couple offered us respite from the wind in their colossal recreational vehicle, a permanent home for them as they had sold their house and been on the road for four years. We were treated to a proper meal with steel cutlery and wine in glasses. Afterwards we received a tour of their thirty-seven feet long camper van that was built on a bus chassis. There were reclining armchairs and a sofa, a king-size bed, shower, toilet, fridge, freezer, oven, microwave, stereo and *two* televisions. This leviathan that guzzled fuel to the tune of seven miles per gallon was more of a mobile-mansion than a mobile-home. Terry and Ruth were retired psychiatrists and now offered voluntary counselling after accidents and emergencies, such as the recent Oklahoma bombing. They could not have imagined in their worst nightmares how their services would be required later in the year, after 9 September 2001.

We rode out of Arizona into Utah through desert wilderness void of plants apart from cacti and tumbleweed, only sandstone buttes punctuating the horizon. I was reminded of the Western films I watched as a boy and half expected the Lone Ranger to ride into view on Silver, his trusty white stallion, his faithful Red Indian friend, Tonto, by his side. In my mind's eye I see them surrounded by hostile, warlike Indians.

"This looks dangerous Tonto, what are we going to do?" the Lone Ranger asks.

"What do mean *we*? Paleface!" replies Tonto as he urges his pony towards the warriors.

The San Juan River, after Mexican Hat, was our destination, but the campground had no water. Mormon missionaries came to our rescue; Marion and Gary gave us water, 'white gas' (Coleman's fuel for our stove) and a lift in their car, which they tow behind their RV, to Bluff for groceries.

During the night I was woken with a start by the sound of an animal under the flysheet ransacking our newly bought groceries. "Bloody racoons again" I thought. I unzipped the inner tent ready to chase the thieving creature away but was faced, not with the bandit mask of a racoon but with a beautiful black and white skunk! It raised its bushy tail ready to defend itself with a squirt of evil-smelling liquid. I froze, skunk stink, we had been informed, was all-pervading and obnoxious. "Nice skunky" I cooed in as unthreatening a manner as I could manage, "Shoo, shoo, off you go." The skunk looked at me, saw nothing threatening or of interest, lowered its tail and squeezed out under the tent flap – thankfully without leaving his "calling card," phew!

The Rocky Mountains could now be seen standing proudly on the horizon. From this distance, they looked to be a white-capped impregnable barrier and sent shivers down my spine. Soon they were to be our trial, a testing ground as we attempt to cycle over those lofty passes. However, first of all we had to cross barren tracts, bare of the interesting outcrops and valleys that had featured earlier. Gophers or prairie dogs and soaring raptors were the only signs of life under a shade-less temperature in the nineties Fahrenheit. The National Monument at Hovenweep offered us some sanctuary, ancient ruins of impressive stone structures built over a thousand years ago by the Pueblo Indians – but why build anything here in the middle of nowhere?

On our way to Cortéz in Colorado, we hoped to stop for provisions at a small settlement called Ismay. Small was an understatement for Ismay consisted of just one building, that being a dilapidated and seemingly closed shack. The windows were boarded up but as we stood disconsolate outside, the door creaked open and we were greeted by two toothless old timers, sporting white stubble and dressed in baggy dungarees with battered old Stetson hats. They beckoned us into their store where we could have been stepping back seventy years. Apart from a fridge and soft drinks, the shelves were stocked with cans and packets of indeterminate age, all coated with a layer of dust. We made do with a tin of fruit cocktail and a packet of fig rolls. The old timers followed us to look at our tandem. They were not impressed. "Don't ya know that you can get one o' them thar contraptions with a motor these days? Yer behind the times!"

We chuckled for the next ten miles. Then followed an unexpected treat as we pedalled down the Elmo Creek Valley and found ourselves in a fertile, green oasis amongst the surrounding harsh desert. The valley was irrigated and grew wheat and hay for the cattle, horses, sheep and even a few llamas. There were neat homesteads with vineyards and fruit orchards. We had forgotten how beautiful green grass and trees could look. We take it all for granted back home!

In Cortéz we found a campground that was full of folk who had taken the old timers' advice about motors for their bike. We found ourselves in the middle of a thousand strong Honda Goldwing motorbike rally. The friendly guys treated us like poor cousins due to riding a push-bike. Secretly, I think that they quite admired us, albeit a bit eccentric.

A cycling rest-day was needed; so, we pedalled out to the Mesa Verde National Park, then hitch-hiked up the table-top mountain to visit the remarkable buildings that were constructed in caves and under overhangs by Pueblo Indians in the twelfth century. Dark, ominous rain clouds loomed over the San Juan Mountains where we were to cycle tomorrow. It was raining over Cortéz but not a drop reached the ground. Humidity was so low that the rain evaporated before it hit the ground. We enjoyed not having a tent heavy with dew each morning and not perspiring profusely in spite of the temperature.

The San Juan Skyway, advertised as the most scenic road in the USA, lived up to its billing. Pastures edged the river valley with an occasional flash of bare rock-face showing between the green cloak of spruces and aspens. As we climbed, the temperature became less intense. We stopped for a drink at Stoner, pop 5. I was fascinated by the population statistics shown on many town signs, they were always seemingly so exact. In a large city they must have births and deaths every day, so were the signs corrected on a daily basis?

Our adventure in wonderland continued. We spent hours struggling slowly up roads carved through snow drifts to reach mountain passes, where we then hurtled down the other side, often at speeds up to fifty miles per hour. We crossed the Great Divide several times and enjoyed the treat of real ale at the mini-breweries we found in the ski resorts of Telluride and Breckenridge. The going was tough and sometimes at the end of a hard day we would argue, especially when looking for somewhere to camp for the night. Often a campground would allow "No tents," RVs only. It was very, very frustrating when you were tired and weary. This would be about the only time when Maggie and I would have cross words and they were soon forgotten once we were fed and discussing the day's events. Events such as our detour to the Black Canyon, so-called because little sunlight was able to penetrate the deep and narrow grey schist and gneiss walls of the fourteen-mile-long gorge. We cycled around the perimeter with two thousand-foot sheer drops to the rushing Gunnison River below: this was not a place for vertigo sufferers. In the nearby campground we saw signs warning us of bears. We knew that we needed to suspend food out of their reach but according to this notice one should also refrain from sexual activity. No need for headaches Maggie!

A twenty-three-mile climb took us to over the highest paved road in mainland America. The Trail Ridge Road at 12,183 feet was our fifth crossing of the Continental Divide. It took us six hours because at every viewpoint we had to stop to absorb the splendid scenery. We climbed past beautiful meadows in stream-fed valleys into Alpine country with the road lined with spruce, aspen and ponderosa pines. Up into tundra territory above the tree-line, the earth was scoured from eons of wind and ice. Elk wandered on the mountainside, while marmots and picas lounged in the sun. Maggie commented that if she was reincarnated she would like to come back as a pica. "Lazing around in the sun, eating and having sex in the summer, then sleeping all winter" she remarked. Actually, these tailless, mouse-like rodents worked quite hard during the summer by collecting and storing food to sustain them through the winter. Nor would Maggie be so keen if she realised that picas had to get every last morsel of nutrition from their food by eating their own faeces. Although picas do not hibernate, they did sleep a lot during the winter: and Maggie was very good at sleeping! If snoozing were an Olympic sport, Maggie would represent Great Britain. She had the ability to sleep anywhere at any time. Considering our chosen lifestyle that was a big advantage.

At the top of Trail Ridge Road, a man who had earlier passed us in his pick-up said, "Wow, you guys gotta be strong!"

"Not strong" I replied, "Just patient."

In Walden, the "Moose Capital of Colorado," we detected an error on their signs: 'moose' should have been spelt 'mosquito.' We saw one moose but *felt* swarms of mosquitoes. At least the sign did not claim to be 'Moose Capital of the World', for on our journeys through the United States we continually saw signs claiming to be "World Capitals." For example, we had passed through the "Cherry Capital of the World," the "Apple Capital of the World," the "World's Smallest Harbour', the "Kite-Flying Capital of the World." The list seemed endless but we assumed that "the World" being referred to was just the United States.

We cycled north-west past a sign reading "Welcome to Windy Wyoming"; actually it didn't, but if the signs were to be truthful, it should have; through a rolling scrubland seared by the sun and relentless wind. There were few signs of wildlife apart from gophers, prong-horned deer and ominous turkey vultures wheeling high overhead. This land used to be grazed by enormous herds of bison before they were decimated by the arrival of the white man.

On the 13 June, in Rawlins, we were forced to rest for a day because of an unseasonal blizzard. We took shelter from the snow, ice and freezing cold wind in a motel and had a look around Wyoming State Prison. Maggie was able to rest in the electric chair which was introduced when the gallows were thought to be too inhumane!

The following day it was still cold but we decided to move on and met a fellow cycling traveller and namesake, one Gene Pendleton from Atlanta, Georgia. Together we battled against a ferocious gale along an arrow-straight road with no trees for shelter. The wooden snow-breaks offered no shelter either. There was no wildlife, just a boring straight road over a sage-bush prairie. No wonder this State was one of the most sparsely populated. At the end of one day we arrived at a designated campground only to find that it had been taken over by Mormons, who were in the process of converting it into a visitors' centre. We were on the route the early Mormons travelled with their handcarts to Salt Lake City in the mid-1800s. As Gene and I had a couple of beers earlier, Maggie was sent to ask if we would be allowed to camp there. Not only were we allowed to pitch our tents but were fed and feted like long-lost family. One of our benefactors was a world age-group triathlon champion. In the morning, sixty-nine-year-old Wayne McSheeny supplied us with pancakes, fried spam and hot chocolate for breakfast while we swopped triathlon tales.

During our short but pleasant stay with the Mormons not one word was uttered regarding their beliefs. I reviewed my previous animosity towards the faith; a faith borne because of the rejection of a lay-preacher by a protestant church in Upstate New York. In the 1820s an angel directed the self-made prophet Joseph Smith to a location where he found golden tablets on which were written a text in an ancient language. Smith translated, 'with the gift and power of God', what was to be known as *The Book of Mormon*. No one else was allowed to witness the golden tablets, not even Smith's wife. After the translation was completed, angels took the evidence back to Heaven! However, Joseph Smith acquired some followers which caused friction with other religious communities, resulting in the death of Smith by a mob. The Mormons sought a new leader and a safer place to practice their beliefs. Brigham Young became the new prophet and led his people on an epic journey to find solace in Utah. Mormonism did have its attractions such as having more than one wife and, on your death, a place in the Celestial Kingdom as you were in your prime!

Wind, wind, wind! Will it never end? We struggled on to the aptly named Wind River, following the canyon to Crowheart, so named because the Shishonie Indian Chief Washakie held the heart of an enemy Crow tribe warrior after a famous battle here. The canyon grew narrower with beautiful sculptured sandstone cliffs, like a mini-Bryce Canyon, but by this time we were beyond caring! Pedalling into a strong head wind is tough. You are battered relentlessly; the noise makes conversation impossible, words snatched away in the gale. You must fight for every yard, each pedal revolution is a huge effort, there is no respite, no chance of a brief freewheel, no summit to reach with the rewarding downhill plunge. The only way to end the torture is to 'stop'. Even then shelter has to be found to escape the buffeting. To really rub salt into our wounds, shortly after Crowheart, four touring cyclists flew effortlessly past in the opposite direction, winds on their backs, smug smiles on their faces. I hated them!

"Everything comes to he who waits." The Togwotee Pass at 9,658 ft, our eighth crossing of the Continental Divide, left the exposed Wyoming ranges behind us with the Teton Mountain Range ahead, offering us, at last, some

Never Say "If Only"

protection from the constant wind. The Jenny Lake Campground was full but, being on a bike, we were found a 'hiker/biker' pitch. Many State Park campgrounds guarantee a camping site for walkers and cyclists. We were now in 'grizzly' country, metal bear-proof lockers were provided for campers' belongings.

After walking in the lovely Tetons we continued on to Yellowstone National Park. The devastation caused by the catastrophic fire of 1988 was immense. Much of the park had been ablaze leaving behind only charred trunks. The skeletal remains of the forests allowed fine views, especially of the Lewis River churning away hundreds of feet down in its canyon. Likewise, we were in awe of the power and intensity of the Yellowstone River Waterfalls. A visit to 'Old Faithful' was an imperative but the gravel road on which we were pedalling was encroached by a herd of buffalos. We were forced to stop and quickly were surrounded by the mighty beasts. The American bison weighed a ton and could run at 35 mph. "Don't look them in the eye" implored a very nervous Maggie. It was with some relief that we found a gap and passed through unscathed.

Boiling mud pools, steaming geysers, dramatic waterfalls and even 2,000-pound bison can become a little wearing after a while; especially when confronted by a ceaseless headwind and a road that always seems to be going up! Late one afternoon, as we crawled past a parked big red Chevy, a fat guy chomping on a wad of gum, looked at us, guffawed and in a deep southern accent, laughed, "She ain't pedalling on the back."

Maggie turned in the saddle, looked him in the eye and blurted out, "Oh, fuck off!"

I had never before heard as much as a *damn* or *blast* pass her lips. That afternoon my girl was *not* a happy lady. I just kept my head down and pedalled on.

Further along the way, major road works were in progress causing traffic jams and long queues. Parts of the road were closed to cycles and so we accepted a lift on the back of a flat-bed truck, already loaded with a giant caterpillar excavator. The driver took us to our next campground at Madison Junction where we met Jim Damico, a white-bearded chap from Kansas City who was cycling the length and breadth of the United States. Jim became our pedalling companion for the next few days.

We had a lovely ride into Montana; the sun was out, the wind behind us, rolling hills, big skies, a bit like a sunny Scotland. We followed a river with fishermen standing thigh-deep trying to lure cut-throat trout onto their hooks, and into a valley which became a lake, Earthquake Lake. In 1959 massive tremors caused a landslide that blocked the valley thus creating the lake, and, sadly, completely buried a campground killing twenty-eight people.

Two days later at the Big Hole Battlefield site, we were given another opportunity to mourn loss of life. This time, however, it was man's inhumanity rather than a natural catastrophe. In 1877 the Nez Perce Indians were fleeing to Canada to avoid deportation to reservations. The US Army caught sight of the Indian encampment near the Big Hole River. At dawn on the 8 August the soldiers attacked the unsuspecting Indians killing indiscriminately, including women and children. Somehow the native warriors fought back and, leaving their dead and injured, managed to escape. Regrettably, just forty miles short of sanctuary in Canada and after a trek of over one thousand miles, Chief Joseph's brave tribe was finally defeated and forced into reservations.

We rode through the Bitterroot Valley into Missoula, home of the *Adventure Cycling* magazine and the producers of the excellent maps we were using. We visited their headquarters, where all passing cyclists are given free ice cream and photographed for their gallery. It was also 4 July, Independence Day. In a City Park we were treated to speeches, prayers, "God Save America," the Star-Spangled Banner and bagpipes, yes bagpipes, before one of the best firework displays we had ever seen. The Americans certainly know how to pat themselves on the back.

The Flathead River gushed along in the valley beside our road. We watched an osprey swoop down to take a trout from the river, and as it struggled to gain height with the weight of the fish in its talons, an aggressive bald eagle attacked it. With a screech, the osprey dropped its catch and flew to safety. The bald eagle immediately plummeted and miraculously caught the fish before it hit the water. Wow! This was an event we would never forget.

Our day of raptor rapture had not ended for, as we stopped for a rest under a dead tree, a massive bird of prey rose from the wizened branches and circled effortlessly above our heads. It soared for a minute or two on broad dark brown wings, wondering whether we were a threat or tasty, it decided that we were neither and returned, to our delight, to its perch... It was a golden eagle. It had a two metre plus wingspan, with a golden-brown neck. We just stood mesmerised and stared in wonder. Eventually, with stiff necks, we pedalled away thinking how lucky we were.

From Montana we rode through the Idaho Panhandle and then into Washington just south of the Canadian border. Nearby severe forest fires were raging resulting in the deaths of four young fire-fighters, including two females. Near Winthrop, a town rebuilt as in the pioneering days of the 1890s, we visited a "smoke jumpers' centre" – so-named because in an attempt to take early control of forest fires, fire-fighters were parachuted into the fire zone, places they could not normally easily reach.

It was semi-desert in the rain-shadow of the Cascades but as we climbed into the mountains, the previously parched ponderosa pines looked a lot healthier. One day's cycling took us from cacti to snow-drifts. We followed the North Cascades Highway, which was closed from November to April due to snow obstructing the Washington Pass to the aptly named Rainy Pass. From here we felt much more at home as the weather became very English; cool, cloudy and wet. Waterfalls plunged down the snow-pitted walls of Skagit Gorge into the turquoise water of the river; the stunning blue was a result of particles carried down in glacier-melt.

The weather was grim and I was feeling fragile and not fully appreciating the stunning glacial scenery. Since reaching Washington State I had an aching back. I felt lethargic and when not on the move just wanted to sleep. Now, as we toiled over the Cascades, I had developed a rash. Maggie diagnosed 'shingles', a doctor in a medical centre near Seattle confirmed it and prescribed some very expensive tablets. We continued at a leisurely pace and I began to recover.

Once over the mountains, the countryside, as well as the weather, had become much more like home with potato fields, apple trees and cabbages. We finally reached the Pacific Ocean at Puget Sound. We explored Seattle, the Olympic

Peninsula and took a ferry over to Victoria and Vancouver Island, then on to Bellingham for our boat to Alaska.

We embarked onto *MV Columbia* for what was billed as the "longest ferry ride in the world." The deck was covered with free-standing tents crushed together like an English campsite on a bank holiday. We occupied a small clean cabin but spent much of the three-day voyage on deck watching orcas, porpoises and hump-back whales. We cruised between the mainland and a myriad of islands with spectacular scenery through channels known as The Inside Passage. As we sailed north, the rounded conifer-covered slopes became jagged, dusted with snow and divided by glacier-filled valleys. Wispy clouds adorned the mountains like necklaces, even the throbbing of the engines seemed muted, like a heartbeat. Everyone spoke softly as if not wanting to disturb the tranquillity and natural beauty that unfolded in front of our eyes. For once the American overused word "awesome" was appropriate.

On disembarking in Haines, Alaska, we were met by our friends Pat and John Ashwell, who were there with one of their cycling groups. They were happy for us to tag along with their bunch of sixteen, which was great for us because they had a back-up vehicle which carried much of our luggage and it was good to have some company. Our first night of Alaskan camping was at Mosquito Creek Campground, appropriately named after the insect that was regarded by many as the Alaskan State Bird. Thick applications of deet were required and mesh face-masks were worn by those who owned them and coveted by those that did not.

We cycled into the Canadian Yukon territory, through a native-Indian fish-trapping site and past a rock glacier. This "glacier" was formed by stones and boulders, shattered by eons of freezing and thawing. It flowed down the mountainside like an ice glacier. There were even "waves" on the rock slope caused by immense pressure. Along the famous Alaskan Highway, which was 1500 miles long and built in 1943 in case the Japanese invaded during World War II, we pedalled beneath mountains that boasted the highest number of non-Arctic Circle glaciers. The highway was under reconstruction making the cycling dusty, dirty and difficult. Apparently, Yukon and Alaskan roads were often under repair during the short summer months as the winter weather played havoc with paved roads.

Near Beaver Creek, we stopped at a grocery store for some triple-A batteries for our head-torch. The store stocked just about everything: fuel, tools, fur hats, animal skins complete with heads, gemstones, fossils, you name it, they had it – except for AAA batteries. "But don't you worry," we were told by the proprietor, "they will have some in the store just down the road!" Which we were informed was 153 miles away! Distances had a different meaning in the Yukon. Although Beaver Creek was only two miles from the Alaska border, it was four thousand miles from Newfoundland on the Canadian east coast; further away than Newfoundland is from Britain!

We rode on, back into Alaska and onto the Denali Highway comprising dirt, gravel washboard and potholes. Here it rained, turning the road into a mucky track. Passing trucks and pick-ups sprayed us with mud as they sped past unknowingly or uncaringly. The group had a hotel booked for that night but we found a log shed in which we could erect our tent.

Six days further on, we entered Denali National Park. An eighty-five-mile ride took us on an unpaved road to Wonder Lake Campground immediately to the north of the highest mountain in North America, Mount McKinley, over 20,000 feet. En route we saw caribou, moose, an arctic fox, Dall sheep, which are a rare species of mountain goat and, thankfully in the distance, a grizzly bear. A thunder storm drenched us and blotted out any sight of the mountain, but after a wet night we awoke to gorgeous views of Mount McKinley basking in early morning sunlight, towering over the valley like a huge white guardian, reflecting the sun's rays like a massive beacon.

We said goodbye to Pat, John and their intrepid group and headed south for Anchorage. On our own again we talked more to people we met rather than only our friends. Alaskans were an interesting breed. Many had come to escape; possibly from failed relationships, uncertain careers or were just fed up with the rat race. Life in Alaska was certainly different and many returned home within a year or two. The long winters, with temperatures dropping to minus forty degrees and very little daylight, were very testing: only the most resolute remained.

Troublesome Creek Campground was near the spawning grounds of the Susitna River where we watched huge salmon leaving the main river for the smaller tributaries that were their birthplace. For three or four years the salmon lived out at sea, then at spawning time, they returned to their freshwater birthplace to lay their eggs, then die. Grizzly bears liked to come here at this time of the year to feast on the fish. We met a park ranger who pointed out signs of frequent grizzly presence. We returned cautiously to our tent and made sure that all our food and toiletries were well stowed in the bear-proof box.

Approaching Anchorage, we dropped in at the Iditarod Centre where the famous 1,100-mile dog sled race starts. The sixteen-dog teams haul sleds from Anchorage to Nome on the Bering Sea. The race takes from nine to fifteen days or more. It is held in early March when blizzards, white-outs and gale-force winds can cause wind chill temperatures as low as minus 100 degrees Fahrenheit: not an event for the faint hearted.

In an Anchorage bike shop, we managed to scrounge a couple of boxes for our double bike and flew home via Minneapolis. Pat and John were not so lucky, for after ensuring that their group had departed safely, they decided to enjoy a few extra days in Alaska on their own before flying home on 11 September. The 9/11 atrocity put paid to that! Their flight was delayed for a number of days before they were allowed to return to England.

CHAPTER 20

India

"Travel leaves you speechless, then turns you into a story teller."
Ibn Battuta *"The Travels of Ibn Battuta"*

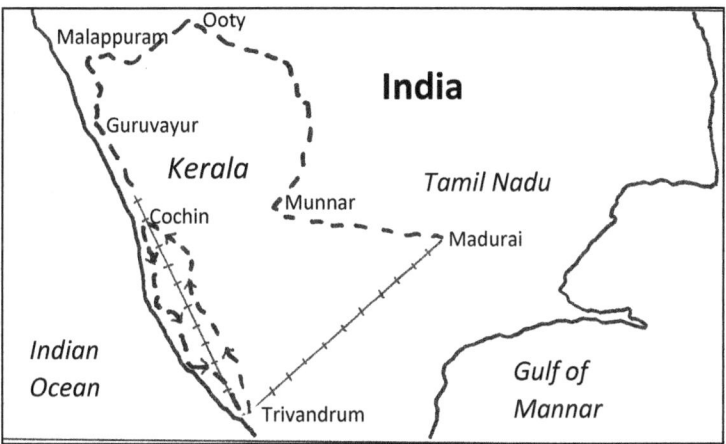

Feb-March 2002. 650 miles

There was a tropical feel to the air when we landed in Trivandrum, capital city of the south-west Indian state of Kerala; warm but, at 4 am, still dark. Since 9/11 2001 security was quite tight, even here in India we were subjected to a thorough check of baggage and passports. By the time we exited the airport the sun had risen giving us a foretaste of the heat to come. We were part of a cycling group run by the Cycle Touring Club and were met with warm smiles by our friends and tour leaders Pat and John Ashwell. Our route through town to our hotel exposed us to the laid-back chaos of Indian town life. People everywhere: on foot, on bikes, inside tuk-tuks, on motorbikes. The cars were all hooting as they overtook or undertook through streets lined with chai stalls and shacks that teemed with sellers, buyers and beggars. The Indian women, however, dressed elegantly in colourful saris, were able to glide effortlessly through all this mayhem.

As part of an organised group we were able to enjoy luxuries unknown to us on our previous trips, such as a rice boat cruise on the Kerala Backwaters. Rice boats were initially used to transport rice and spices to Kochi (Cochin) but had now been converted into house boats to take tourists through the network of rivers, canals, lakes and lagoons. It was a meeting of two worlds; rich westerners gliding by in motorised comfort sipping cold beers, past hand-propelled barges being loaded with mud, for use as fertiliser, by men and boys diving into the murky depths with tin buckets to scoop the sediment of the lake bed.

Also on our agenda were visits to a brick works where all the work was done by hand. This included digging, carrying and moulding – all with no mechanical aids. Many of the workers were women, still in saris but knee-deep in mud. We found similar archaic conditions at a factory where floor mats were woven by hand on ancient wooden looms using coir, coconut fibre.

Back on our bikes we pedalled through the countryside alongside paddy fields dotted with hundreds of women toiling in the sun, past men and women breaking rocks by hand. There were women in saris waist deep in stagnant pools or muddy rivers, scrubbing away at clothes At a graveyard, men were busily digging up old graves to deposit the skeletons of those long dead into a rubbish skip, making room for those not so long dead. However, it wasn't all hard labour, for Indians love to party. Many of the towns and villages were adorned with flags and bunting to celebrate one occasion or another. The Elephant God Ganesh seemed to take pride of place with many effigies made in his honour. The festivals often included a parade of gaudily decorated elephants followed by troops of bands. These consisted of drummers and other percussion instruments, and hoards of followers and dancers in elaborate costumes. Many were fuelled by toddy, an illicit locally produced alcohol made from palm sap.

At Alappuzha we studied a snake boat; one hundred and thirty feet long and propelled by a crew of one hundred and ten paddlers and singers. It was being prepared for the annual snake boat races held every August.

We rode into Cochin which, at first, appeared to be just another bustling, congested metropolis. Towards the harbour things thinned out and we emerged into a green, relatively tranquil area with a cricket field, match in progress, on one side of the road and the Malabar Hotel on the other. The five-star Malabar Hotel was our home for the night and the most luxurious accommodation we had yet experienced. There were air-conditioned rooms with antique king-sized beds and furniture, a swimming pool, fantastic food and Kathakali Dancers to entertain us. Close to the hotel at Fort Cochin we were able to observe Chinese Fishing Nets in action. Ten-metre high structures supported long bamboo poles from which hung huge nets. The nets were lowered into the water then hauled up with ropes by a team of six fishermen. Their catch was meagre, but entertaining for tourists.

All too soon the two weeks of our group holiday was over. On our return to Trivandrum we bade our new friends goodbye as they returned to England while we prepared for further Indian adventures with Pat and John.

An overnight train with pre-war rolling stock took us out of Kerala into the Tamil Nadu State Capital of Madurai, a 2,500 year-old city at the heart of which is Meenakshi Temple, shortlisted as one of the *New 7 Wonders of the World*. The complex houses fourteen Gateway Towers up to 170 feet high and two golden shrines. Extremely impressive, but inside we found it rather bizarre with pilgrims prostrating themselves, others walking nine times around statues, one statue gave good luck while another promised fertility if bombarded by butter fat balls and covered with milk and rice flour. There were 'followers' with shaven heads coated with sandalwood paste. It was all very unusual to our way of thinking.

We escaped to the streets teeming with tourists, but, following 9/11, not many Westerners. Struggling through the crowds, we ignored hawkers, avoided the eyes of beggars, dropped a few rupees into the laps of cripples, and, not looking where I was going, I got stabbed in the ribs by the horns of a cow, which, apparently, is deemed holy and granted right of way. Undaunted, we explored a fascinating market in part of the old temple and ventured down alleys, each of which catered very specifically. One street was full of book sellers, another consisted entirely of tailors, each with a treadle sewing machine.

A long bike ride and a hard climb up the Western Ghats took us from Kodaikanal to Top Station and Munnar. Maggie and I nearly didn't make it! Halfway up the hill we were approached by a large lorry descending too rapidly and taking up most of the highway. I steered towards our side of the road, close to the edge. Too close! As the truck was almost upon us our front wheel slipped off the road pitching us sideways into the path of the juggernaut. I remember looking up as I fell and seeing massive tyres towering above me as I was about to be crushed. But as I hit the ground I instinctively jack-knifed my body and the screeching wheels of the truck missed me by barely an inch. Maggie, miraculously, had a similar escape. The driver, belatedly, hit the brakes and a hundred yards down the hill, to the smell of burning rubber, the lorry squealed to a halt. The driver jumped out and ran back towards us wondering how he would explain squashing a sahib and ma'am sahib. To his profound relief he saw that we had not been flattened, but he was the whitest Indian we have ever seen!

He might have been pale but we were both shaking uncontrollably, it was possibly the closest we have come to being killed. It took some time for us to pull ourselves together and resume pedalling up the hill. To this day I am very wary about being close to the edge of the road, especially when there is a drop-off.

From this point we became very wary of the traffic, especially the buses and overloaded trucks that overtook on blind bends and had no consideration at all for pedestrians or cyclists. The rule of the road was "Might is Right!" In Britain car horns are underused; in India, however, the opposite is true. Drivers use their horns all the time. Our caution on the roads was well founded for I later read in the *India News* that there are over one million deaths in India each year caused by road accidents, forty per cent of which are pedestrians or cyclists. Aware of this the authorities erect many caution signs, such as *"Left is Right"*, *"No hurry, no worry"* and *"The death of safety is the birth of accidents"*.

We descended to the industrial city of Coimbatore before climbing again to Coonoor and Ooty in the Nilgiri Hills were we relaxed for a few days in the Hill Stations. The days of the English Raj may be over but the boating lakes, botanical gardens, houses, late opening hours and the huge tea plantations that are immaculately maintained and roll down the slopes like vivid green lava, still give a Colonial feel to the area.

Mr. Mortee, Pat and John's agent and our hotel host in Trivandrum, was a bit of a entrepreneur and had invited us to test his latest venture, Tree Houses. A very rough road and two river crossings over precarious wooden bridges took us into relatively untamed jungle. The unpaved track ended at a clearing and large log cabin. This was the reception area; we had to strain our necks and look up to see our accommodation. Perched ninety feet above our heads, like a giant eagles nest, was an elaborate tree house. Access was gained by a large bamboo cage which was hauled up by two or three strong men using ropes, pulleys and a huge bag of water which acted as a counterweight. The water came from a stream that gushed over a nearby cliff. The ascent was a bit scary but worthwhile. Inside the tree house there were three floors. On the first was a bedroom, bathroom (complete with shower, flush WC and sink) and sitting room, on the second floor another bedroom and en suite bathroom, while at the top of the house was a sun deck and viewing platform. What a paradise! After a meal in the log cabin below, we spent the star-lit evening watching fireflies and listening to cicadas, unknown jungle noises and the trickling of the brook far below.

We woke to the dawn chorus but lay in bed for a couple of hours just revelling in the unique feeling of being in bed one hundred feet above the forest floor. Later we reviewed a second tree house which was even higher at one hundred and twenty feet. This also was a two-bed-roomed, three story residence, but access was gained by way of a swaying bamboo and rope bridge that spanned the gap from the nearby cliff.

Fantastic experience, lots of wild life too. There was a rat in the log cabin's dining room, a lizard on our bed, a snake in the grass and a leech that got rather attached to Maggie when we went for a walk while some Italians were viewing *'our'* house.

All good things must come to an end and it was with regret that we had to leave the tree houses. The only useful advice we were able to offer in return for our free accommodation was to suggest that fire extinguishers, in wooden houses a hundred feet above the ground and lit by paraffin lamps, might not be a bad idea.

We headed to the Arabian Sea and followed the coast south, stopping at a variety of hotels on the way. At Guruvayor, north of Cochin, we planned to spend a lazy afternoon by the pool at Hotel Sopanam. Maggie went to the changing rooms but all of a sudden ran out half-dressed screaming "There's a rat the size of a cat!" A waiter heard the commotion, fetched a broom and sack and bravely entered the ladies changing rooms. A series of thuds and thumps echoed across the pool before the waiter emerged clutching the bag which now contained something bulky. He turned towards us, smiled and said "mouse!"

While at Guruvayor we visited the Temple, dedicated to the God Krishna and one of the most important Hindu Pilgrimage Centres in India. Non-Hindus are not allowed in, and as I sat watching the comings and goings of the Faithful I was approached by an old man, bearded and wearing the traditional dhoti. He said that he was a healer and suggested that I was an asthma sufferer. I was impressed for I do indeed have asthma! He went on to claim that he could cure me if I followed his advice. He placed his hand on my head and asked me to meditate for ten minutes while he murmured a mantra. He then promised that my asthma would be cured as long as I abstained from: eggs (possible), beer (not so easy), and sex for at least three months (well, my asthma wasn't that bad anyway).

Time was running short so we took a train back to Trivandrum where we detected a feeling of unease and sectarian unrest. We were informed that in the north western Indian State of Gujarat a train fire in Godhra had caused the deaths of 58 Hindu Pilgrims. Arson by Muslims was suspected and in the ensuing riots 790 Muslims and 254 Hindus were murdered, with rape, the burning of children, looting and the destruction of property. Some estimates put the death toll at over 2,000. It was time to go home.

CHAPTER 21

France and Spain

"If you think adventure is dangerous try routine, it's lethal!"
Paulo Coelho

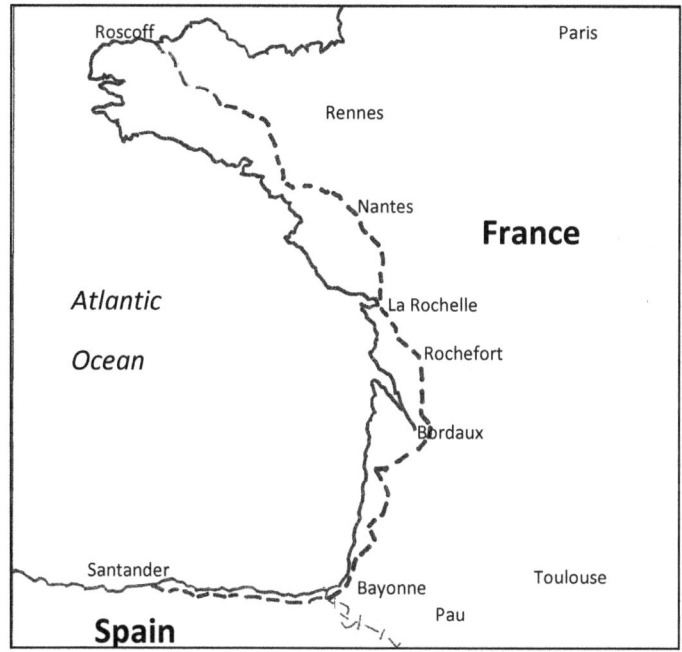

Sept, 2002. 955 miles

Our ferry from Plymouth arrived in Roscoff at 3pm., time enough to pedal the few kilometres to Morlaix and the campground clearly shown on our large scale Michelin map. It was clearly shown on the map, but not at all apparent on the ground. In fact there was no campsite in this French village. We had no alternative but to pedal on. As light was failing we found ourselves followed by a car, and felt a little bit uneasy. After a while the vehicle drove past then pulled in just ahead of us, the sight of children in the back of the car relieved our fears slightly. The driver, probably in his forties, jumped out and flagged us down.

"Where are you going?" we think he asked in a strange French accent.

"The next town to find a camping spot" Maggie replied in her long forgotten French. He shook his head, *"N'est pas"*.

He gestured for us to follow him, jumped back into his car and drove off at cycling pace. We shrugged, thought 'why not?' and duly followed along the main road before turning down a side lane and stopping at an old barn bedecked with scaffolding and obviously being renovated. Our good Samaritan unlocked the barn and quickly showed us round, invited us to have a coffee and help ourselves to anything we could find in the fridge, then he shot off to take the children home. This old building was obviously nearing the end of alterations and was fully, and luxuriously, furnished. We put our bags in the 'guest room' that we had been shown and took a shower in the en-suite.

Our host returned and helped us to use his cooking facilities and prepare a meal. He was very proud of the refurbished barn, which dated back to 1638, and showed us 'before and after' photographs. Evan, we think that was his name, was German and spoke poor French and no English. But with my spattering of Deutsch and Maggie's grammar school Francais we had a very enjoyable evening, an evening cut short when Evan suddenly announced that he had to leave. Apparently it was time to put the children to bed in his town house where he was currently living with his wife. They had not yet moved into the 'Barn'. Our kind host again encouraged us to help ourselves to food and drink, and requested that when we left in the morning we put the key under the mat and made sure that the cat was out. With that he wished us "Bon voyage" and departed, leaving us, total strangers, alone in his new, beautiful house.

This was a very unexpected and pleasant start to our trip along the west coast of France on our way to Spain. In the morning we found the Nantes-Brest Canal, built by convicts in the 1820s, with a cycle path for traffic free riding but unfortunately not designed for tandems. At every road crossing there were chicanes, built, we suppose, to prevent motor bikes. The only way we could pass through the barriers was to tip our tandem onto its back wheel and push it through the gate, or to lift it manually over the fence. Both required unloading the bike! After crossing eighteen roads, and negotiating thirty six chicanes, we decided to abandon the Canal in favour of minor roads. These passed through pretty villages with bustling markets and splendid churches with tall spires, and provided enjoyable cycling. We were especially pleased by the courteous driving, a polite 'honk' warned us of cars approaching from behind and we were always given plenty of room. Very different from some drivers in England who never give any prior warning before rushing past, sometimes with only inches to spare or an aggressive blast on their horn!

After St. Nazaire we encountered sand and pines and estuaries crossed by towering bridges. There were herons and egrets in abundance, and we saw coypu which took me back to my childhood in the Fens. Here the South American aquatic rodents were bred for their fur, but before long some of these beaver-sized animals escaped into the wild, causing untold damage to the banks and habitats of the indigenous wildlife. Most were culled and now a coypu is a rare sight in East Anglia.

We cycled through picturesque La Rochelle and across another massive bridge at Rochefort, which took us to Brouage, a 16th century village surrounded by ramparts and a moat and with ancient cobbled streets. Then more paved cycle routes through pines and sand dunes, a ferry across the River Gironde to avoid Bordeaux, round the largest freshwater lake in France, Lac d'Hourtin-Carcans, to the highest sand dunes in Europe, Dunes du Pilat. We skirted the Atlantic Ocean which looked wild and did not invite us to take a dip. There were many signs warning of dangerous rip currents which helped to absolve our cowardice. However, at Contis Plage where, many years before we had camped with our daughters among the cork oaks, a hot day tempted us to go for a plunge. This rash moment of bravado was nearly our last, for once out of our depth we found ourselves being rapidly swept out to sea. With a massive effort we made it back to land, albeit several hundred yards further along the beach, where we lay for some time, panting and exhausted.

Biarritz offered a friendlier beach, after which the Pyrenees beckoned and we pedalled up our first big climb of the tour, Puerto de Otxonde, and into Spain. Our route followed the undulating Bay of Biscay coastline and one evening we camped on a high headland quite near to a group of youths. They were having a barbeque and sat around drinking and laughing and generally having a good time, noisily! Everyone seemed to be talking at once and in a range of languages. We were kept awake, and at 1:30am I got up and wandered over to ask for a bit of hush. The group, which consisted of Belgians, Dutch, two German surfers and a Basque girl, profusely apologised but had a better idea. Why don't we join them? So we did, and they all switched to speaking English on our behalf. We discussed travel, the Euro, education and, this being just two days after the anniversary of 9th September, terrorism. Very enjoyable, but at nearly three o'clock in the morning the camp host/boss/ commandant came across and insisted that we all turn in.

The following evening, tired from the long night before, we camped in a site above Mutrika. We went to bed early but before long were awoken by ear-shattering blasts of explosions and detonations from the town below. It was an impressive fireworks display. We sat outside our tent and enjoyed the free spectacle. When it finished we were about to return to our sleeping bags when a brass band struck up. The shape of the valley somehow directed the sounds to our campground, distorted but still loud enough to prevent sleep. Eventually the noise from the marching band ceased; peace at last? No chance, now an all-night Pop Concert sprang into action. From our perch, high above the performance, the electric guitars, drums and crooning reverberated around the surrounding hills, it was loud and sounded terrible.

Never Say "If Only"

Tired and weary we continued on through beautiful Basque countryside and the less attractive apartment-block towns that serve paper and log mills. We crossed the river to Bilbao by cable car but had to push the bike a mile through extremely soft sand to access the ferry to cross the estuary at Laida. Finally we rode into Santander and, for a couple of days, enjoyed its beautiful beaches and panoramic headlands before lining up with the motorbike boys for embarkation onto the ferry. We spent the voyage sitting in the sun on the deck before rolling out our sleeping bags onto the floor between seats in the lounge. In the morning we woke to see that the blue sky to which we had become accustomed had been replaced by grey, ominous clouds. It was good to be home.

CHAPTER 22

Australia

"Why do you go away? So that you can come back. So that you can see the place you came from with new eyes and extra colours. Coming back to where you started is not the same as never leaving."
Terry Pratchett, "A Hat Full of Sky"

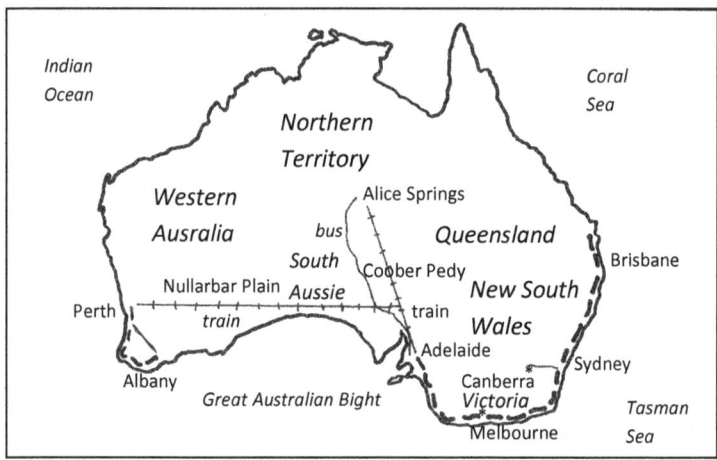

Dec. 2002-April 2003. 2,800 miles

It was Christmas Day and 35 degrees Centigrade as we pedalled through public parks, every shady spot frequented by a family enjoying barbequed Christmas dinners. We had been woken early by a combination of squawking parrots and jet-lag. We were exploring the "Round the Rivers" cycle route which led us from Perth to Freemantle by way of scenic parks and a river rife with brightly coloured parrots, curlews, pelicans and black swans. We had arrived "Down Under" the previous day. Perth is the most remote state capital in the world, and possibly the sunniest, as we could verify when we returned, sweaty and sunburned, to the Central Caravan Park. Maintaining the Australian theme, we cooked ourselves a festive feast of kangaroo steak washed down with Aussie red wine before wandering down to the '*Good Shag*' pub for a couple of cold *stubbies*!

From Perth we headed south along the coastline of the Indian Ocean, into a steady, unrelenting headwind, through a dry, scrubby landscape with little growing, no crops, no orchards, a few sheep, even fewer horses although there was a paddock of camels. Mainly just barren scrub, but plenty of 'roadkill', snakes, lizards, even a kangaroo. Maggie wanted to stop to check that there wasn't a Joey alive in the pouch.

We got rained on in Bunbury, said by scientists to have the "best climate in the World for human existence." The wind intensified but it helped to repel the flies. Whenever we sheltered from the wind we had been plagued by flies and had developed the 'Aussie Wave', that is a swipe across your face with an open hand. Head nets, even when cycling, were essential.

Near Dunsborough we had pitched our tent in a eucalyptus grove before going down to the beach for a swim. However, wind-driven sand and stinging jellyfish, for which 'wee' did little to ease the pain, forced us to beat a hasty retreat back to our tent.

On New Year's Eve we rolled into a large campground near Augusta in the extreme south-west corner of Australia, where the Indian and Southern (Antarctic) Oceans meet. Here we encountered two laid-back Aussies sitting on a veranda, wearing shorts, vests and bush hats, no corks, but with their thong-clad feet on the guard rail. They greeted us with "G'day mates. Yer on a bike! Good on yer. You can put yer tent up anywhere, no worries."

We showered and got all dressed up in clean tee-shirts and shorts, then went downtown for a New Years Eve 'bash'. Augusta had a population of only about a thousand residents so there wasn't much choice of where to dine. But we got lucky and found an unbooked table in town in a cafe next to a garage. It was a 'bring your own' so we raced off to the liquor store for beer and wine. We ate a "Two Oceans" platter which consisted of every sort of fish and seafood you could think of, and some that you couldn't. Plus salad, dips and bread followed by fruit and coffee. Our eyes had certainly been bigger than our stomachs with regards to both food and booze. We drunkenly wobbled back to camp and failed to see-in the New Year.

On New Year's Day 2003 we were too stuffed and hung-over to think about moving on, so we had a lie-in before staggering to the laundry and then the museum. There we read and saw pictures of the biggest stranded whale saving operation in history. In 1986, 116 false killer whales became stranded on the beach. False killer whales looked and acted very much like their namesake, the real killer whales, or orcas, attacking and killing fish and other aquatic mammals. Anyway, these stranded whales had to be transported individually by truck to an enclosed cove at nearby Flinders Bay where they were kept until they could all be released together. Singly they would have returned to the pod only to become stranded again. Ninety-six whales were saved.

After Cape Leeuwin, the most westerly point of Austalia, we headed inland, as did most of the Brits who tried to create a settlement here in 1830, but found conditions so hard that almost everyone left. The trouble was the acid soil, only good to grow vines as was later discovered. A permanent settlement was finally established in Cape Leeuwin in 1860 but just two generations later the population was decimated by the Great War. A Memorial showed the same family names repeated over and over again. During World War One Australia lost more men as a percentage of their population than any other country.

We cycled through rolling green striped hills of wine plantations, then into the eucalyptus forests with jarrah and karri. Jarrah produced a tasty honey but the wood from these forty-metre-high trees was mainly used for cabinet making and panelling. Karri, on the other hand was the second tallest hardwood in the world and towered to a height of ninety metres and as such, had been used as fire lookout towers. The Bicentennial Tree near Pemberton was one of these. In 1988 several hundred metal spikes were hammered into the poker-straight trunk to climb spirally all the way up to a platform that was seventy-five metres above the forest floor. Ascending was not for the faint-hearted and I suffered from nausea and double vision as I attempted to keep the spikes in focus while nervously clambering to the top. However, once I had made it to the viewing platform, the wonderful panoramic view over the forest canopy made all the palpitations worthwhile. The surprising thing was that anybody was allowed to climb it! There was no safety harness, nor supervision, just a sign stating that, "Your safety is our concern but _your_ responsibility" and that thongs (flip flops) were not ideal footwear for the climb.

Further through the forest, towards Walpole, we came across a 420 metres walkway stretching forty metres precariously above a red tingle gulley. Red tingle trees were another type of eucalyptus which could grow to a height of seventy-five metres, with a girth of twenty-four metres at the base and a lifespan of 400 years. Fires often caused massive hollows in the trunks creating huge tent-like shelters. Overall, the "Valley of the Giants" was quite an amazing place.

Albany, our final destination in Western Australia, was first settled by the British in 1826 by the military to house convicts transported from England. It also served during World War I as the final dispatching point for ships carrying the ill-fated ANZACs (Australian Imperial Force and the New Zealand Expeditionary Force) to Egypt in 1914, many of whom never returned.

We visited the whaling station, now an interesting museum. Prior to 1978 whaling had been a major source of employment for the local population, and it was the last operating whaling port in the southern hemisphere.

At this stage on our trip we had cycled over a thousand kilometres, and having not the tiniest inclination to pedal across the Nullarbor Plain, happy to leave that type of masochism to the likes of Mark Beaumont or lone Japanese, we took a bus back to Perth then a train, the Indian Pacific, to Adelaide.

Before leaving Western Australia however, we spent a few days on Rottnest Island which was just off the coast at Fremantle. We stayed at a YMCA hostel and had a relaxing time sunbathing, swimming, snorkelling and watching quokkas. Quokkas? Well, a quokka is a cat-sized mammal that has a tail like a rat's, a face like a koala's, a pouch and back legs like a kangaroo's, it can climb trees and is constantly having sex. Maggie can keep her picas, I think I'd rather be a quokka!

We spent our final day in Perth by taking a free tram ride around the city centre before going to Kings' Park, located on a bluff overlooking the city. The park was a mixture of botanical gardens, lakes, water gardens, children's play areas and war memorials. There were long avenues of trees, each one dedicated to a lost Western Australian soldier. It was very moving and enhanced with splendid views of the city and Swan River. There were six weddings being conducted while we were there. It was really a fabulous place but also, with so many reminders of wars, a place for contemplation. With a touch of sadness, we rode home on the South Bank and enjoyed final panoramic views of the city.

East Perth Rail Terminal had check-in counters like those in an airport. The tandem was whisked off and we were ensconced in a small cabin with a loo and shower next door. Now we could sit back, relax for the next two days and watch the scenery flash past as we travelled over 1,000 kilometres to Adelaide. After nine hours we stopped at Kalgoorlie, went to a pub and watched TV as England lost to Sri Lanka at cricket. Back on the train, the beds had been pulled out in our cabin but it was a bit of a squeeze even for us 'little-uns.' When we woke we were on the longest straight section of railway line in the world – more than 300 miles over a flat, arid, treeless desert. The enormous limestone expanse was the Nullarbor Plain. When peering out of the window, it was like staring at a dull painting because all we could see was low scrub stretching to infinity. The train stopped to take on water at Cook which, until 1998, was an active community with a hospital, school, swimming pool and golf course. That was before rail privatisation. Cook now had a population of four! The nearest grocery store was at Kalgoorlie, 300 miles away. As the sun was sinking, blood red, below the horizon, we saw a kangaroo, then an emu! Such excitement – I needed a beer to calm me down.

We pulled into Adelaide at 6am, had breakfast then found a very helpful Tourist Information Centre. There we reserved a ten-day expedition into the Outback to visit Ayer's Rock and Alice Springs. This was to be followed by a return train ride on the famous Ghan railway, supposedly named after the Afghan camel drivers who helped build the railway in the late 19th-century. We also booked a bus trip to Mount Gambier and a campground for the next three days. We purchased tickets to watch England hopefully gain revenge on Sri Lanka in a One Day Cricket International at the Adelaide Oval. Well satisfied we pedalled through the city with its many parks awash with a multitude of runners, cyclists, cricketers, rugby and tennis players. I liked Adelaide.

The next two days were spent watching the cricket, which England won, just! We cycled beside the Torrens River and along the coast to Port Adelaide and generally had a laid-back time. We swam in the sea and in a lake where, on leaving, we saw a notice board that welcomed swimmers but, in small print at the bottom of the sign, warned that this lake was a breeding area for the blue ring octopus whose sting could be *fatal!* Luckily, we did not see a blue ring octopus but did see lots of less-threatening creatures including egrets, pelicans, ibis, large white and small green parrots, and, on a plate, snapper, which was very tasty with fries and a beer.

Five Swiss, two Japanese, a German couple, two English female backpackers and seven Korean teenagers with their American teacher joined us in the 'Wayward Bus' for the ten-day excursion to Alice Springs. On the first day we covered 430 kilometres to arrive at the end of the sealed road at Wilpena Pound, deep in the heart of the Flinders Ranges', after which we had to endure rough, dirt roads – so rough that the tow bar snapped! Leaving the trailer and most of our belongings behind, we continued to the old copper-mining town of Binman with a population of fifty. There we were lucky to find a blacksmith of sorts and a pub. While the bus was being repaired we visited the pub to escape the heat. We drank beer and watched England lose to Australia in a one-day test match.

The heat was intolerable, over forty degrees Centigrade. Australia was experiencing a severe drought and had not received any substantial rain for three years. Continuing along the Oodnadatta Track we passed the biggest cattle ranch, actually the largest privately owned property, in the world, the Anna Creek Station of 22,000 square miles; and stopped whenever possible at water holes until we reached the settlement of William Creek. In spite of the heat it was overcast with ominous clouds looming on the horizon. Tony, our driver and guide was worried about the possibility of an impending summer storm that could cause the roads to become impassable and strand us here in the Outback. Not an unfounded fear, for in 1998 a young lady died when trying to walk back to William Creek from her bogged down vehicle.

William Creek, pop. 20, is hot, dry, plagued with flies and is hundreds of miles of dirt road to anywhere. If the residents are not insane when they go to live there they most probably will be when they leave! The William Creek pub is one of the most remote pubs in the world with the ceiling festooned with signed ladies knickers. After a couple of pints and gratefully unable to see any panties with my daughter's name on, she had passed this way a year or so earlier, we retired to our tent as a glowing red sun was replaced in the sky by an equally crimson moon. It was too hot and with no breeze inside the tent we slept outside under stars dulled by a bright, full moon.

During the 1880s the world's longest fence was built across Australia. It was called the Dog Fence and was constructed to keep dingoes out of the sheep breeding southern areas. It was nearly 3,500 miles long and had been relatively successful at keeping dingoes in the northern territories. It did not keep us out however, and we continued on to Coober Pedy.

Coober Pedy is known as 'white man's hole' by the indigenous Australians, or 'the opal capital of the world' by the white inhabitants who, like the opals that are mined there, are usually found underground. Due to the scorching daytime heat, the locals tended to spend most of their time in man-made caves where the temperature remained constantly at an acceptable level. Houses were excavated out of the hillsides, as were a museum, two churches and a pub which, when we went for a cold beer, had refrigerator problems and therefore had none. 'A pub with no beer', in Australia! At least we were able to have a good night's sleep in our cool, windowless, subterranean dormitory.

A huge, red, rock rose up from a barren landscape. It was, of course Uluru, or Ayer's Rock in white man's language. Soaring 350 metres above the ground and extending even further below ground it was the world's largest monolith. We camped nearby and early next morning I set off to climb the 1,000-foot rock while Maggie walked round the nine-kilometre base and watched the rock change colour as the sun rose. She was also entertained by a large aboriginal woman who cooked and then ate, witchetty grubs. These were large moth's larvae and when cooked are said to taste like scrambled eggs and to be high in protein. However, Maggie was unable to verify the claim as she turned down the offer of a taste.

There was more imposing scenery, wild walks and stunning swim holes on the way to Alice Springs. We were amazed that any wildlife could exist in such a harsh environment. We witnessed a giant sand monitor lizard stalking a black-footed wallaby with a joey in its pouch. There were also emus and feral camels. The camels were introduced into Australia in the 19th-century during the colonisation of the interior. As transport became motorised the camels were released into the wild and proliferated so that a culling programme was introduced limiting the camel population to around 300,000.

A thousand miles after leaving Adelaide we finally reached Alice Springs. We were sad to see many overweight and inebriated Aborigines. After a millennium of witchetty grubs, the almost overnight arrival of Big Macs, Coca-Cola and Foster' beers had played havoc with their constitutions. Their bodies had not evolved to deal with Western food and drink; consequently obesity, diabetes and alcoholism were rife.

After scrummaging with fellow backpackers at the ticket office, we climbed aboard the Ghan for our thirty-six-hour air-conditioned recliner journey back to Adelaide. The Ghan which now, incidentally, continues all the way to Darwin, meant that Alice Springs was approximately just the half-way point. Half-way was far enough for us and it was with some relief that we returned to Adelaide. We collected our bike and promptly visited the Botanical Garden for a green 'fix.' Living in 'the green and pleasant land' of England we take the abundance of green for granted. After ten days of fifty shades of brown in the Outback we were suffering from withdrawal symptoms. To make us feel even more at home, it was now raining!

The next day we loaded our tandem on a bus bound for Mount Gambier, 280 miles south of Adelaide. Gambier was built on the flanks of a volcano and had many caves and sinkholes. It was popular with cave divers with a death wish! We camped at Blue Lake, which was cobalt blue in summer but steel grey in winter. We then explored a park at Valley Lake, which was another drowned volcanic crater. The park was fantastic; it was more a zoo than a park, but a zoo with no cages! The perimeter fence was electrified but all the animals ran, swam and flew freely. We saw boxing kangaroos, wallabies, emus, aquatic tortoise and loads of other species including a pottaroo, which was a cat-size marsupial and was one of Australia's most endangered species.

We started cycling properly again and headed east along the Southern Ocean to the delightful little wooden bungalow town of Port Fairy, where we found one of the best campgrounds ever. There were barbeques, cookers, microwave ovens, a boiling water dispenser, flowers in the urinals and we were even able to have a bath, all for less than £5.

Near Port Fairy was Griffiths Island a breeding ground for short-tailed shearwaters. These birds choose to make a 30,000-kilometre round trip each year to Alaska. At dusk there was not a bird to be seen but then within minutes the sky was filled with thousands of them. Also known as mutton birds, they swooped in, silently like giant bats, to feed their young in metre-deep holes in the ground.

It was very hot, even after nightfall. We left off the flysheet, very un-British I knew but with little risk of rain we needed it to be as cool as possible. Until dusk the flies were a perpetual torment. A continual 'Aussie wave' was a must, but even then they hovered inches above your head waiting for your aching arms to tire. As soon as your guard was lowered, the fearless plague of insects mounted a Kamikaze assault and crawled all over your head and face attempting to gain access into any orifice. Why do tourist boards fail to mention these national pests? Alaska's national bird, the mosquito, seldom received a mention in the advertising leaflets; nor did Quebec's black flies, or Patagonia's giant horse flies called tabanos. New Zealand remained strangely silent about their sandflies, and are midges recognised as being as much an integral part of Scotland as whiskey? I thought not! However, here Down Under, while the flies go to bed at night, ants, spiders and mosquitoes have no fear of the dark and make it impossible to sleep under the stars and force a retreat into the stuffy tent, door zipped tightly shut.

The Great Ocean Road ran dramatically for over 400 kilometres along the south-eastern coast of Victoria. The road was the world's longest war memorial and was built in memory of those killed in the Great War of 1914-1918. Construction began after the war using thousands of returned servicemen. This massive task was undertaken with picks, shovels and horse-drawn carts. It wound through varying terrain and included some vantage points for views of outstanding natural beauty, including the limestone stacks of the Twelve Apostles. It was impressive but, in my opinion, not a touch on our South-West coast in England or the Pembrokeshire coast in Wales. We are spoiled in Britain.

Bush fires were causing havoc in the Interior and sending strong, hazy winds down from the mountains smudging the skyline. Pedalling into the face of the enemy into Victoria, it was with some relief that we finally reached the outskirts of Melbourne. We camped at Frankston from where we were able to take a train into the city, then a tram to the St Kilda Festival. It was a gathering of art, music and sport. Wanting part of the action, I entered

Never Say "If Only"

an open water swimming race to be held in the bay. I was the only one *not* wearing a wet-suit, and they say the Pommies are soft!

Like Adelaide, Melbourne was a hive of sporting activity. We visited Melbourne Cricket Ground which was the Olympic Stadium in 1956. It was currently being revamped for the 2006 Commonwealth Games. The city centre was compact and easy to get around. There was a fascinating mixture of buildings from the 1850s and new skyscrapers. The River Yarra was home to plenty of rowers and canoeists. Grey-headed fruit bats, flying foxes, hung from trees in the botanical gardens in their thousands. They had a one-metre wingspan and fluttered about so noisily that at first we thought they were parrots. At 11am we paused at the cenotaph, a huge memorial to the victims of World War I, and listened to a short service that omitted God, and to the Last Post played on a bugle. Australia did not forget those lost in the wars and in every town and city there were memorials to soldiers, sailors and airmen, with the Last Post still being played daily at 11am in the Returned Serviceman's League (RSL) clubs. Consequently, there seemed to be much hostility concerning the threatening behaviour of Bush and Blair towards Iraq.

Back on the road again we forsook the paved road for the dirt and hills of the Great Ridge Road to Tarra- Bulga National Park deep in the Strzelecki Ranges. Riding through a strand of eucalypts and almost as comatose as the koalas that sat, like stuffed toys, in the trees above our heads, we almost ran over a strange animal. It had the snout of an ant-eater, looked like a hedgehog and had fur between it's spines. It was an echidna. Echidnas are marsupials and extremely rare, not surprising considering their lack of road sense, and are one of only two egg-laying mammals. We carefully moved it a safe distance from the highway. Feeling quite smug and self-satisfied, we continued onward.

En route we camped at a youth hostel, with a bar! There was a television screening England playing football against Australia. There were many young Aussies watching and I felt confident that Beckham, Rooney, Scholes et.al would regain a little of the pride that we had lost during the current cricket tournament. However, catastrophe! We lost 3-1. Never in the field of English endeavour has there been such a humiliating occasion. Needless to say, it cost me quite a few pints that night.

Allan Pendleton

At the Ferndale Campground in the Tarra Valley we got up at the crack of dawn to see both a wombat and a duck-billed platypus When the platypus was first discovered and a specimen sent to England, scientists believed they were the victims of a hoax. They thought it was a combination of several other creatures, a duck (bill and webbed feet), a beaver (tail), and an otter (body and fur). Apart from the echidna the platypus is the only mammal to lay eggs. Male platypuses are also venomous.

Rolling, leg-sapping, Devon-like terrain and an evil headwind welcomed us to New South Wales. In Bateman's Bay we threw in the towel and hired a car for the 300 kilometres round trip to Canberra. The capital city was awash with war memorials; ANZAC Parade, Tomb of the Unknown Warrior, statues, a light and sound show of the Japanese attack on Sydney Harbour, WWI dioramas and most impressive of all, the War Museum.

The grass-roofed Parliament House had a small tent village where campaigners for aboriginal rights loitered in a hut which they claimed was the Aboriginal Embassy. In the visitors' gallery we witnessed Prime Minister's question time. Very much in the British tradition, John Howard cleverly avoided giving direct answers. The speaker had an unenviable task of keeping the hecklers in order. The main issue of the day was the pending war in Iraq. Like the British, the Australian government voted to go to war against the will of the people. Sitting next to me in the spectators' balcony was a very angry and indignant anti-war campaigner. Feeling betrayed he stood and yelled obscenities at the prime minister. I edged away and hunkered down keeping as small a profile as possible, for although I tended to agree with my neighbour, I did not want to be found guilty by association and consequently spend the night in the cooler!! Two bulky security men quickly appeared, grabbed the offender in an arm-lock and frog-marched him, still protesting, out of the public gallery. Interestingly, the main entrance of Parliament House leads directly along the memorial-lined ANZAC Parade to the War Museum, deliberately designed to be a constant reminder to those in power of the human suffering caused by war. I imagine that the current Government was using the back door.

At the city library we checked our e-mail, only to find that Julie and Dean had lost their unborn child. With war declared and our daughter's miscarriage this was not the best of days!

Having to return our hire-car we were unable to partake in any liquid antidepressants but instead had to endure three sober and sombre hours driving back to Bateman's Bay. What awful parents we were, gallivanting around on the wrong side of the world when we were needed at home! Self-flagellation was required; therefore, the next day, irrespective of the head wind and hills, we rode hard along the Princes Highway to Sydney. There was a lot of traffic, motorists whom seemed to have an intense dislike of cyclists, not unlike their English cousins. We experienced a few near misses and blaring horns, but in hindsight it was probably our own self-destructing attitude that was to blame.

After "doing" Sydney, including the Harbour Bridge, the Opera House and Bondi Beach in the rain, we continued north for another thirty days covering about 1,000 kilometres, experiencing on the way more hostile drivers, thunderstorms and a bevy of beautiful beaches. Whenever we were able, we took side roads which were often no more than dirt tracks; tough enough in the dry but in appallingly wet conditions they became a quagmire. Consequently, much puffing, panting and pushing was required. However, the sparklingly blue sea and squeaky sand beaches more than compensated for each day's efforts. The crystal-clear water was ideal for snorkelling. It was a joy to float above huge stingrays and literally rub shoulders with dolphins. Meanwhile, sea eagles and pelicans skimmed inches above the waves seeking out their lunches. We also met a number of interesting people, both locals and foreigners. A young French-Canadian couple were bicycling around the world looking for the place in which they would like to live and bring up their children. When we asked them if they had a favourite place they unhesitatingly stated it was Patagonia. Not to live in, they emphasised but a fantastic place in which to travel. Mmm...interesting, a destination for the future perhaps?

At Port Macquarie Maggie needed assistance from a very hunky lifeguard when she swam precariously close to some jagged rocks; she was not normally a reckless swimmer so I questioned her motives. That evening she shared a shower with a snake! Apparently, halfway through her dousing she looked up to see the two-metre long reptile gazing down at her from the rafters. With supreme calmness and composure, according to Maggie, she finished her shower before leaving the cubicle to the snake.

Allan Pendleton

In spite of the violent rainstorms the countryside had become more tropical as we travelled north into Queensland with bananas, avocados and oranges; and mosquitoes replacing flies in equal abundance. Noosa Heads was as far north as we could manage before having to return to Brisbane for our flight home. On our way back, we took an incredibly quiet road through the Glass House Mountains National Park. We said goodbye to a kookaburra, avoided snakes and had a live fat kangaroo bound across the road inches in front of us. Also, a dead, flat kangaroo lay fermenting in the sun. On a road where all day we had hardly seen another vehicle, it would seem amazingly stupid, or exceedingly unlucky, to get run over by a truck! We rode straight to Brisbane International while luck was still with us.

CHAPTER 23

Patagonia

Chile and Argentina

"Quien no ha visto los bosques de Chile, no conoce el planeta. "He who has not seen the woods of Chile, does not know the world."
Pablo Neruda

Jan-Feb, 2004. 830 miles

On our left, to the east, the Andes reared up. Snow-covered peaks rose from damp, green forests to merge with a slate-grey sky. Mighty glaciers crept down the mountains' flanks, imperceptibly grinding out steep-sided valleys before finally meeting and crumbling into the Pacific Ocean. Volcanoes, white-capped and perfectly cone-shaped, complimented the landscape; as did waterfalls, fjords, lakes and turbulent white-water rivers. The scenery was incredible.

Regrettably, while cycling on our newly purchased Thorne tandem I was unable to enjoy the stunning views; instead, all my powers of concentration were needed to manoeuvre the tandem around the potholes and rocks that littered the trail. Only by stopping was I able to enjoy the splendid panorama. We were riding

145

on the *Carretera Austral del General Augusto Pinochet* in Patagonian Chile. It was an unpaved road, or *ripio* as it was known locally, which consisted of rocks, gravel and dirt. It was a cross between a shingle beach and a dry river bed and demanded my undivided attention. Luckily there was little traffic; any that did appear left us shrouded in a mantle of dust and created a washboard effect that further rattled our bones. The building of this road started in the 1970s under the dictatorship of Pinochet and was a testimony to man's ingenuity as it cut its way through impenetrable rainforest, zigzagged up the lower Andean slopes and skirted around lakes and fjords. For decades Chile's southern territory was accessed by way of Argentina but during the 1970s a dispute about the possession of islands to the south of the mainland created tension between the two countries. This not-so-neighbourly antagonism was seen as the main reason for Chilean support of the United Kingdom during the Falklands War of 1982. In order to strengthen Chilean presence in this remote area, the Chilean Army built the road using more than 10,000 soldiers, many of whom lost their lives in the process.

In 2000, Pinochet was rewarded for his alliance with Britain during the *Malvinas* conflict when, thanks to Margaret Thatcher's support, he was given specialist medical care in England and allowed to return to Chile, in spite of requests by Spain for extradition to face charges of human rights violations during his 17-year regime. The charges included personal enrichment through embezzlement, illegal arms and drugs trade, the murder of over 2,200 people and the torture of at least 30,000 Chileans. As I sat writing this in January 2016, there was news that the British Government had spent more than £12 million keeping guard on the Ecuadorian Embassy in London where the Australian WikiLeaks founder, Julian Assange, was receiving asylum. The British Government wanted to extradite Assange to Sweden to face rape charges. The problem for Assange was not the dubious rape charge but the fact that Sweden would then send him to the USA to be persecuted for revealing secrets of which the United States were not proud. Thus, it would appear, the British government, who were happy to help an alleged mass murderer to avoid justice, were now willing to spend millions of pounds trying to extradite a purveyor of the truth.

We hit the *ripio* just twenty kilometres after leaving Puerto Montt which was our starting point in Patagonia. We had flown there by way of Sao Paulo in Brazil and Santiago de Chile. As we shuddered, slipped, struggled

Never Say "If Only"

and skidded precariously along the *carretera*, averaging little more than eight kilometres an hour, I realised that we did not have a spare tyre! We always take a spare tyre, but this time on the roughest road we have ridden, no spare! Am I stupid or am I stupid? With trepidation we soldiered on to La Arena, a river port of clapboard and shingle buildings. After the ferry crossing the road deteriorated further. Unable to gain traction on the hills, we had to dismount and push!

This was an area of dense rainforest and camping sites were hard to find. A German couple travelling in a multi-terrain camper, which looked like an armoured personnel carrier, stopped to inform us of a stream a little further down the road. Rivers provided the only break in the vegetation. We managed to pitch the tent on a seemingly impossible rocky slope but with a plentiful supply of cold, crystal-clear water. This was not our ideal camping spot but it was very popular with large horseflies called *tabanos*. These insects sounded like, and were as big as, bumblebees, and with a bite to match! They were our constant daytime companions, our only defence being a liberal layer of deet.

In the virgin rainforest of Parque Pumalin containing 1,000 year-old alerce trees, we did, however, enjoy a beautiful campground overlooked by the massive snow-capped and dormant, but not extinct, Volcan Michimahuida (2,404m) and adjoining glacier. There we were joined by a gaunt cyclist in his fifties, a sculptor by trade named Osvaldo Pena. Osvaldo's English was limited, on a par with our Spanish, but we did ascertain that he had been jailed and tortured under the Pinochet regime and that his family had been thinned out. Why do dictators often seem to have problems with intellectuals?

A field of waist-high grass scattered with cow dung but with a fantastic view of the surrounding mountains, provided an acceptable camping site at Villa Santa Lucia. This was an old *pueblo* with an adjoining army base. Our host was an ex-army *caballero*. This former mounted soldier told us that he had to go to Chaiten where his father had died the previous night. We felt sorry for him until he proudly showed us his army medals and photographs of himself with Pinochet's henchmen. We wondered what gruesome tales he could tell.

More mountains, *ripio* and llamas, and while we were taking an icy dip in the aquamarine glacier-melt waters of the Río Palena, our new *amigo*, the pedalling sculptor Osvaldo, rode by. We cycled together to the settlement of Puerto Puyuhuapi on the banks of Lago Ventisquero. Many early German pioneers had settled here and quite a few sought sanctuary after World War II. There were large Dutch-barn type buildings, with *cafe und kuchen* for sale. German music at the cafe gave a distinct Deutsch feel to the place. There was no camp site, so Osvaldo booked into a *hospedaje* while we put our tent up on the grassy shore of the lake and enjoyed a litre of Chilean red.

During the night it started to rain. I lay half-asleep in my sleeping-bag listening to the pitter-patter of rain drops and fighting the call of nature. As I lay there semi-comatose, I felt a fluid-like movement beneath my sleeping mat, as if I were lying on a waterbed.

"What the...!" Suddenly I was wide awake, I fumbled for my head-torch and unzipped the tent door. This was a big mistake! As I unzipped I was hit in the face by a wall of freezing water, which immediately filled the tent a foot deep, waking and drenching Maggie in the process. Everything was inundated, our sleeping bags, panniers, clothes, everything! I looked out and by the feeble light of my head-torch could see nothing but a sea of icy water. Then, at a distance in the mist, I made out an island, or at least a small hummock that promised an escape from the freezing waves. We waded over to the mound and sat shivering in the teeming rain. I stuck sticks into the ground by the water's edge to check if the tide was still advancing. When satisfied that it was not, we made several journeys in thigh-deep water to salvage our tent and belongings. Stuffing our saturated kit into the panniers and wrapping ourselves in a London Marathon space blanket, we sat and shivered until dawn.

At first light we wrung out our kit, loaded it onto the bike and pushed it into Puerto Puyuhuapi. With our sodden equipment our tandem was much too cumbersome to ride. This is where our luck changed. Not only did Puyuhuapi have the only hotel, *Casa Ludwig*, in the vicinity, where Osvaldo had wisely taken up residence, it also had a tumble-dryer, possibly the only one for 100

Never Say "If Only"

kilometres in any direction! We spent the day drying out. It was still raining, so our room was festooned with lines pegged with clothes, peseta and dollar bills, passports, maps, airline tickets and documents. Downstairs, in the lounge, we were allowed to surround the log burning stove with our sleeping bags and boots. Apparently, Lago Ventisquero, the lake beside which we had camped, was not a lake at all; it was a fjord! The water did not taste salty when we had washed in it the previous evening because it was fed by many rivers and glaciers. Camping on the grassy bank had seemed a safe option. However, torrential rain and snow-melt in the mountains above had caused a tidal surge and we were well and truly 'Puyuhuapied!'

Later that day, Osvaldo continued on his journey while we still had a lot of drying out to do. We enjoyed Señora Louisa's hospitality for a day longer. When we did leave, feeling buoyant after our lucky escape, we continued south along the main highway. The weather had now become typically Patagonian with cloud and rain, although the strong winds, of which we had been warned, had yet to make an appearance. After a short ride we pulled into the camping area for the *Ventisquero Colgante*: the name of a hanging glacier in the Queulet National Park. This beautiful site with covered picnic tables and fire pits was overlooked by snowy canyon walls with 150 metre waterfalls plummeting into a lagoon.

The next day when stopping to hike to a nearby waterfall, for some obscure reason and more through habit than necessity, I locked the tandem to a metal bridge. Not that anyone was likely to steal it, or indeed that anyone was there to steal it. On our return Maggie went to open the combination lock but could not. "Silly woman, let me do it" I said shouldering her to one side. But I also failed. Then followed what seemed like an age of frantic fumbling, trying all order of combinations. I felt hysteria rising, for, after our dunking a few days previously, to lock one's bike irretrievably to a steel bridge when miles from nowhere verged on complete and utter incompetence. While contemplating whether to throw myself off the bridge or simply break-down and cry, Maggie suddenly exclaimed, "Done it!" The lock snapped open to the combination I'm sure we had tried a hundred times before.

It felt good to climb onto the bike and ride again, no matter how rough the *ripio* or how steep the climbs. The forthcoming climbs were steep, including twenty hairpin bends zig-zagging nearly a thousand metres up the *Cuesta de Queulat*. We were rewarded with the best views yet of glaciers, waterfalls and tree-covered slopes extending to the snowline. However, there was no sign of habitation. We had not seen a house all day, let alone a cafe or store. Consequently, we were famished and were running on empty. Luckily a car with four Germans stopped for a chat and they gave us a banana each.

Ventisquero Colgante

Ripio

That was our last full day of dirt as paved sections were rapidly being laid. One hundred kilometres of asphalt cushioned our ride to the main town of Patagonian Chile, Coyhaique. Here we met another British cyclist, Huw, a Welsh rock climber from Newport and his French partner Gwen, who were also riding a Thorne tandem. We chatted until the early hours sharing wine and swopping tandem tales. They were having problems with their locally bought tyres and yesterday had to hitch-hike eighty kilometres back into town after their newly purchased tyres had expired, despite having only covered a short distance. They were now experimenting with *two* tyres on each wheel, one inside the other. We, on the other hand, had been more fortunate and did not suffer a single puncture throughout our Patagonian adventure, although we had now acquired a spare tyre. Huw and Gwen were also impressed with our Rohloff fourteen-speed internal rear hub gear which had proved absolutely perfect for multi-terrain cycling. The ability to select any gear at any time was ideal. Many of the cyclists we encountered had experienced transmission problems in the dust and dirt. After a day in Coyhaique we spent another evening in the campground with our new friends drinking and discussing climbing, politics and drugs; their uses, abuses and the case for legalisation. Regarding climbing, Huw claimed to have met many old climbers and numerous bold climbers; but rarely any old *and* bold climbers!

We pedalled down the Rio Simpson valley in bright sunshine to Chacabuco. This part of the world only expected a handful of sunny days each year and luckily we had grabbed one of them. The weather has been very kind to us so far. At Chacabucu we watched the unloading of *MV Puerto Eden*, an old cargo boat converted to a ferry and to be our home for the next few days. It disgorged its cargo of livestock, trucks and containers before we were finally allowed to board. We were shown to our 4-bunk cabin along with a young couple from Santiago. Andres and Marsela were treating this trip as a belated honeymoon, it being the first vacation they have been able to take since getting married several years previously.

The ship sailed through a flotilla of icebergs to Laguna San Raphael, 200 kilometres south of Chacabuco. There we were all loaded onto lifeboats and taken to the face of the San Raphael Glacier. Huge chunks of ice calved off the glacier creating a mini tsunami which caused more than a murmur of alarm from the passengers, until a roar from our outboard motor aligned our small craft to safely ride the wave. Dolphins enjoyed our company, while the crew fished out lumps of the sapphire-coloured ice that originally had fallen as snow high up in the mountains a thousand years ago. This crystal-clear ice sparkled like diamonds and was broken up to be placed in glasses of whiskey, one for each passenger. We all toasted *"Viva el Chile"* and sang their national anthem with our whiskey and Millennium Ice. Overnight we sailed back to Chacabuco where the rear deck was loaded with trucks full of cattle and horses. We then continued north to Puerto Montt. It is supposed to rain 360 days a year in this neck of the woods but we were sunburned! A beautiful full-moon lit our passage through narrow channels between steep uninhabited tree-clad cliffs, occasionally rent by glacier-formed fjords, with a backdrop of volcanoes. We sat on deck under a star-lit sky talking to Keith Clarke from Yorkshire who had ridden three-times as far as us in Patagonia and on a horse! He planned to continue across the Argentinean Pampas.

On our return, Puerto Montt looked a lot livelier and more upbeat than it was two and a half weeks before. The sun was shining, the fountain in the plaza was working and there was a fiesta-like buzz in the town. Stall holders selling trinkets lined the esplanade. On the short pier there was a book fayre and a stage was being set-up for a pop-concert. Puerto Montt was about to swing!

Left-wing slogans pledging unity with Cuba and remembering the former president Salvador Allende adorned many buildings.

Salvador Allende was democratically elected as leader of Chile in 1970. He tried to restructure Chile along socialist lines while retaining democracy, respecting civil liberties and the due process of law. His government expropriated American-owned copper companies, started to purchase several other mining and manufacturing companies and to take over large agricultural estates for use by peasant cooperatives. This, of course, did not encourage foreign investment and caused hostility from the land and mine-owning middle class. Although Allende retained the support of lower classes, his government was overthrown in 1973 by a military coup led by Augusto Pinochet with United States encouragement. During an attack on the presidential palace, Allende died. Suicide claimed the aggressors, murder cried the populace. Rumour had it that the hands of the CIA were not squeaky clean.

The plan for the second part of our Patagonian odyssey was to cycle to Argentina. Regrettably there was a barrier in the way, namely the Andes. Not letting a little mountain range spoil our plans, we set off regardless. Our exit from Puerto Montt was relatively easy, if pedalling on the Pan American Highway in horrendous traffic and fumes could be called easy. At Puerto Varas we were able to leave the Pan American Highway for fifty kilometres of delightful cycling along the shore of Lake Llanquihue with the daunting Osorno volcano becoming ever closer. A campsite on the shore of the lake presented us with the opportunity to swim in what must have been one of the world's most idyllic locations. Dark, volcanic sand led into the clear water of the lake and was overlooked on one side by the perfect cone of Volcán Osorno. The pointed summit of Volcán Puntiagudo was just visible over Osorno's shoulder, while on the other shore stood the older Volcán Calbuco. Older but with a more recent history because in April, 2015, with just one hour's warning, Calbuco erupted sending a plume of volcanic ash ten kilometres high that caused much airline disruption and the evacuation of 4,000 people.

Eleven years earlier, and with no thoughts about erupting volcanoes, an early rise was needed for us to catch the ferry at Petrohue. The ferry, a foot-passenger, walk-on catamaran, was full of package tourists each touting a cam-recorder attempting to capture on film the beautiful vistas. The volcanoes and steeply wooded mountains reflecting mirror-like on the surface of the emerald-green Lago Todos los Santos did indeed make memorable pictures. Ahead was the port of Peulla, backed by a wall of snow-clad mountains guarding our route into Argentina.

On landing we got directed to the *aduana,* to get our exit permits from Chile, and eventually found the customs shed but we were sent next door. There an official took our passports back to the building from where we had just departed to get them stamped, then returned them to us! That's the way it works in Chile!

The boat-load of tourists crowded into Peulla's hotel, while we climbed aboard our trusty steed and pedalled into the sunset. Not only was the trail *ripio* but it was steep! Up and up we climbed, slipping and sliding, our wheels finding it difficult to get a grip on the loose surface. Occasionally, I have to admit, we dismounted and pushed. But pushing a loaded tandem uphill was not easy and soon we were looking for somewhere to take refuge for the night. A grassy bank beside a rushing, murky, grey and very cold river offered a good option. But after our Puyuhuapi experience Maggie decided it was too close to the water and we had to make do with a rocky, sloping ledge among brambles, which we shared with a battalion of hungry horse flies.

Never Say "If Only"

We slept quite well considering the rocky mattress and after two more uphill kilometres we came to Chile's border control, but there was nobody around. Maggie's repeated knocking on the door of the neighbouring house roused an official who, dressed in his morning uniform of carpet slippers, shorts and a pyjama top, checked our documents then, looking at us with pitying eyes, gesticulated that the next eight kilometres were seriously UP!

Two and a half hours and just five miles later we reached the top of Paso Perez Rosales and the border with Argentina. There was no relief as the road became even steeper. It was still the same dry river-bed type surface but the incline increased from ten to fifteen percent. It was impossible to find purchase or avoid the boulder-like rocks and pebbles. It was either get off or fall off! We resorted to pushing again. However, there were magnificent views of Mount Tronador standing at 3,491 metres being the highest in Parque Nacional V. Perez Rosales through which we were riding and pushing. Peels of thunder greeted our arrival at the top of the pass and we freewheeled into Argentina and the ferry, and more border officials, at Puerto Frías. During the seventeen hours since we left Peulla, we had only seen two vehicles: both were tourist buses.

Two more lakes and two more ferries eased our tired legs on the way to Bariloche, which had been a popular destination for German speaking immigrants in the late 19th-century, before it became popular for skiing, trekking and mountaineering. After World War II it became notorious as a haven for Nazi war criminals. For us, however, it was a return to civilisation. There were cash points, internet, supermarkets and facilities you don't realise you have missed until you see them again. There were garden centres, children's nurseries, ski slopes, beauty parlours and coffee shops! We had a chatted with an Italian couple, who were in their forties and had been cycling around the world for seven years! Verana and Lucano Pavoroti said they did not really like cycling but loved the experiences such as the freedom, people and places it revealed to them. After pedalling and pushing over the Andes we shared those sentiments entirely. Maggie was most impressed that, after seven years cycling, Verana still managed to have immaculately varnished toe nails!

It was a very windy day as we set off into the Nahuel Huapi National Park and so different from the Chilean side of the Andes. Here we saw brown, scrubby hills with short, stumpy trees, caused, perhaps, by the decreased precipitation. But I was inclined to believe that the wind was the culprit. The ferocious wind limited us to ten kilometres per hour *downhill!* The gale was as noisy as standing next to a loudspeaker at a pop concert. We had to yell at the tops of our voices to be heard. Eventually, in the lee of a mountain, the wind abated. At a lakeside campground the water tap was labelled *El agua no es potable*. No drinking water, so we waded into the lake to seek out some semi-clear water with which to cook. However, our food and drinks tasted horribly of the iodine tablets. The red wine we carried in our bottle holder was an excellent antidote!

All too soon the paved road metamorphosed into dirt, black volcanic ash that had us slipping, sliding and frequently falling whenever the road had a camber. Dust from passing traffic coated us head to foot. Luckily the cold, clear water of the *Siete Lagos* – the Seven Lakes, provided regular washing stops. Eventually the road returned to a paved surface as we passed through thickly wooded hills that had bare, smooth rocky summits like monks' pates. We crested a pass beneath the 2,393-metre high Mount Chapelco. There was a river running down its flanks that divided into two steams: one of which meandered west into Chile and the Pacific Ocean, whilst the other flowed east to the Atlantic. By the time we had reached San Junín de los Andes we were exhausted and were well pleased on the discovery that a bus ran from here into Chile. It departed four days later which gave us time for a little rest and recuperation.

Our sojourn coincided with a carnival where we were treated to clowns, jugglers, music, a rodeo and a barbeque, Argentinean–style, where complete cow carcasses where roasted on spits above a dug-out trench of burning logs. We ate more beef that evening than we ever had before. The next day featured a procession which followed the customary dignitaries' speeches. First to march by were small groups representing social services, kindergartens, schools, fire brigade, forestry commission, fire fighters and the like. These were followed by local council trucks, snow ploughs, dirt graders etc, each group carrying a national flag. Then came the military and jack-booted police complete with weaponry, ranging from hand guns and automatic rifles to anti-tank missiles, their formal march a refined goose-step. Finally the highlight of the parade, *los gauchos,* well over a hundred horsemen, many Mapuche Indians dressed in black hats, spurred boots, baggy trousers, knives in wide cummerbunds with silver jingling everywhere.

Shaking his head, the bus driver looked at the tandem and said, *"La bicicleta es muy grande"* implying that there would not be room in the bus for it. While Maggie pleaded with him to wait, I quickly unscrewed the S&S couplings and divided the bike into two; much to the curiosity and amusement of the other passengers. With a shrug of his shoulders and a wry smile, the driver opened the hold where we easily stowed the two pieces inside. We were glad we took the bus as the route was rough and steep in places, which would not have been much fun on the bike. We passed through spectacular scenery, first through scrubby mesa country, then up into monkey puzzle woods. The Argentine border was guarded by the giant, cloud shrouded, Volcán Lanin. After thirty minutes at the border post it was then over the pass into Chile and forests coated with Spanish moss. An hour was spent queuing in the rain at the Chilean customs where the whole bus was unloaded of baggage and passengers. The only item left in the hold was our two-piece bike.

We left the bus at Curarrehue and a short ride took us to a campsite with a thermal pool. The hot spring was in a cave and we had it to ourselves, as we did the whole campground. There was nobody around except pigs that were snuffling around looking for windfalls in the plum and apple orchard. The following day easy and smooth riding took us past the steaming Volcán Villarica which last erupted in 1970. At the tourist hub of Pucón we found posh houses, outdoor gear outlets, tourist and adventure establishments, cafes, restaurants and a golf course. This was a part of Chile that we had not witnessed before. A further twenty-five kilometres took us through an avenue of *cabanas* and hotels to Villarrica. From there we pedalled on to the Pan American Highway with its frightening traffic in oven-like heat. Now we were on the coastal plain where it was unseasonably hot at thirty-five Centigrade or more. We had not been on the motorway long before we came to a very recent and upsetting accident. A small boy was lying dead on the road; his school bag and packed lunch were scattered around him. The police had just arrived and were rapidly cordoning-off the accident scene. We were allowed through and for the rest of the journey to Temuco we had the carriageway to ourselves.

Temuco was a big city with not a lot to recommend it, except that, on that very evening, the city was hosting the South American Boxing Championship. We secured tickets and I, at least, thoroughly enjoyed an evening of fisticuffs. Sadly, the Argentinean champion was too good for the home-town favourite. We were lucky to be introduced to a local hero, Martín Vargas, who was an Olympian and professional world champion contender. We realised that with our time in Chile rapidly running out we could not possibly cycle the 600 kilometres to Santiago to catch our flight. We decided to hire a car but unfortunately the only available vehicle was a small Ford Fiesta. Luckily it was a hatchback and by removing the rear seats we were able to squeeze-in the two-part tandem and all four panniers.

There was a lovely, friendly campsite at Lago Lanalhue, then miles of eucalyptus plantations and logging stations before Lota. This town used to be a big coalmining area until the mines closed in 1997. It had now become a South American version of the Welsh Valleys. We found a deserted camping ground just north of Coronel with a green, slimy pool. In the morning we awoke to an all-pervading smell of urine! We frantically examined our sleeping bags but thankfully they were dry. Outside the tent the ammonia stench persisted, perhaps that was why no one else was camping here. We hastily breakfasted then set off. However, the urine smell continued and we guessed that it probably had something to do with the local industries.

We drove through Conceptión and on to a toll-road, where there was hardly another car, and up surrounding hills into fresher air! Another hot day but we did not care, we had air-conditioning! We joined the Pan American Highway Route 5 with lots of traffic and tolls and drove through the wine-producing

Central Valley of Chile. At San Bernardo we thought that we might find somewhere to camp but, like Lota yesterday, the town was a rabbit warren of similar, unmarked streets and very few signs. The streets were dusty and dirty, the houses small and poorly maintained. Nevertheless, and more by luck than judgement, we found ourselves heading for Cajón del Maupo where rich Santiago residents spend their weekends, rafting, horse riding, hiking, or just sitting by a pool barbequing. Anything to get out of Santiago, the second most polluted city in the world.

Just before we reached San Jose del Maipo, we spotted a camping sign. Owner, Juan Carlos and his son Louis, greeted us and showed us their run-down facilities which included a cold shower and a pool in which the water was not green! However, they charged a huge 5,000 pesos per person. This equated to £5 but with no alternative we had to agree. There was a distant roll of thunder as we put up the tent and had a brew. Then, as an alternative to the cold shower, we went for a swim as the first patter of raindrops fell. Before we had time to dry and dress, the patter turned into a deluge with thunder and lightning crashing around the surrounding hilltops.

"It will only last a few minutes" Juan Carlos assured us as we sheltered in a hut. But for over an hour the torrent continued – rain interspersed with hailstones. The campground was quickly becoming a lake, our tent marooned in the middle. Still dressed only in swimming trunks, I made a dash for the tent to belatedly check our possessions. The panniers stood in inches of water but luckily the ground sheet and inner-tent had repelled most of the water. Our equipment was just damp, not soaked. Juan Carlos suggested that we might like to cook and sleep in a little 'A-Frame' shelter that he had erected for the children. Now the 10,000-peso rent did not seem so bad.

It was time to go home. After an emotional *adios* with Juan Carlos and his family, we left with plenty of time to spare. One of the highlights of this tour had been the friendly and helpful people: *"Viva el Chile."* We drove to Santiago ready to take the ring road to the airport. "You can't miss it" we were told. What ring road? There were cars everywhere, no signs, so we followed the trend which took us into Santiago. We stopped repeatedly to ask for directions but in each case, we were only able to follow the instructions for a short while because of the congestion and lack of signs. Finally, on a one-way street, we stopped to ask a policeman. He told us that we were going the wrong way but

Allan Pendleton

"No problema" he intimated and obligingly stood in the middle of the road and with a raised hand stopped all the oncoming traffic. We made a three-point turn and drove to the intersection where we were able to head back. After about ten kilometres we took a right turn and hallelujah, there was a sign, *al aeropuerto*. At last we were on the illusive 'ring road'

The men at Avis car-hire were aghast when we handed back the Fiesta, *"Donde esta los asientos?"* they exclaimed, "Where are the seats?" Luckily, in Temuco, I had anticipated a difficulty in explaining the absence of the rear seats and had requested an explanatory letter.

There was no departure tax and Maggie found some Chilean pesos she had stashed away six weeks earlier. Consequently, we were able to enjoy a final restaurant meal with wine. Ten minutes after take-off we once more crossed the Andes, this time effortlessly.

CHAPTER 24

Slovenia

"One's destination is never a place but a new way of seeing things."
Henry Miller

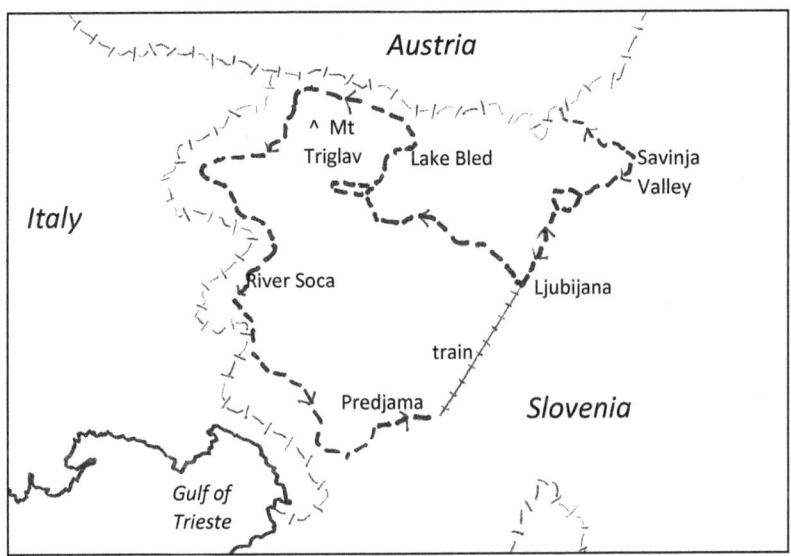

Sept, 2004. 465 miles

Pat and John Ashwell met us at Ljubljana airport in Slovenia, a country in southern central Europe that was, until 1991, part of Yugoslavia. Pat and John had invited us to join them to do a reconnaissance ride for a tour they intended to lead there for the Cycle Touring Club. The route led us through a beautiful countryside of meadows and forests, hayricks, cowbells and quaint Alpine houses, each with a flower-covered balcony. We rode into the Julian Alps, up passes and through a ski area before descending to our destination for the day – Lake Bled. The picturesque lake was sandwiched between mountains and forests with a medieval castle standing guard on a rocky promontory on the north shore. The castle overlooked a small island on which stood a pilgrimage church with a fifty-two-metre high tower. The lake frequently hosted the World Rowing Championships and provided an excellent swimming environment of which I was happy to take advantage.

The sun was rising behind the church tower as I took an early morning dip before we set out on a quiet dirt road through the Radovna Valley. In a village we passed a World War II memorial that included the names and ages of many children. Was this the scene of a Nazi massacre, a reprisal for defiance? The power for the village was sourced entirely from a small hydro-electric generating station. The River Radovna also powered a much older water mill and saw mill.

In the Julian Alps, Mount Triglav at 2,864 metres was Slovenia's highest peak and cast an ominous shadow as we sweated up grades of twenty-five percent to Aljazer Dom. This was the base camp for climbing parties. We froze on the descent as the mountain hid the sun. Our next challenge was Vrsic Pass, the highest in Slovenia, with nearly 1,000 metres of climbing and twenty-four hairpin bends. On the descent we had a blow-out of our front tyre. The constant breaking as we descended another 26 zigzags made the rims red-hot.

Julian Alps, Slovenia

We then followed the emerald waters of the River Soça, famous for kayaking but also popular for canyoning and rafting. The valley was the scene of major battles during World War I with over 300,000 Austro-Hungarian and Italian soldiers being killed. Hemingway's, *A Farewell to Arms,* depicted these battles. We spent a long time in the Isonzo Front War Museum and learned that this part of Slovenia was actually Italian until after World War II when it was shared out between the victorious Allies.

The next highlight of the trip, or more accurately the low point, was the UNESCO World Heritage Site of the Skocjan Caves. These caverns were huge, especially Martel's Chamber with a 150 metres high roof and with a volume of 2.2 million cubic metres, it was the largest underground chamber in Europe.

The following day we visited the Renaissance Predjama Castle which was built under and into a massive natural rock wall thus making it virtually impregnable. In the 15th-century the owner, Lord Erazem, a sort of Robin Hood figure who had upset the Holy Roman Emperor Frederick 3rd, found himself besieged in his fortress. However, Erazem had a secret tunnel which led from the castle to the nearby village enabling him to collect supplies and then taunt his adversaries from the safety of his lofty towers. There was only one room that was slightly vulnerable, the privy on the top floor. One of Erazem's servants was bribed to reveal when his master was answering a call of nature. A strategically placed candle prompted the besiegers to fire a cannonball into the toilet killing Erazem whilst he was on the loo. It was literally a case of "being caught with your trousers down!"

Slovenia is a very green country, eighty per cent is forested with abundant pastures. Many houses had orchards and vegetable gardens. Wood piles often took pride of place outside homes, often under roofs but always delicately stacked, each log the same length as if merits were awarded for the neatest wood pile.

The weather became dark and menacing, thunder peeled as we headed towards the Slovenian Alps. One morning, after a night of rain, we had to beat a hasty retreat from our campground as it slowly submerged. We escaped only slightly *Puyuhuapied*, others were less lucky. We cycled into the Savinja Valley in low cloud with poor visibility. At a junction with no road signs, we gambled on a road that headed roughly in the right direction. We were assured by a youth, and later by a farmer, that this road did indeed lead to Luce, our destination. However, it quickly deteriorated into loose gravel and became exceedingly steep but nevertheless we stalwartly soldiered on. Upwards ever upwards, and by the time the track had steepened to thirty-three per cent, we had dismounted and were pushing. Eventually, in the cold, dank atmosphere with steam rising from our sodden shirts, as if we had been rucking and mauling in a rugby scrum for the last eighty minutes, we reached the top! As we stopped to recover we saw, through the mist and just below us, the roof of a car glide quietly past, cruising by on a velvety tarmac surface. At least we had a smooth descent.

At the Austrian border we turned around and headed back towards Ljubljana. We were tired and it was time to go home but we had thoroughly enjoyed the Slovenian experience. The country is beautiful and so are the people. They are benign and helpful, surprisingly so considering their turbulent history, the area so often being the hub of one conflict or another.

CHAPTER 25

Southeast Asia

(Vietnam, Cambodia, Thailand)
"Hope means hoping when everything seems hopeless."
Gilbert K Chesterton

Jan-Feb, 2005. 1,470 miles

We pedalled in the drizzle through family graveyards and past spirit houses, the wet sand plastered our bike and bodies with a bloodlike redness. It was eerily appropriate, because this was My Lai, scene of the 1968 Vietnam War massacre. But of the museum, commemorating the 504 villagers, mainly women and children, killed by the Americans, we could find no sign. This was not the only time we found ourselves frustrated when looking for evidence of the American War, a war so recent yet, in the eyes of the Vietnamese, so long past. Apart from the occasional US Army Jeep or truck, we saw very few reminders of the conflict. The Vietnamese appeared to be content to just get on with their lives and apart from specific tourist destinations such as the Cu Chi tunnels, did not dwell on the past.

We had flown into Bangkok barely a week after the devastating tsunami that had inundated most of the landmasses bordering the Indian Ocean, killing 230,000 people in fourteen countries. Sitting next to us aboard the Thai Airways 747 was a middle-aged couple with grief etched onto their faces. They accepted in-flight meals but ate not a crumb, they held books but turned not a page. Perhaps their son or daughter had been enjoying Christmas in the sun or were taking a gap year when the giant tidal wave struck. Maggie and I felt that we should have spoken but we were shy, no, afraid, to intrude into their obvious pain. It was an uncomfortable journey, we often wondered about them. The tsunami was again in evidence at Bangkok International Airport where piles of medical and emergency equipment were stacked.

A connecting flight took us from Bangkok to Da Nang where our plane-load of thirteen passengers were the airport's only clients. This was the airport that during the Vietnam War was one of the busiest in the world!

We were soon exposed to the bedlam that was the traffic in Vietnam. Once we had got used to the vehicular chaos it did not seem too bad. There were hardly any cars but a multitude of trucks and buses belching out clouds of black smoke and thousands of bicycles, mopeds and small motor bikes. Because there was so much traffic, it was not able to travel too fast. But, what it lost in speed it made up for with noise! Road junctions were fun but if we had waited for a gap in the traffic we would have still been there; so, we just went, held our line and most importantly, our nerve. Then we were just absorbed into the flow, the traffic divided and swooped round us like a murmuration of starlings. Road rage was non-existent and tolerance was absolute.

We mainly kept to National Highway 1 on our way to Ho Chi Minh City, with a detour to the hill town of Da Lat. As we travelled south the weather became hotter and more humid. We tried to be on our way by first light, but the roads would already be teeming and the paddy fields dotted with the conical hats of rice planters knee-deep in mud and water. Most fields had a water buffalo, each with an egret on its back. Sugar cane stalls became our refuge when we sought solace from the sun. Our Thorn Raven tandem caused an amazing amount of interest, surprisingly because the locals often had three or even four people on board their own bicycles, to say nothing of the fully-grown pig strapped to the luggage rack, or the dozen or so chickens hanging from the handle bars. Our 14-speed Rohloff hub was hardly noticed, presumably because it looked little different from the local single-speed bikes.

At Hoi An, after changing some American dollars, we became *dong* millionaires. But such wealth did not stop my larium induced nightmares. I later abandoned the pills feeling that a bout of malaria would be favourable to the fear-filled sleep. Vietnamese food was delicious and we enjoyed many inexpensive feasts using chopsticks, which meant that each meal lasted an age. There were few tourists and in restaurants we often found ourselves to be the only customers.

Many roads were under repair and when it rained we got coated in mud. However, the locals on their "sit-up and beg" bikes, especially the school girls who were immaculately dressed in white blouses and baggy trousers under long, split skirts, always looked cool and clean.

Arriving early at Doc Let we spent the afternoon on the beach where a bevy of beautiful girls were offering body massages. Maggie, seeing my eyes lustfully glaze over, asked me if I would like a massage. No reply was necessary so she added, "As long as I can choose the masseuse." The chosen nymph looked at least ninety years old, had skin like wrinkled cardboard and possessed a mouthful of chipped, pointed, black teeth. Her knobbly fingers were as hard as iron and the massage was painful: not passionate. We keep her photograph to remind our grandchildren of the consequences of not cleaning their teeth!

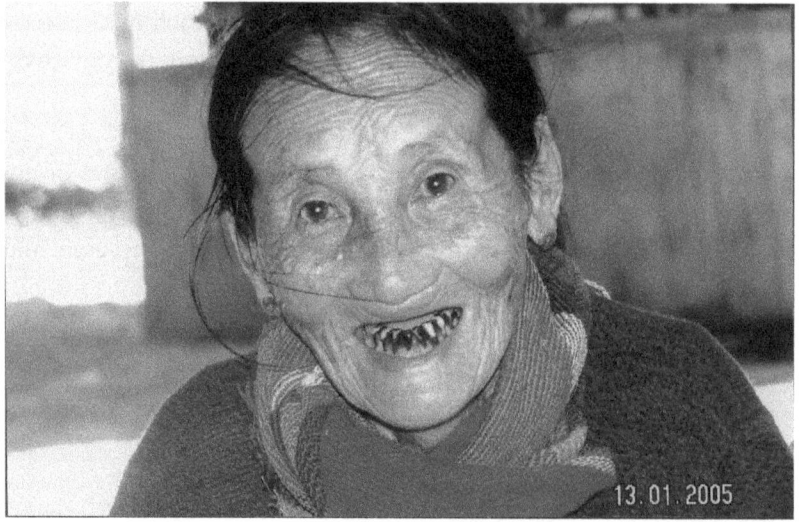

My masseuse

In Ho Chi Minh City – formerly Saigon – we visited the Reunification Palace, previously called the Independence Palace, very much pro Uncle Ho and anti the old southern Vietnam Regime. Even more anti-American was the War History Museum. After two hours of photographs and accounts of the Vietnam war from a Vietcong point of view, we had to admit that the museum had been aptly named when it was previously known as the Museum of Chinese and American War Crimes. Robert McNamara, the US Secretary of Defence, stated, "Human beings will not tolerate such a disaster happening again, either in Vietnam or anywhere else on our planet." Mmm, so how come Iraq ?

In Ho Chi Minh City there were one million bicycles, and three million mopeds and motorbikes. When we left the city they were all on the road at the same time, or so it appeared. They used their two-wheeled vehicles as we would a car or pick-up truck; three or four passengers or a cargo of livestock, furniture, groceries or whatever else that required transporting. Bicycle rickshaws were also popular and were the Vietnam equivalent to a container lorry or removal van. We saw one with a three-piece suite of furniture on board and another with a double bed! We enjoyed Ho Chi Minh and our departure was also fun as we just allowed ourselves to be swept along with the flow.

At Mytho we were intercepted by a freelance tourist guide by the name of Tung and cajoled into going on his moonlight boat ride. An unofficial boat ride as the government had a monopoly on tourist excursions. We were given a motorbike ride on his Honda Dream, all three of us aboard, then a fascinating boat ride across the Mekong to an Island which we explored through narrow waterways beneath canopies of palm and coconut trees. We netted our own dinner, an elephant fish which we consumed with noodles, greens and banana wine. By the time we had finished it was dark and fire-flies illuminated the trees much as fairy lights do at Christmas time.

After the trip, Tung invited us back to his place for a beer and to meet his family. His home was little more than a garage. He pointed across the road to a much finer house. "That used to be our house" he said. His father had been an officer in the South Vietnamese Army, was wounded and the victorious Vietcong confiscated his house and gave it to a communist sympathiser. Tung was denied a proper education and fled to the hill tribes to avoid conscription. He trained as a tailor but then became an unofficial tour guide. In the meantime, he had made three attempts to leave Vietnam by fishing boat. However, each time he was intercepted by the communist authorities and sentenced to a year in prison: the last incarceration with his entire family. Was Tung bitter and twisted about the unfair hand he had been dealt in life? Apparently not judging from the friendship and smiles he gave to us.

Near the Cambodian border was the Cao Dai Temple. The exterior was decorated with multi-coloured dragons of all shapes and sizes while inside there were statues of Jesus, Buddha and the Hindu God, Brahma. Above the main entrance was the all-seeing eye, the symbol of the Cao Dai religion which combined Buddhism, Christianity, Taoism and Confucianism. We watched as some incredibly old believers prayed and chanted to bizarre string music.

Next, we visited the Cu Chi Tunnels. Vietnamese soldiers constructed these tunnels during the French occupation in the 1940s. This elaborate underground labyrinth was used by the Vietcong to escape from American bombing. With a total length of more than 200 kilometres they contained everything needed to evade capture, including some evil-looking booby traps. There was a complete village underground with living quarters, hospital, command centre, school and even a weapons factory. These tunnels were literally under the feet of the Americans with the entrances well concealed and tiny. We had to squeeze through the trapdoor although it had been doubled in size in order to accommodate Western tourists.

On our way to Cambodia we visited a snake farm which bred snakes for the pot. Rows of cages of pythons, some were thin with a nervous duck trembling in the corner, others were fat with duck-shaped tummies. We were introduced to another form of wildlife in our hotel in Cantho – bed bugs! We itched and scratched all night but it made the 5am get-up easier.

After the usual light breakfast of noodles, rice, spring rolls, fish and snake, we took a long-tailed boat ride to visit the floating market at Cai Rang. Like the name suggests it is indeed a floating market. Just about anything you might need, and a lot that you wouldn't, is for sale from boats, often single-handed punts. Bamboo poles are used to hang samples of the traders' wares such as fruits or vegetables, fish or poultry. We saw mangoes, coconuts, melons, dragon fruit, turtles, snakes and even a pot-bellied pig for sale. There were also house boats with families and livestock, and floating take-away restaurants.

Cai Rang floating market

We criss-crossed over numerous bridges and pedalled alongside the waterways of the Mekong Delta, on which there appeared to be as much traffic as on the roads. Everywhere people were boating, fishing, weeding, washing, or, for some reason or other, grovelling in the muddy water. On the road there was a constant flood of people travelling, shelling coconuts, drying rice, making bricks and pots of clay, conveying merchandise and selling anything and everything. Many folks lived adjacent to the highway, often in tin or coconut leaf huts framed with bamboo and on stilts reaching out over the river. It was very hot and humid, we would regularly stop to rest at which point we were immediately surrounded by people, mainly women and children, smiling and laughing at our sweaty pale skin and sunburn.

Ho Chi Minh City

From Chau Doc we took a boat and then a bus to Phnom Penh, Cambodia and enjoyed its relative tranquillity. In Vietnam we were never out of sight of another human being. But in Cambodia the Khmer Rouge had wiped out almost half of the population in the 1970s. This created a little more space for those who had survived. In those bad, sad days of the Khmer Rouge having an education or holding any type of office was not good for life expectancy. During our visit, half the population were under 15 years of age. At one point the capital, Phnom Penh, was emptied of its entire population, the people were sent to work in the fields as slave labour.

We journeyed north to Siem Reap and Angkor Wat through a flat, barren landscape. The rice had been harvested leaving patches of stubble in the fields ready for burning. This looked to be an area of extreme poverty. Children played naked in the dirt beneath their bamboo, wattle and banana leaf houses. These dwellings were all built on stilts which suggested that with the forthcoming monsoon rains this stark, flat and dry landscape might change to a lush, green and abundant rice bowl on which the country depended. In the meantime, the people waited listlessly but never too weary to mark our passing with a cheery, 'Hello!' These shouted greetings echoed ahead of us demanding increasingly tired responses.

The stunning temples, ruins and monuments of Angkor Wat, which once formed the heart of the Khmer Empire, had now largely been reclaimed by the jungle. It was the most extensive religious monument in the world and we were thankful to have the tandem as a means of transport. This allowed us to escape from teems of tourists and discover temples seldom seen. The ruling Khmers built Ankor Wat as a Hindu temple but it became Buddhist towards the end of the 12th-century. Ankor Wat, which means City of Temples, had, at one stage, one million inhabitants and was sacked by the Chams, the traditional enemies of the Khmer, then abandoned to the ravages of time. In the 20th-century the French rulers in Cambodia started reconstructing the temples. However, restoration was halted in the 1970s by the civil war and the Khmer Rouge taking control of the country. Evidence of the restoration attempt was obvious by the piles of masonry, each brick carefully labelled with a specific code. The work had started again but was hampered by the loss of the plans and the code that was needed for the reconstruction. It resembled a massive 3D jigsaw puzzle.

One day a young girl, ten or eleven years old, approached us and asked if we had any foreign currency for a school project. We found a small collection of English coins and gladly gave them to her. Two days later the same girl, not recognising us, asked if we would like to buy some English money because she couldn't spend it in Cambodia!

After three days we were "templed-out." We returned to Phnom Penh by bus. From the capital city we continued by bike south to Sihanoukville. We passed a rather grand house that was constructed for one of Pol Pot's henchmen who, on completion, had all the builders executed so as not to reveal the secret escape routes. Pol Pot became leader of the Cambodian Communist Party, the Khmer Rouge and between 1975 and 1979 his attempt to form a peasant farming society resulted in the deaths of twenty-five percent of the country's population from starvation, overwork and executions. During the Vietnamese war, the United States had invaded Cambodia in order to expel North Vietnamese fighters but instead drove them deeper into Cambodia where they allied themselves with the Khmer Rouge. From 1969 until 1973, the Americans intermittently bombed North Vietnamese sanctuaries in eastern Cambodia, killing up to 150,000 Cambodian peasants. Consequently, the peasants fled the countryside by the hundreds of thousands and settled in Cambodia's capital city, Phnom Penh. By 1975, America had withdrawn its troops from Vietnam. Cambodia's government, plagued by corruption and incompetence, also lost its American military support. Taking advantage of the opportunity, Pol Pot's Khmer Rouge army, consisting of teenage peasant guerrillas, marched into Phnom Penh and seized control of Cambodia.

Once in power, Pol Pot began a radical experiment to create an agrarian utopia inspired in part by Mao's Cultural Revolution which he had witnessed first-hand during a visit to Communist China. All foreigners were thus expelled, embassies closed and any foreign economic or medical assistance was refused. The use of foreign languages was banned. Newspapers and television stations were shut down, radios and bicycles confiscated and mail and telephone usage curtailed. Money was forbidden. All businesses were shuttered, religion was banned, education halted, health care eliminated and parental authority revoked. Cambodia was sealed off from the outside world. All Cambodia's cities were then forcibly evacuated. At Phnom Penh, two million inhabitants were evacuated on foot into the countryside at gunpoint. As many as 20,000 died along the way. Millions of Cambodians accustomed to city life were now forced into slave labour in Pol Pot's 'killing fields' where they soon began dying from overwork, disease and malnutrition on a diet of one tin of rice, just `180 grams, per person every two days. Workdays in the fields began around 4 am and lasted until 10 pm, with only two rest periods allowed during the eighteen-hour day, all under the armed supervision of young Khmer Rouge soldiers eager to kill anyone for the slightest infraction. Starving people were forbidden to eat the fruits and rice they were harvesting. After the rice was harvested, Khmer Rouge trucks would arrive and confiscate the entire crop. On 25 December, 1978, Vietnam launched a full-scale invasion of Cambodia seeking to end Khmer Rouge border attacks. On 7 January, 1979, Phnom Penh fell and Pol Pot was deposed.

It was exceedingly hot as we rode south towards the Gulf of Siam. Here we were constantly bombarded with cries of, "Hello" from ubiquitous children. "Hello, where you from?" echoed from the houses, fields and trees. Many moto-riders also regarded us with interest, often cruising just behind us or alongside, studying either the bike's mechanics or the shape of Maggie's backside. This was all conducted with smiles and good humour.

From Sihanoukville we boarded an overloaded ferry to the Thai border. We loaded the tandem unsecured on top of the boat and hoped that the sea would not be too rough. However, since all the seats were taken, many people climbed onto the roof; it was more likely that some of them and not the bike that would fall overboard. At departure time we were jam-packed with two persons per seat, plastic stools in the gangway, the roof was full and still people were trying to climb on board.

Four hours later we arrived safely at Krong Koh Kong and were met by a mad scrum of moto-taxis all touting for fares. They scrambled on board, grabbed bags and rucksacks then, on finding the owners, attempted to get them to travel on their motorbikes. We had a hard time because they could not understand that we had our own transport. It was not until the bike was retrieved from the boat roof that they eased off the pressure. Even then we were persuaded to follow a moto-rider to a guest house. We accepted a room and were requested to pay in advance; on doing so, we were short-changed in Thai bhats. Grabbing back our dollars, we re-loaded the tandem and rode off looking for honest accommodation. It was the Chinese New Year, Year of the Rooster. I got too near to a fire cracker and had a ringing sensation in my ears for days. Chinese or not, the kids here planned to have a good time. A charming Cambodian customs official offered Maggie the use of their staff toilet. Maggie did not stay long for she had to share the squat loo with an enormous crab! Rather than crap on the crab she left, mission unaccomplished.

In Thailand there was an immediate diminishing of noise, litter and people and also of friendly spontaneity. The roads improved and there were ATMs, McDonalds and other signs of Western culture: not least the increasing girth of the Thai people. Upon entering Thailand, we remembered to switch to the left-hand side of the road. We cycled under a remorseless sun. The sea was on one side and dense forest inland. After many hot miles we saw a resort sign and decided to see what was on offer. After five kilometres down a side road and completely lost we stopped to ask for directions. Upon miming our needs to a lady on a scooter, she beckoned for us to follow over a narrow concrete raised walkway, through a fishing village on stilts, to the resort. We would never have found it ourselves, the only access was by boat, bike or on foot. Someone was sent to the village to buy a fried rice meal for us and we were shown to our room, a hut on stilts. The owner had recently returned from Massachusetts and was developing this property; we were his first European visitors. He told us that when he first went over to the States he took his pet with him, a pot-bellied pig. On returning to Thailand a few years later, he brought, at great expense, his pig with him. Regrettably the pig, used to bustling New York streets and not familiar with Thailand's ways, got rolled on by a water buffalo and died. Our host was distraught.

At 6:20pm precisely, it was as if someone had turned on a badly tuned radio with loads of static as the cicadas started their evening chorus accompanied by the croaking of frogs. It was a memorable moment.

We took a ferry over to Koh Chang Island, a beautiful jungle-clad mountain. There was a lot of puffing, panting and pushing before we found a place to stay but then we remained for a couple of days of swimming, snorkelling, sunbathing and sundowners of Singha beer.

Back on the mainland we continued north and decided to take a look at Pattaya. The city's reputation as a sex capital was well deserved, with hundreds of beer bars, go-go clubs and massage parlours. We booked into the Sawasdee Hotel, where we found many sad-looking middle-aged men, often accompanied by young Thai girls. We were glad to leave and with time running out, we took a bus to Bangkok. This was still my favourite city in spite of, or because of, the traffic, the smells and the pollution. It was just so exotic, there was always something new to find in Bangkok.

During the eight-week expedition our accommodation ranged from three-star hotels to a hut in the mangroves. We always ate out, mainly a diet of fish, noodles and rice, with some of the most delicious food coming from roadside stalls. Including boat and bus excursions and the daily pint or two of cold beer, excluding airfares, we returned home only £1,000 poorer, that is less than £20 per day, but with a host of fantastic memories from a trouble-free and worry-free adventure.

CHAPTER 26

Yucatan, Mexico

"Life is like a bicycle, to keep your balance you must keep moving."
Albert Einstein

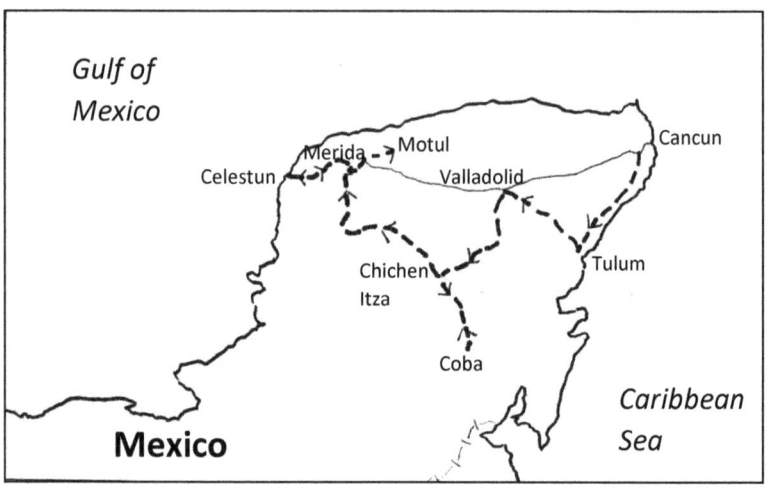

Jan-Feb, 2006. 620 miles

We arrived in Cancún on the tail of a devastating season of hurricanes. The city was still recovering from the most recent, Hurricane Wilma. The few hotels that had not been demolished were still closed. The beaches were strewn with smashed coral, flotsam, up-rooted palms and debris. Sun-beds lay empty. Diggers and other heavy machinery were busy trying to repair the devastation to enable Cancún to once more attract the tourist trade on which so many depended. However, at that moment the sea front resembled a cross between a war zone and a building site.

Our first challenge was to survive the 130 kilometres of motorway between Cancún and Tulúm. In the Tourist Office we had been warned that it was very dangerous with many deaths. There was a wide hard shoulder but we had to share it with the lorries and buses that raced along the Tulúm Corridor and used the shoulder as an overtaking lane. A ten-wheel truck blew a tyre just as it was passing us. There was an enormous, deafening bang and rubber flew in all directions. Luckily, the driver kept control and managed to pull in just ahead of us.

We celebrated our lucky escape with a visit to Gran Cenote, an underground lake. Long ago parts of the cave roof had collapsed creating a magical subterranean swimming pool full of crystal clear water containing many small fish. The only light came from the opening high above but the white limestone walls reflected this meagre light, especially underwater. I explored some of the adjoining tunnels, careful not to bang my head on the cave ceiling and ensuring that I had air-space for my snorkel. It was a magnificent and unusual experience to dive under stalactites.

We peddled to the ruins of Coba, one of the largest Mayan settlements of its time. During 800-1100 AD its population was estimated to be 55,000. Like Ankor Wat and Machu Pichu, Coba was lost to the jungle for centuries and there was still much to excavate. We climbed the pyramid of *Nohoch Mul*; at forty-two metres in height this was the second biggest Mayan structure in the Yucatan.

In the Spanish-style town of Valladolid we stopped to buy some fruit and to people-watch. It was a typical Sunday morning street scene. Everyone was out walking; the ladies and children in their Sunday best. A few men talked to us but were really just in pursuit of a few pesos. We were sitting at a table in the market when suddenly we were attacked by a swarm of flying ants. As quickly as possible we gathered our possessions and beat a hasty retreat. However, later that evening in a youth hostel room, I opened up our bar-bag and quite literally opened up an ants' nest. Thousands had encamped in the bag which was under the table when we were invaded and made themselves at home alongside my wallet, passport and camera. I had a hell of a job to get rid of the ants from the bag, the majority dropping to the floor, free to further torment us through the night.

Chichen Itza was our next pyramid where a sound and light show portraying Mayan culture and history entertained us. We moved on in overcast, sultry, steamy conditions along straight and flat roads. There was slightly less jungle but the foliage remained very green with a wall of yellow daisy-like flowers bordering the road. We turned left at Dzitas, consumed a Coca-Cola at Quintana Roo then met a weather-beaten old man in a bar at Tunkas who had quite a story to tell.

He was either a Polish or German; either way he was one of the few survivors to escape the allied bombing of Gdansk in 1945. The Free City of Danzig was overrun by German troops in 1939 thus provoking the beginning of World War II. Anything remotely Polish was destroyed and thousands were executed. By 1944 and with the fortunes of war altering, Gdansk became a major transit point for the thousands of refugees fleeing from the east. In 1945, with the Red Army fast approaching, the population had reached 1½ million. Suspected deserters were strung up from trees and lampposts as allied bombers devastated the city slaughtering Nazis and civilians alike. Those that survived the bombing had the avenging Soviets to confront. Polish and Red Army troops finally entered Gdansk on 30 March. Gdansk, where six years earlier the first shots of WW II were heard, had become a ruin of rape and slaughter. Apparently, our Polish-German acquaintance had managed to steal a ride on the last boat to leave Gdansk before the city's capitulation; he travelled to the United States then spent thirty years in Alaska. For the last four years, his wife had lain in a coma while his daughter was recently killed when her car collided with a moose. Our aged veteran was now trying to create a new life in Yucatán, Mexico.

As we approached Merida the damp jungle smells were eclipsed by the stench of road kill, sewage and fly-tipping. The city, however, more than compensated for the unpleasant aromas of the journey. A city of a million people, Merida offered museums, markets, murals, modern art, musicians, magicians and much more. There was a huge cathedral and interesting colonial buildings. Impressive murals by Fernando Castro Pacheco in the Palacio del Gobierno depicted Yucatan history. The raucous din from the thousands of birds flying in to roost in the *Zocalo, the* city square, at twilight left indelible memories. We spent a week cycling round the Merida region. There were more Mayan ruins at Uxmal where we shared the site with numerous iguanas, until the tourist buses arrived. At the white sand beaches at Celestún, pelicans swooped low over the waves, while frigate birds and gulls fought over any left-overs.

Uxmal

We also had a look round the old sisal manufacturing estate or *hacienda,* at Ochil. Sisal, or henequen, was a variety of cactus and was used to make rope, cord and twine which was exported in the 19th-century for the booming shipping industry. The production of henequen was very labour intensive involving hundreds of men working in the fields and processing buildings. *Haciendas* were run like the southern plantations of the United States with the landowners as masters and the indigenous people as workers. Each *hacienda* had a chapel, school, infirmary, jail, store, workers' huts and cemetery. The grandest building was always the *Casa Principal,* a mansion, where the master lived. These estates were not dissimilar in many ways to the British coalmines of long ago, when the workers were housed in company houses and paid in tokens that could only be redeemed in the company store.

It was stiflingly hot as we pedalled through thick forest, past Mayan ruins and fields of maize, cocoa beans and squash and orchards of bananas, oranges and avocado. It must have been a never-ending battle to stem the spread of the jungle. Undergrowth rapidly covered anything that was not permanently tendered, which was why the fantastic Mayan pyramids and structures remained hidden for so long. There are possibly more to be found.

At intervals we passed through scruffy villages, *pueblos,* where the children always seemed to be either going to, or returning from school. Either way, they filled the streets and greeted us, or taunted us, with *"¿Hola gringos, tienen pesos?"* Meanwhile the majority of menfolk sat smoking in the plazas while the women wandered and gossiped in the streets with toddlers permanently perched on their hips. Dogs were everywhere, most were emaciated, mangy and flea-infested with most of the bitches either pregnant or with pups. Posters for *"Gran Corrida del Toros"* .... a bull fight, were plastered everywhere; on lamp posts, windows, doors, walls, on every spare surface. Based upon the theory that you should not condemn anything unless you have seen it, this was obviously an opportunity too good to miss, plus there would be buses to take us to the bull ring at nearby Motúl. We purchased *sombres,* meaning shady seats but we were still in the sun, although not facing it. Twenty thousand spectators were crammed into the arena waiting for the bull fight to exhibit a display of artistry, pageantry and courage; or so we were led to believe. Alas, it was not to be, for as Maggie recorded in our log:

"A bull was released into the ring to be taunted by four toreadors, including the famed matadores, who were armed with long, sharp lances which they plunged into the bull's neck before fleeing behind the bullring safety fence. The bull at this stage was rather lively and obviously a bit narked at being stabbed repeatedly in the neck. Enter stage left, a picador carrying a long spear and riding a well-padded horse. The picador's task was to implant his weapon deep into the bull's neck causing loss of blood and further weakening the animal. Then it was the turn of the t*ercio de banderillas,* three men each armed with two sharp, barbed pikes that they also endeavoured, cleverly, I must admit, to stick into the tiring bull's neck. By this stage the poor bull was bleeding profusely with its neck and shoulders like a pin cushion and almost on its knees when the matador made his re-entrance alone with a sword and red cape. He strutted his stuff to the adulation of his fawning fans, teasing the reluctant bull and tempting it to charge so that he could make a few daring passes before finally performing the *estocada,* a thrust of his sword to the heart of the bull."

Twenty thousand people, minus two, cheered, waved, *oley'ed* and appeared to thoroughly enjoy the spectacle: just as well as it was repeated a further six times with new bulls. Actually, it was not just the bullfighting that had made Maggie feel uncomfortable, during lunch she had popped a cherry tomato into her mouth and quickly realised that the tomato was, in fact, a chilli, a very *hot* chilli. Rather than spit it out, being a lady, Maggie swallowed it! She was uncomfortably aware of the exact location in her digestive system of that chilli until it made its heated exit some twenty-four hours later.

The bus station in Merida was like an airport terminal with exit gates and big screens showing departure times and gate numbers. Our bus to Cancún was air-conditioned with a toilet and in-flight movies. We watched *Touching the Void,* the true story of climber Joe Simpson's miraculous survival in the Andean Mountains. At Cancún we took a ferry to Isla Mujeres and witnessed more of the damage caused by Hurricane Wilma. There were many large capsized boats including a car ferry to Cuba which, we were told, was picked up by a gigantic wave and deposited on top of a beach restaurant. The eatery was flattened and the ferry left high and dry with ninety cars still in the hold.

We found a hotel that had been less severely damaged than many of the others. Here we spent a couple of days cycling round the island and snorkelling. One two-hour boat trip lasted twice as long when the captain, after our allotted snorkel time, decided to pull in at a beach restaurant for another two hours. The business belonged to his brother-in-law! Sitting in the sun drinking cold beer and enjoying a delicious fish meal was fine for us but for Mark and Candy a young couple from London, it was a worrying affair. They were flying back to England later that day and still had to get back to the mainland and then reach the airport. They earlier thought that they would just have time to fit in one last, short snorkel before leaving for home. I always wondered if they caught their flight.

Forewarned, we left ourselves plenty of time to get to the airport when it was our turn a couple of days later, and had an uneventful journey home.

CHAPTER 27

USA.; New Orleans to Washington DC

Louisiana, Mississippi, Alabama, Tennessee, North Carolina, Virginia, West Virginia, Maryland, Washington DC

"Illegal aliens have always been a problem in the United States. Ask any Indian."
Robert Orben

April- May 2006, 1,685 miles

We were the only white people on the downtown bus apart from a completely loopy chap who continually talked loudly and gesticulated to himself. We had again arrived in the wake of a hurricane. Last August, Hurricane Katrina wreaked havoc on New Orleans flooding eighty percent of the city and leaving 1,464 dead. In spite of concerted evacuation measures, many remained when the hurricane struck, mainly those without access to personal vehicles. The absence of white folk on our bus indicated who they might be. Post Katrina, the authorities received world-wide criticism for an apparent lack of resolve to help *all* of New Orleans residents. After the hurricane there were criminal acts such as the looting of a Walmart store but some of the stories of murder, rape and shooting were exaggerated or untrue. Many buses were lost in the floods, which could account for us having to wait an hour for ours. On board a huge Afro-American woman started shouting and swearing at the top of her voice, to the amusement of some but to the annoyance of others. The driver was put into an unenviable position but eventually coaxed the thirty stones plus lady to get off the bus. In the French Quarter we saw only a few tourists and the locals were busy repairing the damage. This was not the carnival atmosphere that we had hoped for but hardly expected given the situation. We decided to head out of town.

Watching CNN before leaving our hotel, we were informed that tornadoes were imminent and someone had been killed by a bear at Cherokee Campground, one of our destinations. Resolutely, we set off along the William's Boulevard and rode along the levee that should have protected low lying New Orleans. It was, however, a fantastic bike path with two tarmac lanes and splendid views over the Mississippi. Nearing midday, we started to flag in the heat when three guys in a golf buggy blocked our way. They press-ganged us into joining them at their Good Friday barbeque. We were treated to jambalaya, a Cajun inspired rice hot pot with shrimps and catfish, followed by angle's food cake. In return, they trialled the tandem and when the novelty wore off we were allowed to leave. Ten miles later we found that our intended camp ground was "closed for refurbishment." In another ten miles we came to a children's park. While we were reconnoitring the playground with the view of camping between the swings, a young girl in her late teens invited us to put up our tent in the backyard of her mother's caravan. Marilyn's mum welcomed us with a cold Coca-Cola and a gallon of bottled water. Next door, the children's park had a cold tap and a Portaloo which was perfect! Later, as we prepared to cook our pasta, Marilyn arrived with a plate of shrimp po-boys (baguettes) and french fries. Gone were any preconceived notions of Deep South trailer trash. Marilyn's mum's obese boyfriend came out to check us out and, luckily, deemed us as "not too dangerous." "Well, y' all cain't be too careful, what with all them there serial killers from N'awlins!"

Several blood-sucking mosquitoes were intent on sharing our tent. We found the most effective way of exterminating the pests was to squish them between the pages of our books leaving either black blotches on the paper or, in the case of those that had retaliated first, red ones. We were awoken early by the noise from the nearest of many chemical works that lined the banks of the Mississippi, which, together with oil and gas refineries make "N'awlins" second busiest port in the USA. All was quiet in Marilyn's trailer, so we left some English chocolate on the step as a small thank you and continued meandering alongside "Old Man River."

During a couple of long and very hot days we cycled through Baton Rouge and Saint Francisville, into Mississippi State and on to Natchez. It was good riding through rolling countryside and archways of trees, smells of wood and wild flowers and past squashed armadillos and snakes. Normally a Coca-Cola would not rate as one of my preferred beverages but, when we arrived in Natchez State Park after a hundred miles in ninety-degree heat, the caffeine and sugar from a vending machine Coke really hit the spot and was as welcome as any drink I have ever tasted.

A pick-up truck towing a large recreational vehicle arrived alongside our camping pitch. An elderly couple, about our age, unhitched the pick-up and drove away leaving the air conditioning in their RV roaring away. They soon returned with a load of logs in the back of their truck. They lit their camp fire and immediately retired to the cool of the van, emerging at intervals to load their fire with extra fire wood. It was still eighty degrees in the shade but when camping in America one must have a campfire – I suppose. They also used the pick-up to go to the bathroom; well, it was almost thirty yards away.

Maggie was getting painful lower back spasms. Any movement hurt and she found getting on and off the bike exceedingly painful. Our neighbours kept their noisy air-conditioning running all night so we were happy to make an early start on the Natchez Trace Parkway. The Parkway or 'Trace' is a two-lane road that follows an ancient Native American route and extends from Natchez in Mississippi, through the north-west corner of Alabama to Nashville in Tennessee. The surface was silky-smooth, and with a ban on commercial traffic and a speed restriction of 50 mph it made for excellent cycling through conifer and deciduous woods, grassy meadows with birds, insects and spring flowers. A peddler's Utopia.

Never Say "If Only"

We made a detour to Port Gibson for supplies which brought us back to reality as dozens of big trucks roared closely by. In the 1860s during the American Civil War, General U. S. Grant declared that Port Gibson was too pretty to burn, so many grand old buildings remained, including numerous churches. In one street alone, we counted about a dozen churches of different denominations, plus a Jewish synagogue.

Back on the Parkway it was seriously hot again, unseasonably hot for April we were told. At Rocky Springs Campground signs informed us that the water was not suitable for drinking. But needs must, we boiled the water and added iodine and it was fine, if not very tasty. No showers here, but also no fees and no RVs. That evening only bird song, a very busy woodpecker, and the buzz of insects could be heard at our secluded woodland site.

We shared the Parkway with bunches of motor bike riders, often in groups of a dozen or more. There were Harley Davidson battalions, or chapters as they like to be called, and convoys of Honda Goldwings. Each group would consist of only one make of bike, Harleys or Hondas, and never the twain shall meet. We waved to each other as the Harleys rumbled by, lights blazing, and the riders sitting tall with straight legs and sticky-out booted feet, reaching high for handlebars that spurned any thoughts of aero-dynamics. Contrarily, the Hondas purred by, their captains comfortably relaxed in padded armchair-like seats with arm-rests, and feet tucked in. As we were also on two wheels I think that we were acknowledged, but probably looked down on as poor neighbours. We often chatted with resting Harley riders. Most of them were big bearded guys with blond long-haired female pillion riders. We got on well but struggled to understand their southern drawl. Likewise, our English accents were "Kinda funny" and they enquired, "Did y'all bicycle all the way here from England?"

While cycling the 444-mile Natchez Trace we stopped at a variety of campgrounds, ranging from the primitive with only pit toilets, to motor home sites with hard standing pitches and excellent facilities. We preferred the primitive campgrounds every time. Here at least you have peace and tranquillity, while in the mobile home sites there was the constant roar of air conditioning systems or hydraulic hissing and electronic whirring as the owners attempted to level-off their mighty cruisers or extend their living quarters with pop-out bays. They had fitted kitchens, king-size beds, corner

Allan Pendleton

couch units, huge flat-screen and wall-mounted TVs, bathrooms and showers: and were aptly named, for instance, Travel Lite, Wilderness or Roughing It.

After passing some historic landmarks, such as the birthplaces of Oprah Winfrey at Kosciusko and Elvis Presley at Tupelo, the weather became cooler. We pedalled into Alabama and on a damp evening stopped at the Trace Cafe-cum-Grocery Store where, according to our guide book, we would be able to camp for the night. But this was news to the store owner who was in the process of locking up as we arrived. Nevertheless, he gave us permission to pitch our tent on the grass beside his shop. We asked if we could buy some provisions before he left. "Look" he said, "I'm in a bit of a hurry, so why don't you put up your tent before it's dark, then," handing me his keys, "Help yourself to whatever you need in the store. Lock up when you leave and return the keys to me in the morning. Help yourself to coffee and the TV remote control is behind the counter." With that he climbed into his car and drove away. So, instead of shivering in a cold, damp tent we sat inside the warm store reading newspapers and watching television. In the morning we returned the keys to Chris who asked, "What *don't* you like for breakfast?" With that he proceeded to cook us an enormous full American breakfast. When we went to pay and thank Chris for his hospitality and his trust, he brushed our words aside and would only take payment for the provisions that we had taken the night before.

Numerous hills, stops and conversations meant that we made slow progress for the remainder of the Natchez Trace. A burly fellow riding an 1800 Honda Goldwing with a small fluffy dog sitting on the fuel tank pulled in ahead of us and waved us down. Berniel was from Texas and wanted to hear all about us. He was very concerned about our safety and was surprised that we did not carry a weapon. He carried a loaded revolver that he was proud to show us. "You guys are in the buckle of the Bible Belt in tornado alley" he warned us and went on to list a number of dangers we were likely to encounter. Such was his concern for us, that for a number of nights following our initial meeting, Berniel would search for us just to check that we were alright.

Finally, we left the Natchez Trace and rode into Franklin, home of singer-songwriter Sheryl Crow, one-time girlfriend of Lance Armstrong. We booked in at a Best Western motel and enjoyed our first proper wash for a while. We dined at Shoney's, an all-you-can-eat seafood restaurant. Inside, everyone was enormous; we felt that we had landed on an alien planet and being less than half the size of everyone else, were a different species. It was like being in a hive full of queen bees with us being the only workers.

In the morning I had indigestion, served me right for trying to eat like a queen bee. Maggie's back was better but she now had chronic tooth ache. Facing an arduous ride to the Smokey Mountains we decided to try to rent a car. Regrettably, none of the car rentals would do a one-way until Steve, at Enterprise, took pity on us and demonstrated another example of American kindness by bending the rules. The hire charge for our Dodge Neon was just $80, which was less than the alternative bus fare to Knoxville, where we did not want to go. The 250-miles across Tennessee were hilly and windy – we were glad not to be pedalling. We took the car to the birthplace of Dolly Parton; Servierville which was Tennessee's answer to Las Vegas with hotels, motels, theatres, bars, restaurants, neon lights and huge casinos. From there we pedalled, mostly uphill, to the Smokey Mountain National Park then into North Carolina and the Cherokee Indian Reservation, and onto the Blue Ridge Parkway.

The Blue Ridge Parkway was 470 miles long and ran along a mountain chain that was part of the Appalachian Mountains. Like the Natchez Trace, commercial vehicles were prohibited and there were strict speed regulations. It was an area of outstanding natural beauty which we were able to appreciate as we climbed through deciduous forests just coming into leaf. The road rose to over 6,000 feet offering majestic views over deep green valleys and a series of hazy mountains in the distance, each range becoming darker like rows of cardboard cut outs Again, we were having problems finding campgrounds that were open. At Asheville, a park ranger suggested that we tried the Recreational Vehicle Park on Black Mountain Road, "I'm sure that is open" he assured us. It was but they did not allow tents! This was time for Maggie to produce her trump card, standing forlornly, her helmet clutched tightly – all the better to emphasise her white hair – she pleaded, "Please." Sufficiently shamed, the owner relented and found us a small grass patch beside the highway.

The next two weeks saw us riding into Virginia with a deterioration of the weather. The clear blue skies were replaced by cloud, rain and fog with a severe dip in the temperature. No longer were we able to admire the views, indeed on one occasion, we rode past the only refuelling point for miles because the cafe was on the far side of the road: the fog was so dense, we could not see it. The hills seemed never ending. If we were not slogging upwards we were shivering, free-wheeling blindly down. The campgrounds were inevitably closed. However, in a masochistic way we were enjoying ourselves and we were not alone. Many motor bike convoys rumbled or purred past, plus this was a popular training ground for racing cyclists and we were often overtaken by lycra-clad pelotons. On a particularly steep climb, a group of about twenty riders swooshed past but one of the racers slowed down for a chat as we laboured up the hill. After a while I suggested that he should pedal on, catch up with his pals and not allow us to hold him back.

"Not at all" he said, "You are doing really well with all that baggage."

"Do you mind," I retorted, "That baggage is my wife!"

He was aghast, "No, no. I didn't mean your wife, I meant your other baggage. No, your, um, err, kit and stuff." We laughed so much that we nearly fell off the tandem. Still apologising he pedalled on with a shake of his head. Some Americans do not share our sense of humour.

Shortly after missing the cafe in the fog, we found ourselves completely depleted of energy, we had hit the wall, 'bonked' in cycling parlance. Apart

Never Say "If Only"

from some raw pasta in a pannier we had nothing to rectify the situation: no bananas, drinks, chocolate, nuts – nothing. We paused at a junction that lead down to the small town of Buena Vista, just five miles away but 1,500 feet *below*. We debated our options but really, we had none. There was no alternative other than to descend for the necessary rations. But then, a car pulled up alongside and four young people jumped out, two women and two men, they enquired if we needed any food and water. Apparently, they were back-up for some Appalachian Trail walkers and had spare provisions. They gave us Gatorade, water, oranges, fruit cups, Snicker bars and mooncakes: manna from heaven.

"May we pay you something for all this?"

"No, no its surplus, regard it as a gift from God" replied our good Samaritans. What a lucky coincidence; it shakes one's disbelief.

Well stocked we had no reason to descend to Buena Vista, we stayed high and continued up the Parkway. The Blue Ridge really is beautiful, great variety of trees and wildlife; butterflies, including swallow tails, are especially numerous. The trouble is, it is a really tough bike ride, especially on a loaded tandem. The effort can sometimes dampen your appreciation of your surroundings. Today we climbed 6,000 feet, but we have got to get on with it before we are too old, like tomorrow. Tomorrow I am sixty!

I had planned a short ride on my birthday, to Rockfish Gap where we booked in at the Afton Inn with thoughts of a hot bath, a good meal and a proper bed. I was looking forward to a romantic evening. In our room Maggie caught sight of a telephone.

"Look, a phone," she declared excitedly, "We can phone home and check that the girls are okay." However, we were in a hillbilly area and long-distance communication was unusual and therefore, not easy. The operator would not allow reversed charge calls and claimed to be having difficulty connecting us with the outside world. "Please hang up and try again later," which we did, repeatedly, always receiving the same message. After about two hours, I persuaded Maggie to leave it for a while and enjoy a belated dinner. After the meal Maggie, no less determined, continued her fruitless mission of phoning home, again failing miserably. I lost patience and went to bed on my own – so much for a romantic 60th-birthday!

After close on 500 miles we said goodbye to the Blue Ridge Parkway and hello to the Sky Line Drive. This was in the Shenandoah National Park that commanded an $8 entrance fee for cyclists. Having only one bike we got away with just one $8 charge. There was very little difference between the Parkway and the Drive; the former having yellow road markings, the latter white. Occasionally the sun would find a gap between the clouds and illuminate the land as if a giant hand had wiped a cloth across a huffed up windscreen. The weather improved and we were treated to fantastic views and smells of woodland and meadows. "Cycling doesn't get much better than this" declared Maggie as we started a thousand-foot assent. For my part, I was feeling extremely weary and stopped at every overlook for a rest. I wondered if the agony in my thighs, each time we set off again, was worth stopping in the first place.

Finally, we arrived at Big Meadows campground, cafe and store. We ate and bought provisions before continuing up the road to the actual campsite. As we turned the final bend a big sign up ahead shouted "FULL." We could not believe it. Up to now the campgrounds have been nearly deserted. We pressed on anyway hoping that Maggie's white hair might do the trick. It did. We were found a walk-in pitch reserved for hikers.

From the sublime to the ridiculous; from the almost traffic-free, thirty-five miles per hour maximum speed limit on the Drive to sixty miles per hour minimum on the truck-congested Route 340. As we rode down a steep hill into the historic town of Harper's Ferry, we heard and felt, something catching the rear brake. There was a substantial crack in the rear wheel rim. We limped into Harper's Ferry where, in 1859, the anti-slavery activist John Brown of "John Brown's body lies a-smouldering in the grave" fame led an unsuccessful raid on the federal armoury. He was captured and hung.

Cautiously we rode along the C & O Canal path to Leesburg, where we were able to obtain boxes from a friendly bicycle shop and to store our broken bike. Since we had a Rohloff hub it was impossible to get a replacement wheel. We caught a bus to Arlington, booked into a hotel and spent the remaining few days of our trip taking the metro into Washington DC and visiting the

Never Say "If Only"

fantastic Smithsonian museums and zoo. There was so much to see. It was Memorial Day weekend, stars and stripes fluttered everywhere. Thousands of motor bikes paraded on their 19th Rolling Thunder ride, which was an annual motorcycle rally held in recognition of POWs and MIAs (missing in action). This was an interesting end to our trip. We returned to Leesburg, collected our bike and boarded a shuttle bus to Dulles International.

CHAPTER 28

Himalaya: Nepal & Tibet

*"See the world. It's more fantastic than any dream.
Ask for no guarantees, ask for no security."
Ray Bradbury. Fahrenheit 451*

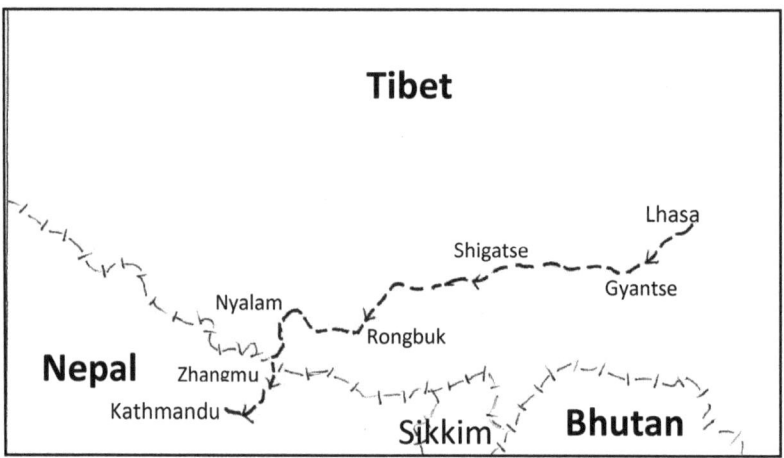

Oct, 2006. 670 miles

I was shaking, partially from the bitter cold but mainly with excitement at standing at the foot of the world's highest mountain. We were at 5,200 metres but Mount Everest still towered another 3,650 metres above us. In 1924, it was from here that Mallory and Irving made their attempt on the summit "Because it was there." I would need a much bigger incentive than that to attempt the climb and felt more than satisfied in just reaching Everest Base Camp by bike.

It had long been Maggie's idea to cycle in the Himalaya and when some Pat and John announced that they were leading a Cycle Touring Club tour to Tibet and Nepal, one thousand kilometres across the Tibetan Plateau

Never Say "If Only"

from Lhasa to Kathmandu, it seemed an ideal way to celebrate Maggie's sixtieth birthday. We flew to Kathmandu via Doha with Qatar Airways who provided excellent service. This included a floor show consisting of several white-gowned Muslims who unfurled their prayer mats in the aisle and offered salutations to Allah. Regrettably, the aisles on an Airbus 330 were not designed for that type of activity and soon chaos ensued with grid-locked food trolleys and queues of agitated toilet-goers. The captain's announcement that it was now sundown, somewhere, and worshipers could now break their fast for Ramadan eased the congestion somewhat.

The exotic smells, sights and sounds of Kathmandu promised an interesting visit but for now, we had to move on, to Lhasa in Tibet. We spent three days in Lhasa to acclimatise, Lhasa was at 3,500 metres and has only sixty-eight percent air pressure compared to sea level. While in Kathmandu I purchased some *diamox* tablets to help to avoid altitude sickness. Maggie has high blood pressure and was not allowed the medication.

Narrow streets surrounded Barkor Square where four huge pot-bellied stone *sangkangs* (burners) spewed clouds of incense over mantra-chanting pilgrims, vendors and tourists, but kept the Gods happy. In the *Jokhang,* the most revered religious structure in Tibet, we entered a world that assaulted the olfactory senses. Being careful not to step on prostrated pilgrims, we jostled with hundreds of worshipers in a veil of smoke speared with shafts of sunlight. The smell was of close-packed unwashed bodies, incense and yak butter.

In the afternoon we visited the Potala Palace. This iconic, massive 7th-century structure, formerly the tallest building on earth was the home of the Dalai Lama and his government. It has since become a museum and mausoleum that housed tombs of past Dalai Lamas made out of gold; each encrusted with precious stones, emeralds, diamonds and sapphires. We saw thousands of images of Buddhas. Scattered on the floor at the foot of these treasure troves was the hard-earned *yuan* of peasant pilgrims, an offering they could ill afford.

Allan Pendleton

At last, we hit the trail, the Friendship Highway. Although Maggie had a bad day with altitude sickness, she was well enough to be the stoker I knew and loved. It was not so good for two other sick members of our party who had to travel in the sag wagon as we headed alongside the River Bhamaputra. We cycled through mud brick villages, past fields tilled by a hand and *dzo*. The *dzo* was a cross between a yak and a cow. It was like being in the Middle Ages or looking at photographs from the National Geographic magazine. Each building had a large clay oven on the roof and yak dung patties plastered the walls to dry, or stacked like log piles, fuel ready for the winter. We passed through the towns of Gyantse and Shigatse, after which the hotels, electricity and other 'gifts' from China, including the paved road, ran out. At the end of each day's ride we found that our crew had set up camp for us, a tent for each pair, a dining tent, toilet tent and kitchen tent. This was camping for softies but I was not complaining. We climbed several lofty passes, each adorned with wind-swept prayer flags, across an unforgiving and hostile environment. Apart from the valley floors, everywhere was arid. It was a desert with very little wildlife. Everything was brown, the hills, the houses even the people. Each afternoon a freezing wind further tormented our lungs that were starved of oxygen, on dirt roads that were, at times, as bad as any we had encountered. At night, everything froze inside our tent; therefore, we dressed up *before* wriggling into our sleeping bags. Somehow, the native Tibetans managed to eke out an existence with little more than water drawn from mountain streams and yaks pulling wooden ploughs. These hardy animals provided much of the Tibetan nomads' needs.

For the superstitious, Friday 13 October lived up to expectations. It was an excessively hard day. It started with a 1,000 metre climb to the pass at Gyatso La at 5,250 metres. It took us four hours and destroyed one of my favourite myths that wind did not blow downhill. There was an icy blast straight into our faces throughout the assent, freezing our toes and fingers and chilling us to the core, even though we were climbing constantly.

After Gyatso La it was Maphu La. We paused for the customary photographs beneath the arch of prayer flags then it was downhill for the next 60 kilometres: but easy it was not! The wind relentlessly attempted to push us back up the mountain. Even the roadside yaks were battered by the gale and looked forlorn and windswept. To make the conditions even more challenging, we had to endure long stretches of road works. The Chinese were paving the Friendship Highway, probably to ensure that tourists would enjoy a comfortable journey to Everest. However, we had to negotiate diggers and dumper trucks on a road that was rough, rocky and at times, soft and dusty.

However remote our campsite, ragged, unwashed children magically appeared within minutes of our arrival. They seemed to be happy just watching. Feral dogs also showed up with uncanny regularity but, unlike the children, they were not averse to brazen theft. We had to be careful not to leave any morsels unattended. Unlike the children, the dogs did not have a home to go to and constantly prowled the site. They corresponded with other mongrels in far-off valleys by barking and howling throughout the night. I now understood why the dogs appeared to be so drowsy during the day, it was because they stayed up and howled all night!

The weather had improved when we ascended Pangla Pass at 5,150 metres, although the zigzag climb up a dirt washboard trail took nearly all day. The view from the top was worth the effort. An 8,000-metre mountain range stood proudly under a blue sky, and, with a wispy cloud like a crown on the king, was Mount Everest. Eleven days after leaving Lhasa we reached the Rongbuk monastery, at nearly 5,000 metres. It claimed to be the highest monastery in the world and was just eight kilometres south of Everest Base Camp. Our camp at Rongbuk was our coldest yet. The last thing John, our team leader, told us before we crawled into our tents was, "No crying tonight!" But it was hard not to cry. I wore two pairs of socks, two pairs of trousers, three upper layers, plus a fleece and a woolly hat and I was still cold.

In the morning we pedalled to Base Camp for a photo shoot. Gordon, from Edinburgh, pulled out some mini-bagpipes and gave us a rousing rendition of *Scotland the Brave*. I bought an ammonite fossil that was, amazingly, once under the sea although it was found at 18,000 feet! We felt satisfied at getting this far, possibly not the first to reach Everest Base Camp on a tandem but very probably the oldest!

Mount Everest

After reaching Everest Base Camp I think we all relaxed a little, but the cycling did not get easier. Initially we took a trekking trail to Tingri which was an off-roader's dream. The boulder-strewn path, loose sandy soil and several river crossings forced us to call it a day on the tandem. However, I was able to borrow Julie's mountain bike as she had, with several others, already abandoned to the safety of the back-up truck. We still had a series of 5,000 metre passes to climb and encountered severe icy winds. I think that the cold and wind contributed to everyone becoming utterly worn-out. After a twisting descent on treacherous soft sand and gravel we had a lunch stop in a disused peasant's house. We were out of the gale but the windows were without glass and we had to sit on a dirt floor. We were freezing. How could people live up here? The environment was hostile and the land barren, yet they survived and bred! Every village we passed through had children that have seldom, if ever, seen soap or had a wash. They stood by the roadside holding out their hands, hopeful that we might give them something. Usually we were met with smiles: occasionally with a rock or other missile. Unable to stop shivering, Maggie and I reclaimed the tandem and left the shelter ahead of the others and set off on the remaining forty kilometres to our proposed camp. The track was awful, it comprised thick sand and deep trenches caused by 4x4s. We passed the grader, an old tractor pulling a wide wooden rake. Although we were heading down the valley, we still had some tough climbs with the icy wind continuing to torment us. The sky ahead looked black and threatening with the occasional peal of thunder. Then it started to snow, a horizontal snow that whipped our faces raw. The surrounding hills turned from brown to white and snow began to settle on the road. With twenty kilometres still to go, the journey looked pretty dire. We were still ahead of the rest of the group, so when the land cruiser and back-up truck were sent out on a rescue mission, we nobly declined and continued unaided.

We passed through the small town of Nyalam, possibly the least attractive and dirtiest town on the "roof of the world." There were ugly concrete buildings on the edge of town with scruffy old stone houses with tin roofs in the centre. The main street was a row of grimy hostels, shuttered-up shops and piles of rubbish. No wonder the Himalayan traders called it "The Gateway to Hell." It was so-named not because of its hellish appearance but because the road to Nepal was so treacherous. It was such a shame because the town had a fantastic location with snow-capped mountains towering above it and was skirted by a deep gorge with a swift flowing river. It was along this gorge that we wound our way out of Nyalam. Our road, now covered with snow, was carved into the sheer wall of the ravine. We were alone and a little concerned as the light was failing. Surely it would not possible to camp on the sheer flanks of this valley. Then, just as we were considering turning back to find accommodation in Nyalam, we saw, through the gloom, pin-pricks of light. As we got nearer, our tents thankfully materialised, small red triangles on a mattress of white. We were the last to pedal into camp, everyone else had been rescued by the support team. During the night, the snow stopped and the clouds cleared to reveal a wonderful starlit sky.

In the morning, we had the most amazing descent ever. We plunged 2,400 metres in just fifty-six kilometres, traversing down alongside the River Bhote Koshi on a trail that was hewed into the vertical rock face of the gorge. Waterfalls cascaded down from the mountains to the white-water rapids in the river far below. The road was steep, rocky and uneven; passing through tunnels and overhangs. Although we were able to free-wheel, concentration was essential. We wore out both pairs of brake blocks but without doubt it was the most spectacular ride we had ever experienced. Also, as we flew down, the landscape changed dramatically. The barren, windswept and snow-covered mountains transformed into green and verdant countryside. We became aware that our sense of smell had returned after being absent in the frozen atmosphere high above. We could also hear birdsong. We came to the town of Zhangmu, on the border between the Chinese Republic of Tibet and Nepal. At 2,300 metres above sea level, Zhangmu had a mild and humid sub-tropical climate. A slabbed road led through the busy, dirty town to the Chinese immigration control. Here followed the usual regulated procedures until we escaped to a sort-of no-man's land for about seven kilometres to the Nepalese border. There was more form-filling and $30 each to pay for an entry visa before we were allowed to continue on our descent down the valley.

Allan Pendleton

The border between the two Countries was the Friendship Highway Bridge that spanned the river. Here all transport had to cross from one side of the road to the other as in Nepal one drove on the left while in China right was right! Further congestion was created by all commercial vehicles having to stop and transfer the goods from one truck to another from the receiving country. This busy route was later closed following an earthquake in 2014 that seriously damaged Zhangmu and required the evacuation of the residents. The town became a ghost town.

Considering that this was the only international crossing point between the two nations the state of the road was appalling. When we were there it had been raining. The road was muddy, potholed, rocky, with trenches either side and was cluttered with trucks. Deluges of water flowed across the road and had to be forded. Gradually road conditions improved as we pedalled our final two days into Kathmandu through dense and lush vegetation and lots of people. The towns were packed and even in the countryside there was a constant human stream. Every few minutes a loaded bus would pass, with people in and on top, hanging on to the roof for dear life. We estimated that up to sixty people could be stacked on top of a bus, including, on one occasion, a goat! One day short of Kathmandu, we encountered a road block manned by rifle-toting Maoists, each wearing distinguishing headbands. Everyone had to pay a fee to be allowed to continue, allegedly in aid of children. Earlier we had noticed that a hydro-electric power station was newly fenced with razor wire and had a heavy and very visible army presence. Our bicycle toll was fifty rupees.

We cruised down in to Kathmandu and the biggest hazard yet – the traffic! Nobody followed the rules of the road, if there were any? It was bedlam; the land of 'might is right' and power to the driver that could sound his horn the loudest and longest. Nonetheless, cycling was fun with no sign of road rage.

Before leaving for home, we took a visit to one of the most sacred sites in Kathmandu, the Hindu Temple of Pashupatinath located on the banks of the River Bagmati. Many elderly Hindus travelled here from all over Nepal and India, to die! It was believed that those who died in this temple would be reincarnated as a human, regardless of how naughty they may have been in this life. This is where the painted, holy men stationed themselves: often with their hands out. We witnessed two funeral pyres already burning, while

Never Say "If Only"

alongside, professional mourners earned their fees with high pitched wailing. Meanwhile, two other bodies were blessed and purified with the mucky river water. It was all very interesting, but we felt a little uncomfortable, too much like voyeurs.

We shared a congratulatory meal with Pat and John on a roof-top restaurant and watched hundreds of kites, both of the feathered kind and those manufactured by man. The human kite flyers attempted to cut the lines of other kites with glass-coated tethers. The kite-flyer on our rooftop claimed fourteen kills.

CHAPTER 29

The Sky Falls In

"Sex is not the answer, sex is the question. 'Yes' is the answer."
AJ McLean, the Backstreet Boys

<u>February 2007</u>

"He picked me up after work on Friday and took me back to my digs on Sunday afternoon when he went to visit his daughter," Maggie told me.

"You mean you stayed with him all weekend?"

"Yes."

"How long did this last?"

"Christmas to Easter."

"Four months! Bloody hell! Why haven't you told me this before?"

Maggie just shrugged. We were hiking in Mallorca and reminiscing about our lives before we met. Nothing new until Maggie dropped this bombshell. I knew that she had been going out with an older man before we had met but as he hardly received a mention when we talked about the past, I had the impression that it was little more than an insignificant brief encounter. Now, after thirty-eight years, she told that me that she had slept with him regularly! This took some digesting. My lovely wife had a life before I came along and she had shared it with a married; albeit separated, man. I was in a state of shock. This was not the girl I thought I had married. My illusion was shattered but there was no going back. How could I deal with this unwelcome knowledge? To my regret and shame, I dealt with it badly. My blood pressure soared and I could not sleep. Bad thoughts and obscene images possessed me.

The darkest hours were just before dawn and it was often at this unearthly hour that I would turn to Maggie and unleash a tirade of accusations and insults. My language was vile. Often these verbal assaults ended with us making love, or rather, having sex. Somehow this eased the tension. The volcano was then passive for a few days but the pressure steadily rose towards another eruption.

"I thought I loved him but didn't know what love was until I met you," she reassured me. This should have been all I needed to know but I continued to wallow in self-pity. How Maggie stayed with me I will never know. I felt cheated and betrayed, yet this was something that had happened *before* I even met her! My jealousy was more powerful than my logic and bloody hypocritical, I've been no saint!

I sought medical help. My doctor referred me to a counsellor. I ended up seeing three! The last one helped. He admitted having a similar experience and it was good to find someone at last with understanding of the hell I was going through. Gradually my outbursts became less frequent and are now consigned to the past. However, even today I hurt and regret knowing. My advice is: do not have secrets, but if you do, then keep them! I love Maggie with all my heart and apologise for my weakness and the torment I put her through.

CHAPTER 30

Thailand and Laos

"If you are not living life on the edge, you are taking up too much room."
Jayne Howard

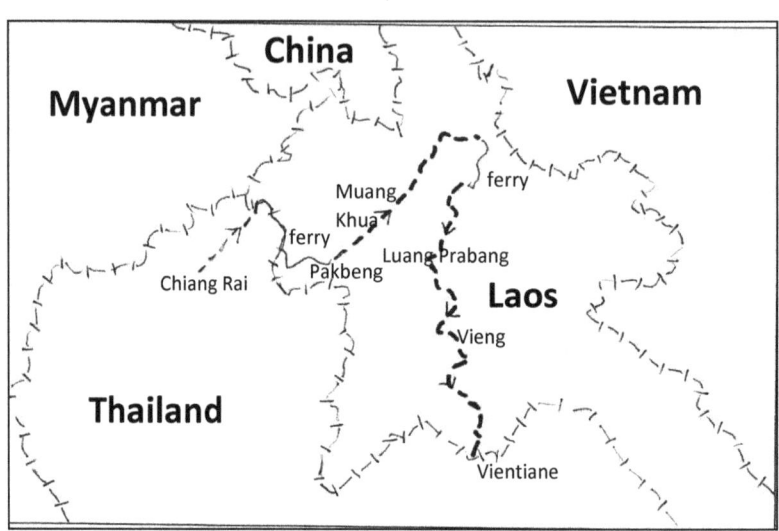

Nov-Dec, 2007. 680 miles

It was early days in my rehabilitation and there was still tension between Maggie and me. The first part of our trip in Southeast Asia was with a cycling group. I would, therefore, be in company and need to control my emotions. We arrived in Chiang Rai, Thailand a few days ahead of the group and explored a small section of the Golden Triangle, the opium-producing mountainous area that overlaps Thailand, Myanmar and Laos. We rode through secondary jungle with occasional clearings exposing thatched and bamboo hill-tribe villages. The hill-tribes used to cultivate opium but now grew other crops, such as cabbages, coffee and fruits. Tourism was encouraged and the long-necked women, who wore bands of necklaces weighing up to eight kilograms were a special attraction. The pedalling was hard, hot and hilly but on occasions, my simmering emotions overflowed and I found the energy to torment Maggie.

Back in Chiang Rai we met up with our group. That night the sky was filled with glowing alien-like space-craft that turned out to be hot-air 'spirit' balloons. We piled our twenty bikes and baggage on the roof of a boat to sail down the mighty Mekong River. This long-boat possessed coach-type seating and a dining table. It was a precarious voyage with rapids, eddies and whirlpools in a strong current with sandbanks and submerged rocks. Occasionally, bamboo stilt houses, roofed with thatch or tin would pop into view on the steep jungle-clad river bank.

We disembarked at Pakbeng in Laos. This country was once a French protectorate. We pedalled through rolling countryside, past communities overflowing with smiling children shouting, *"Sabai dee"* (hello). We stopped at our guide's village, Ban Faen, for a homestay. We were each hosted by a Lao family. Our hosts were an elderly man and his much younger wife, or daughter? After introductions we sat on the floor in their single-room, tin-roofed house on stilts smiling sweetly at each other. We had absolutely no common language. Mime has its limitations, as I discovered when needing the toilet. Our bed was a thin mattress on the floor in the room and our hosts continued to sit and smile as we prepared for bed. Luckily, with only candle light it was quite dark and we were able to slip under the mosquito net quite demurely. Sleep was difficult under our hosts' stare and the roar from next door's generator. A roar that eventually stopped when the cockerels started crowing! We woke at 5 am to find the village in full flow. Work starts early while it is cool.

We pedalled with the group to Udomxai before heading off on our own along a road that was signed in Lao script. Being unable to correlate the place names on our map, written in English, every junction was little more than a toss of the coin. The thick jungle and high mountains were very beautiful. As luck would have it, we found our way to Muang Khua where the pavement ended and a dirt road led to the River Nam Ou which formed the border with Vietnam. The ugly, concrete, Chinese-run Sinaly Hotel offered the only en suite room in town but the electricity supply was restricted. Power ceased at 9pm and in the morning I had to wash and shave by candle-light.

We cycled down to the river to catch a boat downstream. The skipper of the scheduled ferry refused to leave until there were sufficient passengers. There were not, so with three young Americans we negotiated to hire a smaller craft. We managed to haggle down to 600,000 kips ($60) but only as far as Muang Ngoi Neua, which was still well upstream of where we intended to go. The river flowed swiftly through steep, green, tropical rainforest, regularly punctuated with white-water rapids. The voyage was fragmented by numerous stops at stilted villages, cut-off from the outside world except for the river and inland paths. Our pilot seemed to have business in each of these settlements. He would wander off, returning sometime later with merchandise or a full stomach and contented smile. On one occasion, having no transactions to undertake, he stripped to his underwear and proceeded to have a bath and hair-wash in the shallows. We waited patiently.

We travelled slowly with spectacular views of limestone cliffs and majestic karst monoliths. At the village of Muang Ngoi Neua our skipper declared that this was as far as he would take us. Perhaps tomorrow we could catch a proper ferry. With no road access, we dragged our bike, the only wheeled vehicle in town, up a steep hill into the village and found a guest house. Our room was made of woven bamboo and fractionally larger than the bed. The shared bathroom was also rattan and had wafer-thin walls. We slept well in spite of crowing cockerels at 4 am and chanting monks an hour later. We boarded a ferry to Nong Khiaw, jamming ourselves in with another twenty or so *farangs* and not a life-jacket in sight. At our destination we were glad to have the tandem because all the other passengers were crammed like sardines into a local bus for Luang Prabang. Feeling rather smug we sipped a coffee then took a scenic ride to Pacmong. Here our self-satisfaction quickly dissolved at the lack of decent accommodation. Shared squat toilets with bucket and scoop baths, in concrete, windowless garage-type structures were all that was available. However, for just $3 what could one expect? The availability of food was similarly restricted; I was torn between the choice of roasted mole or fried lizard. Actually, I had pad thai, a stir-fried, rice noodle dish, although I was tempted by the bugs kebab!

It was a cool and misty morning as we cycled past streams of children on their way to school. Many were carrying smouldering branches to keep warm and families huddled around blazing bonfires. Obviously having open fires inside their bamboo and thatch houses was not an option. The children waved, pointed and called to us. Laos must be one of the top nations in the league for smiles and waves. We noticed many metal containers scattered in the villages. They were used as plant pots, pig troughs, water holders or just left in piles. On closer inspection, we could see that they were bomb casings from the American war in Vietnam. In *Land of a Million Bombs,* Santi Suthinithet (2010) says:

From 1964 to 1973, as part of the Secret War operation conducted during the Vietnam War, the US military dropped 260 million cluster bombs – about 2.5 million tons of munitions – on Laos over the course of 580,000 bombing missions. This is equivalent to a planeload of bombs being unloaded every eight minutes, 24 hours a day, for nine years – nearly seven bombs for every man, woman and child living in Laos.

It is more than all the bombs dropped on Europe throughout World War II, leaving Laos, a country approximately the size of Utah, with the unfortunate distinction of being the most heavily bombed country in history.

Nearly half of Laos is now contaminated with unexploded ordnances (UXOs), explosive weapons such as bombs, grenades and land mines. Cluster bombs, explosive weapons that work by ejecting hundreds of smaller submunitions over a wide area, make up the majority of UXOs that plague the country. Cluster munitions pose an especially grave danger to civilians, according to specialists in the field of disability, because they are "highly imprecise and indiscriminate" weapons designed to "scatter explosives over swaths of land often hundreds of yards wide."

Of the 260 million cluster bombs dropped by the United States, up to 30 percent of them failed to detonate. These bombs were released on targets in a large shell or casing. Each of the casings contained roughly 600 to 700 small bomblets, or "bombies," as they are often called in Laos.

There are now close to 78 million unexploded bomblets littering rice fields, villages, school grounds, roads and other populated areas in Laos, hindering development and poverty reduction. More than 34,000 people have been killed or injured by cluster munitions since the bombing ceased in 1973, with close to 300 new casualties in Laos every year. About 40 percent of the accidents result in death and 60 percent of the victims are children. At this time, less than 1 percent of the UXOs have been cleared.

Allan Pendleton

Food for thought!

In Luang Prabang we visited the Royal Palace which was built by the French in 1904 for the royal family, but when the monarchy was overthrown in 1975 it was converted into a museum. It was a good example of how the other half lives, or in this case lived, for after the communist takeover, the royal family were dispatched to re-education camps. Anyway, while we were looking at the amazing display of gifts that had been brought by visiting royals or foreign dignitaries, I suddenly noticed that Maggie was no longer by my side. I retraced my steps and saw a group of people gathered around an exhibit. Just as I was about to move on, I momentarily caught site of the artefact that was gripping the crowd's attention – it was Maggie! She was lying unconscious on the floor. She had fainted and fell, luckily not on to a priceless Ming vase. She regained consciousness and apart from embarrassment. Once back in England we never investigated this occurrence. Perhaps, if we had, she may have avoided her cardiac arrest just three years later?

Leaving Luang Prabang at sunrise we witnessed the monks' procession for alms. Local residents and tourists donated gifts, mainly food or money, into the monks' begging bowls. For the next few days, we passed through some of the highest limestone formations in Southeast Asia. However, the high, craggy, green mountains may not have been the only obstacle, for this area was subjected to attack from Hmong guerrillas that had resulted in the killing of two European cyclists. The Hmong were the remnants of a guerrilla army that served the pro-American Lao Government until it fell in 1975. Defeat in Vietnam led to the abandonment of the ragtag army, although some were still in hiding. I had forgotten about this danger until, at the top of a pass, a young man stepped into the road ahead of us. He was scruffily dressed in shorts and a T-shirt but was holding an antique AK-47. He looked up and perused us, then quickly allayed any fears with a big grin and a shared *"Sabai dee."*

Our final destination was back to the Mekong River at Vientiane the capital of Laos. To get there we had more hills, sweat and basic accommodation. This was more than compensated by stunning scenery, smiles, pad thai and delicious baguettes; the latter was one commodity for which to thank the French. Oh, don't forget the beer; seldom a day passed when we did not have a bottle or two of Lao beer; cold, tasty and thirst-quenching and only about forty pence a pint!

CHAPTER 31

Ana

"Insanity is hereditary.... you get it from your children."
Dr David O Dykes

Juliette Morgan (Our youngest daughter wrote this chapter)

I am lucky enough to have come from a family where I know love. I love and am loved by many but until I met Ana, I had never really grasped the enormity of what love was. When Dad asked me to write about our adoption experiences to include in his book I wasn't sure; I wasn't sure how this would fit into his 'travel adventure' genre and I wasn't sure I could articulate our thoughts and feelings. It was clear that Dad was going to write about it if I didn't, I'm not sure if you can tell from reading this but my Dad can be quite opinionated at times: especially on a subject about which he is passionate. Therefore, to save you all from his rant about social services, the legal and justice system and world population, etc; I agreed.

Thinking about it I suppose that the journey my husband Dean and I have travelled over those few years was the biggest adventure of any. We had only one destination in mind – to be a family. It had become clear through a number of miscarriages, ectopic pregnancies and IVF treatment that if we were to become a family we would need to consider adoption. Reaching this point in our lives was a whole different story for another time but it is sufficient to say that those few years of 'trying' were exhausting. The treatments, the excitement, the hope and the loss were physically, emotionally and financially crippling. It was time to move on. Adoption had to be an easier option. How wrong we were!

After applying and being interviewed by Oxfordshire Social Services, they informed us that unless we were prepared to adopt a child over six years old, a sibling group or a child with disabilities, any application would be unsuccessful. As a white couple we were only eligible to adopt a white baby, despite there being so many mixed-race children in care. The fact that we could offer them unconditional love, security and a close loving family was obviously not deemed as important as skin tone! God, I am beginning sound like my dad. They were excited that as a children's nurse, I would be able to take a child with complex medical conditions. I remember feeling extremely guilty that we craved what any new parents want – a happy, healthy baby. Consequently, we started looking at inter-country adoption.

To cut a long story short and for several reasons, we settled on adopting from Guatemala. On 3 April 2006, we had our first interview with the adoption agency that would carry out our home study and UK check before we could start any process abroad. So, after fifteen months, twelve social worker visits, a three-day preparation course, an interview panel and enough paper work to deplete the Brazilian rain forest, we were ready to instruct lawyers in Guatemala to represent us in our adoption. Our names were placed with an adoption agency waiting for a match. That was the easy part.

It was about 8pm on a Thursday evening when the phone rang. I answered to hear Nancy's voice. Nancy was our contact with the agency in Guatemala; my heart was in my mouth as Nancy explained that they had a baby girl looking for adoption and would we be interested. After six years of heartache getting to this point I did not know whether to laugh or cry; of course, we said "Yes!" She e-mailed us seven photos of a five-day old baby girl called Ana Florinda. I don't like to confess how many hours I spent just staring at those photos. I was analysing every minute detail of her face, hair and tiny clenched fists. I have to admit that I was falling completely in love with her!

Ana was placed with a foster mother in Guatemala City and the notarised letters, paperwork, social workers visits and lawyers' instructions began anew. However, with time passing and delays these hold ups meant Ana was growing up thousands of miles away and we were missing her first smile, first tooth, first solid food – and she was missing out on being part of a permanent family. I am not a very patient person at the best of times and found the wait torturous. We received monthly photos and watched her grow. Knowing that her birth mother could change her mind at any time made the wait even more agonising. International adoptions in Guatemala were growing alarmingly uncertain with worrying rumours of child abduction and coercion. The USA was closing all doors on adoptions and Britain was looking to follow suit. I knew I should not let myself get too attached but found it impossible not to. In my heart she was already my daughter.

Ana's birth parents were from a remote highland village. They worked the land, were illiterate and only spoke their native Mayan language. They already had eight children and could not afford another mouth to feed. As part of the adoption process, they had to travel to the British Embassy in Guatemala City, to be interviewed by the British Consulate and for DNA samples to be taken. This ensured all adoptions were legal and ethical. I found this step in the process very reassuring. The problem for the birth parents was that they must find the funds to travel to Guatemala City. Their hand to mouth existence meant that several days off work and care for their other children would be difficult. So, as part of our fees to the adoption agency, we arranged for the birth family's expenses to be met. This was standard practice about which we had no qualms.

To proceed legally with the adoption, we had to now meet our child. In August 2008 we booked our flights to Guatemala, to spend a week with our daughter. Before we arrived, the birth parents were interviewed at the British Embassy. The interview was conducted in English, translated into Spanish and then in to their ethnic Mayan language, and back again. Obviously, there were some language difficulties! During the interview the birth mother mentioned receiving travel and subsistence expenses. The consulate heard this and immediately suspended the adoption as it was felt that the baby had somehow been bought. We were informed of this decision and my world crumbled. The British Embassy were trying to be whiter than white in a Guatemalan system that was riddled with corruption. I could not see any way that they would allow the adoption to proceed now that the alarm bells had been rung, however unjustly. I felt crushed. Despite letters to MPs, embassies, lawyers, the DCFS (Department for children, families and schools), we received very little support or information. We were packed and ready to visit Ana in Guatemala but how could we now spend that week with her when her future as our daughter was so uncertain?

Although so many questions remained unanswered, we still decided to fly to Guatemala, but to meet with our lawyers instead of Ana. They had arranged for the village pastor, who knew the birth family, to be interviewed by the embassy. However, they knew little more than we did, although they were sympathetic and their genuine concern for Ana was apparent. The future for Ana if this adoption failed would be grave. Her return to the birth family was unlikely as their situation had not changed. With no state-run children's homes and the very few charity-run orphanages being closed due to corruption allegations, there were very few options. At this point I would have sold my soul for her but all we could do was wait. After a couple of nights with an empty cot at the end of the bed, we felt we could achieve no more and so cut short our trip to Guatemala.

Finally, on 4 October we received a phone call from the British Embassy asking if we would like to proceed. Of course, we would: what a stupid question! The birth parents were never re-interviewed; so, we assumed that the issue had been clarified and we were overjoyed that by some miracle the adoption was continuing. The birth parents returned to the embassy for DNA testing which confirmed maternity and paternity: now our papers entered the final stage of the Guatemalan process (GPN), the *Proceduria General de la Nación*. This was a notoriously long procedure with some papers taking six to twelve months but it was the last step. Once our papers were finalised, we had officially adopted Ana, in Guatemala at least. There was just one final step: or so we thought! On the 18 January, just over two months later, our papers exited PGN. At last, something was going our way and none too soon as the Government had stopped any new papers entering PGN, effectively halting adoptions from Guatemala.

Four weeks later we flew again, but this time to meet our daughter and bring her home. I would not recommend seventeen hours of travel before your first introduction to parenthood but there was no way we were going to wait a single moment to meet our daughter. Our feet had barely hit the ground before we were waiting in our hotel room for a knock on the door. We did not have to wait long before Suzanne and Rodrigo entered, carrying a stack of documents – and Ana! It seemed surreal. I was handed Ana and Dean quickly examined all the legal documents with Rodrigo before they departed. As the door shut behind them Dean and I just looked at each other and burst out laughing, mainly with relief and joy but also at the absurdity of the situation! Here we sat in a hotel room in a notoriously unsafe city, unable to speak the language, with an eight-month old baby we had known for all of ten minutes, a bottle of milk and a nappy. Welcome to parenthood!

As we hadn't met Ana earlier as planned there were a lot of e-mails and yet more documents to complete before we could bring her home, so we moved base to beautiful Antigua. Although I was desperate to go home, looking back, the two and a half weeks Dean, Ana and I spent together were priceless, just getting to know her and finally spending time as a family.

We were in blissful ignorance that a whole new legal nightmare was about to begin!

Daughters, Joanne and Julie; grandchildren Max, Abi and Ana

With our flight home just a day away, we returned to the British Embassy in Guatemala City to collect Ana's stamped passport. We met with the same official who had been involved with the adoption suspension. He then told us that even though they had approved the adoption, the British visas were issued in the visa application office based in New York and they had refused Ana a visa. When I asked why, he replied it was due to the mention of money during the interview with the birthparents of Ana. We were stunned and asked what our options were. We could return home without Ana and appeal from the UK, or stay in Guatemala. Both options seemed problematic! As it was lunchtime, we were hustled out of the embassy with words to the effect:

"Well it was your decision to continue with the adoption."

How could we now leave Ana? By Guatemalan law we were her parents, but to abandon our lives in England was also a ridiculous notion, we had careers, a house and family. Talk about a rock and a hard place! What were we to do? After some investigating, we learned that Guatemalan citizens can enter the UK as visitors for six months without a visa. Since Ana had a Guatemalan passport, we thought we would fly back to England with her as a visitor and continue the appeal from home. Therefore, on my birthday we boarded the plane to Belize, then the USA and onto London Heathrow, not really knowing if we would be allowed to enter our country with Ana or not? Amazingly we walked through immigration with no hold-ups and were overjoyed to see mum and dad waiting for us. They looked as relieved as we were. Now all we had to deal with was the appeal and UK adoption, but at least Ana was home.

A few days later a 'welcome home' committee consisting of police officers and social workers knocked on our door ready to take Ana into care and arrest Dean and I for child smuggling. I had thought maybe our passage through immigration went a bit too smoothly! Luckily, I had all the paperwork at hand supporting the fact that we had jumped through every single hoop, completed every piece of paper work and possessed every sheet of legal documentation that these officials requested, yet we were still being treated like criminals. It was agreed that Ana was in 'a place of safety' and she could remain with us while we appealed. This would be under the jurisdiction of social services as a 'looked after child'. entailing a weekly visit by a social worker!

So in a nutshell;
a) we needed to appeal the decision not to grant Ana a British visa.
b) We couldn't apply to adopt Ana under UK law until she had a visa.
c) Once we adopted Ana under UK law she would become a British citizen and not need a visa!
d) You cannot appeal for a British visa if you are already resident in the country.
e) It was going to cost in the region of £50,000 in legal fees to run the appeal! Talk about a problem child!!! The whole situation was bonkers.

In total it took another year to fight for the right to legally call Ana our daughter: in our hearts and minds, she had always been that. I would like to say that the legal system always has the best interests of the child as paramount, but regretfully, that just wouldn't be true. I feel confident that if we hadn't had such wonderful lawyers, the courts wouldn't have thought twice about putting Ana into the 'Care' system. How could this ever have been in her best interests? Everyone was 'looking over their shoulders' afraid

Never Say "If Only"

to make any positive decision. It was not until we reached the Royal Court of Justice that sanity was resumed. The Judge quickly signed the documents with a sigh and shrug of his shoulders.

Anyway, it's not just a story of doom and gloom for we met some truly amazing people along the way, like our lawyer Jan and barrister Katherine who did all of our appeal 'pro bono'. Their expertise, generosity and compassion were faultless and I am sure that it is due to them that Ana is with us today.

I write this now and look back at this time and to be honest it all seems a blur, I think I've forgotten how tough it was, but as the saying goes "What doesn't kill you makes you stronger". Bloody stupid saying really, but I now know that as a family we can get through anything. Dean becomes my rock in times of crisis (Mr lazy boy at all other times!)

Ana is now 10 years old, she has a little 4-year old brother to boss around who we adopted domestically. I won't go into it now but it is safe to say, despite the promises given by Government saying adoption is now quicker and easier, it wasn't. His birth family were given chance after chance to care for Mark and each time our little boy suffered, but that will be his story to tell at another time.

Even though I had attended all the adoption preparation courses and study days at the time we adopted Ana I truly believed that love could heal all wounds. I now know that even tiny babies can be deeply affected by early experiences and the trauma for some is carried with them all their lives. That is not to say they cannot overcome, but may just have to work harder at parts of their lives that other families and children take for granted.

Anyway as this is a book about travel I am glad to say our journey has a happy ending, our family is now complete and we are blessed with two healthy happy kids. They now have a world of opportunities open to them, which is a far cry from how their lives might have been if certain decisions had been different.

Best put by Winnie the Poo,
"How do you spell love?" asked Piglet,
"You don't spell it.... you feel it" replied Poo
A A Milne

CHAPTER 32

Life Is Not Fair

"Getting old is hard but it's better than the alternative."
Anon

<u>January, 2008</u>

"I've got it." I shouted to Maggie as I picked up the phone. It was my brother Colin, "Hi Al, dad's in hospital. He has had a stroke. It's a bad one. I think that you had better come!" We hurriedly drove the 240 miles to Bury St Edmunds in Suffolk. Colin was there with his wife, Alison. Our father's stroke was indeed a bad one but not bad enough to kill him. Dad was eighty-three years old but strong as an ox. At his home in West Row, he had an acre of land which he maintained on his own. Regrettably, his strength was to prolong the torment that he was to endure for the next five years.

The stroke paralysed his right side and left him unable to speak. Any communication was extremely difficult which led his consultant, a pompous, bigoted arse in a bow tie, to refer him to the Court of Protection. This legal body was appointed to look after the needs of someone unable to make decisions for themselves, or to delegate deputies to do it for them. Colin and I applied to be dad's deputies; involving, of course, money and solicitors. In theory this was fine and should help to prevent vulnerable people from being fleeced by unscrupulous would-be benefactors. However, for a family to have to account for every penny and justify each endeavour made on their loved one's behalf, did not come easily. To avoid this, and something our dad had *not* done, one should take out a lasting power of attorney. This will enable your kith and kin to take care of your affairs without hindrance and vilification from faceless bureaucrats.

Meanwhile, we had to find somewhere for mum. She was visually impaired with macular degeneration, and had mobility problems. Dad had cared for her at home. Eventually we managed to put mum and dad together in the same care home but he was very depressed. He had been stripped of all his pride and dignity, everything had to be done for him; he had to be washed, dressed and shaved. Our father had been a navy man. He served during World War II as a landing craft pilot on D-Day. After the war, he built his own business and became a county councillor. He was a proud man and found his disability, his loss of independence and lack of communication, so hard to bear. When I was with him, I attempted to maintain a monologue but if I hesitated dad would try to contribute or ask a question. I could never understand what he was trying to say. Consequently, we both got frustrated and angry. It would always end with me hugging him and both of us in tears. Occasionally, dad would make a slashing motion with his good hand across his throat before slumping forwards in his wheelchair. We knew what he wanted but were powerless to help him. His time in purgatory continued.

We had to sell the family home. It was a grade two listed building with an asbestos roof. Back in the early sixties, the original thatched roof needed replacing. My parents could not afford new thatch, asbestos was cheaper and at the time, quite acceptable, in fact dad even received a grant for the project. When we came to sell, however, potential buyers were unable to secure a mortgage, hence, we had to drastically reduce the price and sell to a cash-buying property speculator. Nevertheless, we were finally able to pay for our parents' care.

My mother had once been a keen and talented lawn bowls player and president of the National Bowling Federation. On 21 August 2011 it was she who died first. Eighteen months later my father got his wish and joined her. He suffered another stroke and as he was being wheeled out of his room for the last time, he turned to a picture of our mother on the wall, smiled and blew her a kiss as if to say, "See you soon."

While we were spending much of our lives travelling between Somerset and Suffolk, Maggie's only sister Ann was regularly making a similar reverse journey. Ann lived on her own in north London. She was a teacher and although in her sixties, was a very active sportsperson. She regularly ran cross-country races and marathons. She had an excellent social life but the loves of her life lived in Somerset, namely, her nieces and nephew.]

"Why don't you move down here to Burnham-on-Sea?" we suggested, "You would make new friends and join lots of clubs and societies and your London friends could visit you at the seaside." Ann eventually agreed and started house hunting. She found the home of her dreams: a lovely bungalow with a large south-facing garden overlooking a lake. On the day that she was finally handed the keys to the bungalow she mentioned that she had a stomach ache. "Just nerves and excitement" we said, "You are about embark on a new adventure!" But Ann's stomach ache persisted and just a few weeks later she was diagnosed with pancreatic cancer. She had spent just one night in her new home, in a sleeping bag before her furniture had arrived. Her last week was spent in Weston Hospice. Ann's death was painful but relatively quick. Her funeral was the same week as my father's.

On 1 June 2014, barely a year after my dad and Ann's deaths it was my brother Colin's turn to meet the grim-reaper. Colin had been a type-one diabetic all his life that he controlled impeccably. However, during the night he suffered an acute hypoglycaemic attack which caused a cardiac arrest. He was only sixty-one years old. He had just retired and was expecting his first grandchild any day. It's just not fair!

Colin had, like me, failed his eleven plus and attended Mildenhall Secondary Modern School. However, the nearest school where he could take GCE exams was in Bury St Edmunds, fifteen miles away, where he also took his A Levels. Colin then studied art at the University of Leicester. He did not enjoy the course and after a couple of terms decided to go home. Probably the fact that his childhood sweetheart, Alison, was still at home in Suffolk had a lot to do with his decision.

Colin then turned his hands to a number of challenges. He worked on the RAF Mildenhall Airbase for a while, then for the Water Board at a sewerage works. He helped dad in his decorating business, married Alison and started a family. But his overriding passion, apart from Alison and his two sons, was archaeology. As a child he would spend hours on newly ploughed fields in the Fens searching for flints and other ancient artefacts and he built up quite a collection. In 1980 aged twenty-eight, he returned to education to read for a degree in archaeology at the University of Nottingham. This time there were no distractions because he took his family with him. Three years later he received his bachelor's degree. A year later he was awarded a master's degree, then he gained a doctorate. Colin Pendleton, PHD, returned to Suffolk and purchased a house in Bury St Edmunds where he acquired the post of Director of Archaeology for the County Council.

Sadly, apart from Christmas and belated birthday cards, Colin and I had shared little contact. When dad had his stroke, however, everything changed. We worked together to care for our parents, although Colin and Ali, living much closer, did the lion's share. Maggie and I would drive to Suffolk from Somerset every other weekend and were always offered Alison and Colin's hospitality. We found that we had much in common. We shared many interests and had a good laugh. Their company made these weekends bearable. After our parents died we continued our close friendship and enjoyed a couple of walking and camping trips together. When Colin announced his retirement, we started to make plans about the times and adventures we would share. My brother's funeral was attended by many leading lights in his profession and the Guardian newspaper printed an obituary. I had not realised that Colin had achieved such a high standing in his work and was acknowledged nationwide as a leading authority in many archaeological areas.

CHAPTER 33

The Western Isles and Northwest Highlands, Scotland

"Some beautiful paths can't be discovered without getting lost."
Erol Ozan

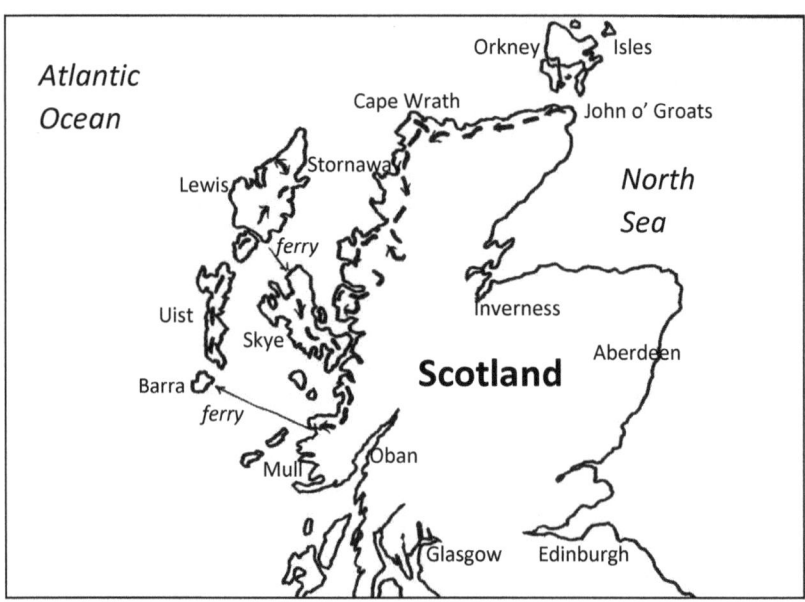

June 2008. 460 miles

We left our campervan in Oban, bought a fourteen-day rover ticket for Cal-Mac Ferries and sat in the sun sipping beer on the after-deck during the five-hour voyage to the island of Barra, in the Western Isles of Scotland. From the port we pedalled over a steep hill to the causeway that led to the island of Vattersay. After more roller-coaster riding, we found an idyllic camping spot overlooking a white-sand beach, near the community hall that had toilet and washing facilities. It was after 10pm but there was still an hour of daylight.

We sat admiring the view and feeling very smug. Cycle camping did not get much better than this!

Famous last words, for in the morning yesterday's sun was hidden behind threatening dark clouds. Furthermore, a bitterly cold wind was building damply from the North Atlantic. It was Sunday and everywhere was eerily deserted, was everyone still in bed or all at the kirk? We cycled up the west coast of Barra and stopped for a picnic at the airport, the only airport in Britain with its runway on a beach and where the state of the tide controls the flight schedule. At the ferry port we found an open cafe and took shelter while waiting for the ferry to Eriskay Island. Continuing north over a rocky heathland with peat bogs and dotted with farmworkers' houses, called bothies, we crossed the Eriskay causeway to South Uist.

Camping outside a crofter's hostel, a converted thatched bothy, we were allowed use of the kitchen and showers. The howling of the wind and constant buffeting of the tent made sleeping difficult, but we stayed in our sleeping bags as long as possible. The weather outside did not encourage an early start. Battling against gale force winds with intermittent showers we struggled past lakes, more rocky moorland and peat bogs to North Uist. Then, another ferry took us to Harris and a wonderful route, an unfenced single-track road traversing the Atlantic coast offering views of beautiful beaches and rocky outcrops being pounded by huge waves. It was perfect cycling country.

From Tarbert we headed north, directly into the wind, and climbed a high pass complete with snow poles. Scary, wet descents led to more climbs: one of which was thirteen per cent in a downpour. We then zoomed down once more on wet roads with red-hot rims at over seventy kilometres per hour to find a hostel at Rhenigidale. Initially, we were the only people there. We chose our bunks and peacefully showered before five wet and tired cyclists arrived, Bob and Sue from Mid Wales and three students from Leeds University. I lit the stove, around which we sat, sharing peddlers' experiences, while outside the wind blew and the rain fell.

It was a severe climb out of Rhenigidale Cove before descending and then climbing again to the snow poles and the pass we had left yesterday. Got rained on again, and the rain stung like pellets as we entered the Isle of Lewis on a rolling and extremely tiring terrain, and headwind all the way. At

Allan Pendleton

Stornoway we foumd a real town at last, one with a TIC, Co-op supermarket and a cafe offering all day breakfasts. We both had a full Scottish breakfast, a fry-up complete with haggis and black pudding. It was still windy and very cold as we set off on a day ride around the north of Lewis. We visited some black houses, primitive thatched buildings constructed of block and turf and used by Islanders until the mid-20th-century.

The next day, after a sleepless night and an awful row, which we continued on the bike, we retraced our route to Tarbert where we took the ferry to Skye. It rained hard during the crossing, so we decided to stop and camp in the port of Uig. Later the skies cleared and we went for a walk around Uig, which took about five minutes. It was another cloudy, damp, windy and chilly morning when we left... We stopped at a crofters' rural life museum at the same time as a busload of Chinese tourists, who were more interested in taking selfies than inspecting the crofters' cottages. Then a beautiful single tracked coastal road with fantastic oceanic views; islands on one side and huge mesa-like mountains on the other. Ominous clouds loomed in the north and the mountain tops were soon shrouded in mist. We stopped to admire the sheer, volcanic formations of Kilt Rocks that resembled the pleats of a kilt, then the impressive rock pillar known as the Old Man of Storr. There were stunning views of the Cuillan Hills. There was a campsite opposite a pub. It was a good day, with our personal vibes improving as the day progressed.

By the evening the wind had dropped and the clouds cleared but swarms of midges appeared. Unable to enjoy the sunset we were driven inside the tent, and in the morning discovered we had burnt a hole in the groundsheet with a mosquito coil. The fly sheet was black with our unwelcome visitors and we dallied in bed plucking up the courage to face the foe. It was obvious from the internationally recognised 'F'-word and other curses flowing from the mouths of our German motor-biking neighbours as they loaded their BMW 1200s, that they were not enjoying this aspect of Scottish Highland wildlife one iota.

From Skye we rode on the bridge over the Kyle of Lochalsh to the mainland. As we continued south, the weather closed in and once again we were subjected to wind and rain. We passed the youth hostel in Mallaig where Maggie mentioned how warm and cosy it looked with smoke billowing from its chimney. "It's only a shower." I replied and pressed on regardless. There were mutterings from the back as we pedalled into the wind and the rain intensified. It continued raining all day. Upon seeing a sign for a campsite, we decided to stop. We cooked and ate dinner inside the tent. The rain eased and the midges made an unwelcomed appearance but we decided to venture out to view the otters, seals, dolphins and sea eagles that frequented these parts. Regrettably, not today, they must have been sheltering from the weather. In spite of the conditions the riding had been interesting with magnificent panoramas of lochs and fells, the sea and sandy coves. We slept deeply, to the soporific sound of rain drops - so well that we missed the ferry to the Isle of Mull. Later, in Tobermory, a whiskey distillery offered a respite from the rain but back on the bike it was more of the same. Maggie, her tolerance pushed to the limit, appealed, "Can we go home now, please?" Turning towards Oban to return to our van we were faced with a bank of black, ominous clouds, like a bully at the school gates promising another drubbing before we were allowed to go home. The scenery had been fantastic, the campsites excellent and the local people helpful and friendly. But the wet and cold, especially the wind, had made it a hard tour. However, this part of the world was simply tremendous and, with more favourable weather, there would be no better place to bicycle tour. We would return.

<u>May 2012. 330 miles</u>

We did return, not to the Hebrides Islands but to the adjacent mainland. This time the weather was kind to us, with clear, blue skies, not a rain cloud in sight. The wind was a brisk and somewhat chilly northerly but it kept the midges away. However, to be on the safe side, we kept close to our van and took circular day rides on the bike sharing the single-track roads with the occasional vehicle, usually a German or Dutch campervan. Initially, we made our way to John o' Groats, the destination of our End-to-End rides, before heading west along the northern coast of the mainland to the remote northwest outpost of Cape Wrath. The coastline was spectacular, big waves crashed on to white sand beaches backed by majestic sandstone cliffs, among the highest in the country. Inland, numerous lochs dotted the craggy moorland wilderness, while high above, skylarks warbled constantly like an agreeable tinnitus. The call of the cuckoo was also a daily occurrence, nowadays a sound seldom heard at home in Somerset.

Allan Pendleton

Further down the west coast, with views over the Sound of Raasay, was the Applecross Peninsular, which, in my opinion, is one of the best one-day cycle rides anywhere. It is a forty-two mile circuit, climbing from sea-level over the highest paved road in Scotland, the Bealach na Ba Pass at 2,053 feet. Much of route is single track road with magnificent views to the Cuillins of Skye. The coast road returning to the excellent pub in Applecross is etched into the cliff, where you cannot help but be in awe of the beauty and grandeur that surrounds you. It was a fine day and the Applecross Circuit provided a perfect end to an enjoyable trip, although we experienced it painlessly in the van with the tandem happily spinning its wheels on the rack.

CHAPTER 34

Quebec, Canada

"Travel makes one modest. You see what a tiny place you occupy in the world."
Gustave Flaubert

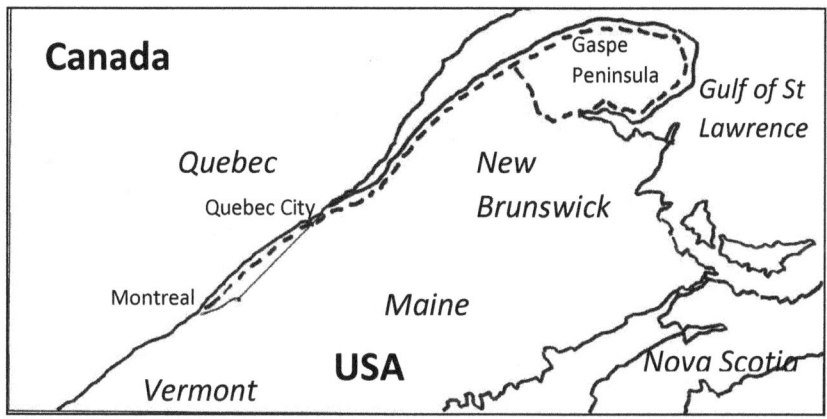

<u>Sept, 2008. 1,120 miles</u>

A delayed KLM flight, an hour-long queue to pass through immigration at Montreal Dorval Airport, then an even longer wait for an airport bus, meant that we checked in at the Comfort Hotel in Montreal eighteen hours after leaving home. The following day we took a bus eastward along the southern bank of the Saint Lawrence River, past clapboard houses with massive log-piles, Dutch barns and grain silos, to the Gaspe Peninsular. At Saint Flavie we started pedalling. Our plan was to cycle anti-clockwise around this peninsular that jutted into the Gulf of Saint Lawrence before riding back to Montreal.

Apart from our multi-fuel stove not working, it all started well enough with fine weather on the quiet ride across the peninsula. It was so quiet that we wondered if some calamity had caused this part of Canada to be devoid of human life, but there was plenty of wildlife. We saw bald eagles, woodpeckers,

229

Allan Pendleton

white-tailed deer, chipmunks, moose and beavers; plus, black flies and mosquitoes! Maggie was particularly vulnerable and was badly bitten. Her face, neck and scalp were quickly covered with red lumps and blotches, with blood in her hair. At a camp on the bank of the Matapedia River, two salmon fishermen gave her some of their favoured repellent. "*Watkins*, the best you can buy" they assured us. Regrettably they failed to tell the black flies and mosquitoes, Maggie's torment continued. Mind you, we became very efficient at speedily erecting and dismantling the tent, our only refuge.

A beautiful ride downstream alongside the river took us to Cambellton in New Brunswick where suddenly everyone was speaking English again, French speakers were the minority. Maggie received pitying glances, for she was well spotty and lumpy, not quite of "Elephant Man" proportions but still very sore plus she was running a temperature. We pressed on along the coastal route, aware that hurricanes were causing havoc in the United States and tracking north. We had experienced hot, sultry weather but now the wind was strengthening and rainstorms were imminent: and rain it did! Steadily for more than thirty hours. We decided to get off the bike and take a boat trip instead. To Bonaventure Island, a National Park with the biggest gannet colony in the Americas. Once on the island it was obvious which way to go. We were led by the obnoxious smell and raucous racket as we walked across the island to the cliff-edge where every ledge, nook, crack and cranny was occupied by seabirds. There were gannets, kittiwakes, gulls and cormorants roosting on Bonaventure Island, totalling a quarter million birds.

Not able to find replacement parts for our stove, breakfast was our main cooked meal. Many cafes offered huge, American-style breakfasts on which we gorged. The local delicacy, *poutine,* provided an ideal afternoon energy supplement. *Poutine* was simply a bowl full of chips covered with gravy and cheese curds. Seldom did we go hungry since most cafes served it, as did roadside vans.

The riding was hard, with many steep headlands and pouring rain. It was to get worse. After leaving Gaspe and turning west along the mouth of the Saint Lawrence River we left the hills, but were met by a ferocious head wind and warnings of an imminent hurricane. During the night the heavens opened and we found our tent marooned in the centre of an ever-increasing lake. Shades of "*Puyuhuapi*" but our little tent withstood everything the elements could throw at it. A brief lull in the storm let us flee to a draughty barn. Dodging drips from a leaky roof we sheltered for the rest of the night. By morning the rain had subsided but not the wind. It took us ten days to pedal the five hundred kilometres to Quebec. En route we saw whales in the estuary; belugas, fin and minke. Plus, honking noisily overhead, formations of thousands of snow geese flew in at sunset to roost in the estuary. Clear skies replaced the rain clouds and we were treated to sunny days and cold, star-lit nights; each morning the tent was encrusted with a film of ice, outside and inside.

Quebec City was once a fortress. A walk round the citadel wall gave us great views of the Saint Lawrence and two gigantic cruise liners docked in the port, the *QE2* being by far the smallest. A great bike path led us out of the city on the north shore, through wooded parks whose trees were donning their autumn coats of red, gold and orange. With the wind on our backs at last, we had a delightful ride to Trois-Riviers then boarded a bus back to Montreal. There were excellent bike trails and we spent our final two days in Canada exploring the city by tandem.

CHAPTER 35

California, USA

"I have found that there ain't no surer way to find out whether you like people or hate them than to travel with them."
Mark Twain, "Tom Sawyer Abroad."

April- May 2009. 1,590 miles

The Southern Tier, from California to Florida, was our original plan. We discussed it via e-mail with our Californian cycling fireman friend, Ed Rodriguez. He persuaded us that a tour of California might be a better option and that he could join us. He even arranged to meet us at San Francisco International Airport and for us to stay the first night with his brother-in-law just across the Bay in Pleasanton. This was a relaxing start to the tour with scrumptious meals of steak and grilled salmon. It took an immense effort to leave Dave and Diane and their generous hospitality.

Our first day on the road led us into wooded hills with many eucalyptus, pastures and lakes, but with hardly a vehicle in sight. That all changed in San Jose a city of one million inhabitants, mostly, it seemed, Mexicans and Vietnamese. After much stopping and starting in teeming traffic, we eventually found a bicycle trail that would lead us out of the city. The path twisted and turned and was busy with cyclists, joggers, skate boarders and walkers. We had a breakfast burrito in Los Gatos, then back onto the bike path which eventually took us to New Brighton Beach. We rode through a flat, fertile stretch with acres and acres of strawberries, cabbages, lettuces, artichokes and cauliflowers, being tended by a stooped Mexican workforce. Ed waved shouting *"Buenos días"* and *"Hola"* as we pedalled past. Most days on the coast road, Route 1 the Pacific Coast Highway, we stopped for the usual breakfast; sausage, bacon, eggs (over easy), hash browns, pancakes (tall stack) and coffee (several refills.)

In Monterey we visited Fisherman's Wharf and Steinbeck's Cannery Row where sardines, in the 1950s, were almost fished to extinction. We rode the famous seventeen-mile drive to Carmel. This was a circuit of the Monterey Peninsula, one of the most expensive areas of real estate in the USA, with multi-million-dollar residences and manicured golf courses lining the spectacular coast. It was home to Clint Eastwood who was once the mayor here.

We continued south along a coast that would rival Cornwall's. At the end of one long day, we arrived at Refugio State Beach campground in the gloaming. There was no one on duty so we found a pleasant little grassy patch, set up our tents and started cooking. Suddenly, a pickup truck roared up, slammed on the brakes and an armed ranger jumped out.

"You can haul your asses outa here, the hiker-biker area's over there." he shouted pointing into the dark. Apparently we were on the picnic area, and although we pleaded and promised we would be gone by first light, rules were rules and we had to move. It was an inauspicious end to a hundred-mile day.

The next day we reached Ed's home in Santa Barbara and spent a couple of days being looked after by Ed's wife Pat and enjoying the sights. Ed used to be Santa Barbara's Fire Chief. He took us to an area which had suffered from a major bush fire last year. The trees were charred and skeletal but green buds showed signs of regeneration. The saddest sights were the empty plots where homesteads had once stood. Sometimes a concrete base or chimney stack remained but often, when the house had been made solely of timber, there was nothing. Strangely, some houses had burnt down while their neighbour's dwelling had escaped relatively unscarred. Ed explained that small tasks such as cleaning the gutters or pruning nearby trees could have made the difference.

Just before Ventura, as we followed the coast road south, a pod of dolphins surfed the waves travelling in the same direction and speed. It was the most amazing experience because they accompanied us for three or four miles before we had to leave the Pacific coast and take to the hills. A ten-mile climb took us to Wheeler Gorge campground, a primitive site with pit toilets, no water and a sign warning of rattlesnakes. We erected our tents, washed in the creek, shared our pasta dinner with a ground squirrel and enjoyed a Napa Valley Merlot, Ed always managed to find a bottle in his panniers! It was so peaceful.

Upwards, upwards ever upwards into the Los Padres National Forest past the 2,000 feet, 3,000 feet and 4,000 feet elevation markers. A short, sharp descent followed, when we reached a speed of fifty miles an hour before climbing once more. It was fantastic scenery of stratified sandstone that lead to mountain pine forests. As we toiled upwards, a large pickup truck, one of the few vehicles we saw that day, slowed down beside us and the driver shouted "Would you guys like a soda?" A man dressed in cowboy gear climbed down and produced cold cans of *Dr Pepper* from an ice box in the trunk. Alongside his ice box were other boxes, or rather, cages. Each cage contained a live snake. Gary was a snake catcher and he proudly showed us his catches: a garter, gopher and a rattle snake. He asked if we would like to handle any of them. We politely declined. Once satisfied that our thirsts had been sated, Gary drove off. We never did discover why he caught the snakes, or what he did with them.

At last we reached Pine Mountain Pas summit at over 5,000 feet, past signs warning of snow and ice, and one pointing to Ozena Campground, that we found to be closed. The only other campground within reach was at Reyes Creek and up a very steep road. We were rewarded with not only a campground but also an unexpected bar. It really was a wild-west tavern with the heads of deer and wild boar decorating the walls, cattle brands burned into the wooden bar and a sign dated 1871. It looked as if the clientele were of the same vintage and could have been extras from a Hollywood western.

In the morning a sheet of ice coated the inside of our tent, with a layer of hoar frost on the outside. Our morning ablutions in the creek were conducted as briefly as possible. However, we enjoyed spectacular views of the lizard-like spines of the mountains to the east, which we had to cross. We set off into an ever-increasing wind through an arid area of deep sandstone gullies, along the San Andreas Fault, where a large coyote padded nonchalantly across the road ahead of us. By the time we had reached our turn-off onto Route 138, the wind had become gale-force. We turned east with the tempest on our backs to receive the most tremendous tailwind; we literally sailed along at thirty miles per hour with hardly a turn of the pedal. Our free-ride lasted for twenty-five miles. We raced the tumbleweed through poppy fields, until a right turn transformed our friend into our foe. Speed dropped to single figures as we were relentlessly battered by the head wind. Our dream ride had become a nightmare. Struggling through Willow Springs, we saw neither a willow nor a spring but battled up the Tehachapi Mountain Range to Oak Tree Pass at nearly 5,000 feet. Such was the wind that we then had to pedal downhill to find shelter for the night.

The wind had relented when we passed the famous Tehachapi Railway Loop. In order for the railway tracks to maintain a negotiable grade, it tunnelled under itself to complete a loop that enabled the engine to travel under, or over, the rear of the train. We struggled uphill at a miserly three miles an hour through wooded valleys. Ten miles and three hours later, all enjoyment and any conversation had long evaporated. A kind lady in a car took pity on us and stopped to give us each a bottle of water. This small act of kindness helped to propel us to Mike's Place where we were allowed to camp behind his store.

We were beside the River Kern, pedalling upstream. Judging from the whoops and hollers, the rafters and kayakers were having much more fun than we were as they sped down the white-water rapids. From Lake Isabella it was more of the same – tough but terrific! We passed through Johnsondale, *alt 4,700 ft, pop 2*, through rugged and arid mountain scenery into woodlands, mainly ponderosa pine and sequoia redwoods. We stopped at the Trail of the 100 Redwoods and walked among the 3,000-year-old trees. Then we visited the Sequoia National Park to look at the General Sherman Tree, supposedly the biggest tree on the planet and estimated to contain enough wood to build sixty, five-room houses. Then it was up to a high point of 7,500 feet with glorious views over valleys thousands of feet below.

"What goes up must come down" and we certainly did, for twenty miles on the Generals' Highway at forty miles an hour with hardly a touch on the brake levers. The grade was perfect and the bends were gentle. We flashed past the last of the redwoods and the elevation markers counted down all too quickly. In less than an hour we had travelled from snow and pines, through deciduous woods and pastures, to bare brown hills and cactus.

Just before Fresco we met Richard, a 71-year-old racing cyclist. He offered to show us a cycle-friendly route through the city. Richard rode a titanium road bike and was garishly dressed in Lycra. Richard was a red rag to a bull as far as Ed was concerned. The two of them continually half-wheeled each other, the speed gradually creeping up. We clung to their back wheels for as long as possible but as the pace increased we had to accept defeat and dropped back. I was not sure who had won but after a while they returned to find us. "Boys will be boys."

While camping beside and swimming in Millerton Lake, we heard on the radio news reports of serious bush fires around Santa Barbara. Thirty thousand people had been evacuated from the hills surrounding Ed's home town. Ex Fire Chief, Ed, was very concerned. He decided to return home to see if he could be of help. It was already hot when we set off with Ed for the last time before he headed for Santa Barbara. Actually, we did not pedal together for long because a pair of racing cyclists shot past at the bottom of a ten-mile hill. Our bicycling buddy took off in pursuit, out of the saddle and throwing his loaded touring bike from side to side. That was the last we saw of him until we reached the top of the hill about two hours later. There he sat, patiently waiting for us with a big grin on his face. A couple of miles further down the road we came to a fork in the road. Ed headed south and we rolled north.

Never Say "If Only"

'bye Ed

We had a day off! Now that Ed had left us, we could peddle more leisurely. We spent a day at the beautiful, blue Bass Lake and its sandy beaches. At Wawona, in the Yosemite National Park, the campground was closed. The cheapest alternative accommodation was a cabin at $240 a night. It was time for Maggie to play her white hair card. A big red pickup was parked outside the Information Office,

"Are you going to Yosemite Valley?" Maggie asked, bashfully. "Sure, we are." replied the driver, "Why? "Any chance of a lift?" she inquired, adding hopefully, "With our bike?" Not only did we receive a lift into the valley but also a thirty-two-mile side trip to Glacier Point for spectacular views over Half Dome and Yosemite Village. All the campgrounds and motor home sites were full but a walk-in area catered for those on bicycles or on foot. The site was packed, like a refugee camp, mainly with young climbers. Bags and boots were strewn around make-shift habitats ranging from tarpaulins and bivouacs to small tents. We squeezed into a small space and were soon recognised as British because of our ingrained habit of always using a fly-sheet. No-one else did; it was May in California, it was not going to rain!

Maggie in the Redwoods

The spring snow melt ensured that the waterfalls were incredible. Colossal amounts of water plunged hundreds of feet, creating huge shrouds of water vapour and a kaleidoscope of colours. Enclosed in canyons with their thousand-foot granite walls, we could feel, see and hear the thunder of the falls. Everywhere, huge boulders and sheer cliffs made this a climbers' Mecca. In the evening at camp, we were entertained by climbers' tales of hand jams and finger holds, of near misses and narrow escapes.

After two spectacular day walks we pedalled out of the Yosemite Valley under the shadow of *El Capitán,* the 3,000 feet vertical rock face considered by many as the Everest of rock climbing. With the aid of borrowed binoculars, we were able to discern two climbers located half way up. The climb usually took a few days to complete. Therefore, the climbers bivouacked overnight in hammocks suspended from the sheer rock face.

After fifty very hot miles, reportedly over 100 degrees Fahrenheit, we rolled into Angels' Camp, the 'Frog Jumping Capital of the World'. It was also the Calaveras County Fair weekend featuring the annual jumping frog championships, as immortalised by Mark Twain. As expected, the town was packed but, luckily for us, a lady who had a reserved pitch on the fully-booked campsite had suffered an accident en route. The, now vacant, lot was a premier pitch no less, with a covered picnic table, chairs, cooking area, laundrette and swimming pool. We decided that it would be an ideal place to spend my 63rd birthday which was tomorrow. Therefore, we set up our tent then visited the fair. It was similar in some ways to English county fairs and resembled Glastonbury Festival. The entertainment included agricultural equipment, live music; pop, country and western, rap and a rodeo. The rodeo started with the pre-school cowboys mutton-busting, followed by teenagers attempting to stay aboard steers, finally bull-riding by the adults. My birthday was also the day of the jumping frog finals. The bullfrogs were about the size of a tea plate and often bred and trained specifically for this momentous occasion. They were placed in the centre of a platform marked with concentric circles. One frog nearly broke the world record; now that would have been a tale to tell our grandchildren.

In Jackson we stopped for breakfast, the breakfast was good. On hearing our accents, two ladies asked where we were going. Barbara, a confessed Anglophile, invited us to stay at her house, where we enjoyed iced tea, a tasty meal with a birthday cake, an interesting conversation and a proper bed!

Folsom Prison was our next stop; voluntarily I'm pleased to say, Folsom Lake actually but we were camped in the shadow of the massive walls of the high security jail made famous by the Johnny Cash album *'Folsom Prison Blues.'* While we were swimming in the lake with some athletes from Sacramento Triathlon Club, some varmints, probably ground squirrels, chewed through a pannier bag. Meanwhile, a skunk sauntered by our tent, along with a million ants.

We followed a green corridor along a paved cycleway through Sacramento that gave no indication that we were pedalling through the capital city of California. Instead of cars and concrete, we enjoyed the company of a multitude of birds including bluebirds, cardinals, egrets, hawks, herons, humming birds and wild turkeys.

At Vallejo, on a cold, grey morning, we took a ferry across San Pablo Bay to San Francisco. It was the first time for weeks that the sun was not shining. From San Francisco Quay, we cycled past Fisherman's Wharf to the Golden

Gate Bridge, barely discernible through the thick sea mist. Then we had a long detour around San Francisco Bay via San José to return to David and Diane's house in Pleasanton. In San José, we chatted with a gentleman taking his son on a bike ride. Miguel told us that he was one of twenty-one children and that his father had eighty-seven grandchildren! I imagine that his Christmas could be rather expensive!

Using Dave and Diane's home as a base, we spent a few days travelling into San Francisco via the Bay Area Rapid Transport underground system, BART, to visit the tourist attractions including the prison island of Alcatraz. It was a good end to a great trip.

A month after returning from the States we decided to cycle Lands End to John o' Groats again. It was ten years since we had previously done the End to End and some of the gang thought that it would be a good idea to repeat it. We have found that return journeys are seldom is as good as the original trip. This ride was no exception. The weather was not kind and the group was much too big with thirty-one riders. Such a large group made it difficult and rather dangerous on the busy British roads, consequently we frequently rode alone. However, we all completed the 990-mile challenge in one piece and I made a pledge *not* to do it again. Famous last words!

For a change we decided to go for a walk and hiked the Pembrokeshire Coast Path in Wales. It was magical. We were lucky with the weather in early May and the scenery was simply astonishing. Beautiful sandy beaches guarded by tall imperial cliffs. The sea rolled in from the Atlantic Ocean to crash violently into base of the cliffs spraying spumes skyward with a boom like a big, bass drum. The footpath meandered along the cliff top with breathtaking views of craggy ledges that are home to puffins, guillemots, razorbills and many more. There was a profusion of colours: daisies, buttercups, bluebells, sea campion, wild garlic, thyme and many others I didn't recognise. Songbirds maintained a continual daytime symphony: blackbirds, thrushes, finches, chiffchaffs, skylarks, even the raucous caw from a raven. No wonder the Welsh regard their homeland as God's Own Country.

CHAPTER 36

Sri Lanka

"The traveller sees what he sees. The tourist sees what he has come to see."
G K Chesterton

Feb-March 2010. 705 miles

A cardboard sign reading Mr Allan / Mrs Maggie was held aloft by a smiley man at Colombo Airport. This was our driver who would take us to our pre-booked, for once, guest house at Negombo, about sixty kilometres away. Outside we were struck by the heat, humidity, honking and traffic bedlam that was so emblematic of the Indian subcontinent. Our excitement was touched with a tad of trepidation when our driver, with a blast of his horn, drove straight out into the heaving mass of traffic on the main road. There appeared to be no driving code; one could pass on either side, yield only to larger vehicles, and there was no slowing down at pedestrian crossings but you always sounded your horn. We saw bicycles with four on board, and motorbikes with six!

Thankfully our accommodation at the Ice Bear Guest House, offered a quiet refuge from the organised chaos outside. We spent two days of relative tranquillity; only relative because I was still possessed by my demons and I tormented Maggie ruthlessly. I really needed to sort out my head. We went for a warm-up ride to a nature reserve and got hopelessly lost. That didn't help, but I began to get it together as we started our exploration of Sri Lanka.

We headed up the west coast as far as the scruffy, smelly and predominantly Muslim town of Puttalam. It was a tired town, like a weary boxer picking himself up off the canvas after a double knock-down; the civil war and the tsunami. A small group of friendly young men with motor bikes helped us to find a guest house. It was here that we received our first real taste of Sri Lankan cuisine; a mountain of rice with a beef, pork or goat curry. This came with an assortment of seven or eight spicy side dishes such as fish, crab, dhal, ladies' fingers, jack fruit, caramelised onions, samosas, melon and cabbage. It was a fiery concoction and definitely not for the faint hearted.

The British Foreign Office advised us not to travel further north into Tamil territory. This was because the civil war that had resulted in 100,000 deaths, had ended less than a year earlier and serious tensions between government troops and Tamil Liberation Tigers remained. Therefore, we rode east to Anuradhapura along the A12, a main road but with a diabolical surface. The previous night's banquet had left me with a touch of Delhi belly and the jolting and jarring did not help.

From Dambulla, we visited Sigiriya, an ancient rock fortress built on the top of a 200 metres tall gigantic volcanic plug. A king's palace stood on top of the rock commanding panoramic views of the surrounding countryside. At the base of the palace were lovely gardens, lakes and, under overhangs, vertical rock walls that were decorated with colourful frescoes of beautiful, topless courtesans. Access to the palace was up a rusted metal staircase and through a gateway built in the form of an enormous lion. Only the lion's claws remained

Never Say "If Only"

and at this point we were instructed to don bright orange, heavy duty rubber suits, including hoods and gloves. Two days earlier, tourists had been attacked by a swarm of hornets so, to be on the safe side, protective suits were provided. It was swelteringly hot so we declined the offer. But no, it was compulsory and we had to take the heavy rubberised onesies. We ended up carrying them.

When we went to collect the tandem, we were unable to unlock it from the concrete pillar. It was a combination lock and no matter how much we jiggled and juggled it would not yield. A group of about twenty young men, mainly motor taxi couriers, gathered around all wanting to unpick the lock. But it was an unbreakable combination. One of the lads mimed a sawing motion, I nodded my approval. Off he roared, returning after a few minutes armed with a hack-saw and made short work of freeing the bike. On our way back to Dambulla in the rain, while avoiding an oncoming bus heading straight at us, we skidded on a muddy patch and crashed. Suffering no more than skinned knees and wounded pride, we were immediately assisted by half a dozen motor rickshaw drivers. They rushed to our aid and fetched water from a nearby pump in order to clean our wounds.

We pedalled through a heavy, cloying atmosphere on our way to Matale. The air was so thick and damp that the simple effort of breathing brought beads of sweat to the brow. The traffic was manic. Earlier in the day, we had to take to the roadside dirt to avoid larger traffic intent on our annihilation. In Matale everyone seemed to have the objective of self-destruction, or they were playing an all-encompassing game of chicken.

Immediately after surviving Matale, we encountered a big hill. Motorbikes and tuk-tuks coming the other way had turned off their engines in order to save fuel letting gravity take over. This was no mere pimple. Hills, heat and heavy traffic could be a toxic trio. Separately they could be managed easily, two out of three were bearable but all three together were no fun at all! A cold Coca-Cola at the top was our reward, before descending into Kandy, the City of Culture.

Kandy was a hill town surrounding a beautiful lake. First we visited the huge Botanic Gardens, gardens with large trees such as the Java Willow which covered an area of 2,500 cubic metres. There were also massive coconuts weighing up to 20 kilograms each, and thousands of fruit bats hanging like black rags from every branch. Some of these Dracula-like creatures fluttered round looking for better roosts emitting a continual squawking din. Below, orderly groups of school children dressed in immaculate white uniforms were the antithesis of the inverted animals hanging overhead. Nandana, our hostess, took us on a guided walk through the city to visit many Hindu temples including the shrine that contained a tooth of Buddha!

We were too weary to cycle so we booked a car and driver to take us to the Elephant Orphanage, and what a scary experience that was! Our driver spent most of the journey on his mobile phone, changing gear with his elbow while his other hand was permanently on the horn swerving in and out of the traffic like a dodgem-car. To be fair, he was probably divinely protected. He murmured a prayer before we set off and had statuettes of Hindu Deities fixed to the top of the dashboard and swinging from the rear-view mirror. I'm not saying he had effigies of *all* the 330 million Hindu Gods, but certainly enough to seriously hamper his vision. We arrived shaken but in one piece to find the Elephant Orphanage was little more than an elephant zoo. Bull elephants were chained and others enclosed. We did watch some being bathed in the river and one three-legged youngster, victim of a land mine. A false leg had been fitted but not tolerated by the poor animal.

Tea-pickers in saris, each with a large white bag suspended from a strap across the forehead, dotted the vivid green, tea plantations as we climbed to Nuwara Eliya, the highest town in Sri Lanka at over 6,000 feet. It was a 19th-century British creation to serve the tea trade. Indeed, we had passed several huge tea factories, many offering guided tours, where we stopped frequently to refresh ourselves with cups of tea, sickly-sweet with condensed milk. In town we visited a gentlemen's Hill Club that dated from colonial times. We were refused admission because of the dress code. Long trousers, a jacket, shirt and tie were the requirements for gentlemen and a dress for ladies. Shorts and sandals indeed, what were we thinking of? In fact, it was as recent as 1970 before ladies and non-white Sri Lankans were admitted. To quench our thirst we went into the Lion Pub but decided not to stay. It was gloomy and little more than a drinking den. Unlike the Hill Club we were overdressed. I was the only white man, no problem, but Maggie would have been the only woman and judging from astonished looks we received, the only woman ever!

It was time for a pilgrimage. We left most of our possessions and the bike at our guest house and took a local bus down a very narrow and rough road overlooking tea estates. They had very British names such as Somerset, Edinburgh and Inverness. Our first destination was Hatton. This was a bustling, busy, smelly and dirty communications hub. Most of the buildings were of uncoated breeze blocks. Several motor rickshaw riders vied for our trade but we took another bus to Dalhousie along even narrower roads. When passing oncoming vehicles, the drop into the valley below looked far too close for comfort. Watching the driver struggling to control the antiquated rust-bucket was an education. The steering wheel was enormous and the three feet long gear stick crunched with every gear change. There were two horn levers, one emitted a car-like beep for over-taking or in acknowledgement, while the other gave out a much deeper and louder blare as if to say, "I'm coming through and I'm bigger than you!"

In Dalhousie we took a scruffy little room but at 700 rupees (£4) we could not complain. We only wanted it until 1:30am. Tomorrow we hoped to climb the solitary 7,360 feet high mountain named Adam's Peak. At the top, was a large foot-like impression in the rocks that Christians and Muslims claimed to be the footprint left by Adam when he was exiled from the Garden of Eden.

Tamil Hindus, however, considered it to be the footprint of Lord Shiva, while for Buddhists, the footprint belonged to the Buddha. Pilgrims of many faiths attempted to reach the peak before dawn so that they can offer their prayers and perform their religious rites in the glorious spectacle of the sunrise.

We were on the trail by 2:00 am after a sleepless night thanks to the constant barking of feral dogs, so loud it seemed that they were howling and rutting on our doorstep. The path wound up the forested mountainside on steps carved into the rock or built of concrete. There were 5,200 steps that took us two and a half hours to climb. Many wayside stalls offered refreshments. Electric light illuminated the entire route. We clanked up the steps in our cycling shoes but most of our fellow pilgrims, young and old, wore sandals, flip-flops or just bare feet. None were dressed for mountain climbing, most wore their everyday clothes, saris and dhotis. As we ascended it became increasingly chilly so the pilgrims wrapped towels and tablecloths around their shoulders. Coats, jackets and jumpers were not part of most Sri Lankan's wardrobes. Early in the climb, there had been much singing and chanting of mantras. At the summit we could hear only gasping and puffing. Many of the pilgrims were far from young and fit and appeared physically incapable of such a strenuous effort. Some folk carried children. All must have been strengthened by their belief in the importance of their quest.

The return bus was even more of a rattletrap than the one before, and we were well shaken by the time we reached Hatton. Rather than another juddering bus ride back to Nuwara Eliya, we decided to try the train. The train arrived forty-five minutes late but we were an hour behind schedule upon leaving. It took fifteen minutes to jam all the people into the already full train. Many of the passengers had boxes, bags and babies. The babies were passed through open windows to any willing pair of hands; then the parents forced an entrance. Eventually, everyone with sufficient determination elbowed their way on board. We chugged out of the station with passengers hanging out of the windows and doors.

We travelled first class where there were spare seats. There were also seats reserved for clergy, while on buses they were saved for monks. The engines, rolling stock, stations and lack of punctuality were so British and reeked of the Empire and a past era that I would not have been surprised if we had been flagged down by children waving a red petticoat.

Never Say "If Only"

Our next port of call was Ella, a pretty little town and popular tourist destination. While there, we tackled Little Adams's Peak, a mini version of yesterday's effort with about 5,000 less steps and a similar absence of pilgrims. Back at the Ella Holiday Inn our beer was served in teacups from a teapot as our hosts did not have a liquor licence.

We went for a day ride to Badulla but became caught up in a political demonstration. Thousands of marchers, nearly all men, shouted and chanted for their chosen candidate who, bedecked with garlands on an open-top truck, waved and smiled benevolently. Wearing the blue and yellow of the People's Alliance Party, boozed activists set off fire crackers and with bangs and smoke presented an intimidating show of force. A sizeable police and army presence increased our fear of being caught up in an ugly confrontation. All traffic came to a halt but we wound our way through the agitators, finally reaching the front of the jam. From then on, it was as if we were lead bike in the Tour de France. We sped away from the demonstration through a corridor of cheering crowds waving their flags and banners.

It was a relief to return to the Holiday Inn for a pleasant cup of beer, but it was not yet time for peace and quiet. Our host requested a ride on the tandem and, although I was knackered, it would have been churlish of me to deny he who had provided teapots of ale. We rode to his parents' house where, while bending down to politely remove my shoes, I was bitten on the arse by their pet dog. It drew blood, left tooth-marks and took a slice out of my shorts. Later my kind wife washed the wound with Dettol while I, through gritted teeth, thought that perhaps I really should have had a rabies injection before we left home.

At Yala National Park we swopped the tandem for a Mitsubushi four-by-four and a guide, a happy guy named Tjula. Bouncing along on rough and rutted roads we made frequent stops to gaze at the wildlife. Around every corner we spied different species; elephants, sambar deer and the smaller chital spotted deer, mongooses, langur monkeys, palm squirrels and monitor lizards. The water holes were especially interesting with water buffalo, wild boar and enormous crocodiles. And so many exotic birds; peacocks, jungle fowl, painted malibu storks, nightjars, hornbills, herons, kingfishers, bee eaters, serpent eagles, brahma kites, spotted billed pelicans and many, many more. Yala has one of the highest leopard densities in the world, but we didn't see one.

Our guide was in the Park when the tsunami hit on Boxing Day, 2004. He managed to escape by driving through a 4 ft wall of water. 250 others in the park were not so lucky. We drove past bare foundations all that remained of houses and bungalows after the Wave. Amazingly, few animals were killed, as if they had a sixth sense they had moved to higher land.

The day was extremely warm and humid as we passed the salt flats near Bundala. We thought that we were hot cycling along in the breeze but wondered what it must have been like for the men and women working in the salt flats. They shovelled and swept the salt into piles as we would shovel snow. Their work was on a huge scale and must have been agony, coupled with the blinding and dazzling effects of the sun reflected from the white salt.

There was evidence of the tsunami devastation everywhere as we cycled along the south coast of Sri Lanka. An open-air cafe with plastic tables and chairs offered a sea view to go with the rotis. This was flat-bread stuffed with whatever you wanted; egg, cheese, fish, chicken and vegetables. We congratulated the young owner and chef on the food and the location. "Yes, but once we also had walls, a roof, doors and windows. Now I just have this." he said gesturing towards the concrete floor. His mother, father, brothers and sister also vanished with the building.

Most days we were slowed, but not usually stopped, by police and army road blocks, just beckoned through the barriers with smiles and waves. More serious obstacles were the feral dogs. At night they slept on the warm tarmac, but during the day wandered across the roads oblivious of the traffic. Occasionally we were barked at and chased, but normally it was too hot and they couldn't be bothered.

It was 'hot as Hell' when we took a diversion to Wewurukannala Vihara Temple where we were unexpectedly given a glimpse of the real thing. A colossal fifty metre Buddha looked down on the dregs of earthly life as portrayed in the Tunnel of Hell. This cave contained life-size models of demons and sinners in Hades. It graphically depicted what might happen if you succumb to temptation and stray from the path of righteousness. You could be disembowelled, immersed in a boiling cauldron or hacked to pieces by fanged demons. A hundred paintings each illustrated a different sin such as gambling or not respecting your mother, with the resulting punishment in Hell. Talking of hot places we had to leave our shoes at the ticket office and to reach the 160 feet tall Buddha, crossed a wide, tiled court yard in bare feet. It was like walking on burning coals and I narrowly avoided stepping on a scorpion. Not only had we been shown what Hell was like, we were also given a feel of it!

Allan Pendleton

The traffic was again quite manic as we rode into Galle and we experienced a number of near misses. I think that earlier I suggested that in Sri Lanka there are no rules of the road. I was wrong. There is one: *overtake,* at any cost. Even if you are turning or stopping in twenty metres, something is coming the other way, it is a blind corner; no matter – you must overtake! This rule also applies to bicycles. We passed a bike today carrying two young men, one sitting side-saddle on the crossbar. They immediately accelerated and sped past us. After a while, as the peddler tired and we caught up, they swopped positions. The lad on the saddle jumped off and ran alongside to jump sideways onto the crossbar while his mate had taken over pedalling. This was performed without stopping and so efficiently that, with a fresh engine, they pulled away again.

A gracious lady showed us round her bamboo and palm tsunami photograph gallery that illustrated the harrowing event. This exhibition was constructed on the foundations of her original house. As we rode to Hikkaduwa railway station, we noticed many similar bare foundations that once were homes. Ninety thousand Sri Lankan buildings had succumbed to the tsunami. We stopped at the memorial built in respect of the 1,700 passengers killed when the Colombo train was swept off the tracks. This was the world's biggest train disaster. The same train, not literally, that we will be taking tomorrow. Out of the quarter million deaths in the 2004 flood, 53,000 were from Sri Lanka.

The 09:43 train for Colombo was a slow train, a very slow train. It took us over four hours to travel the eighty kilometres. Upon our arrival and armed with tickets and a goods receipt, we proceeded to the goods van to collect our so-called double bike only to be told to go to the parcel office which we could not find. Whoever we asked, pointed in a different direction. Back at the baggage van, we could see our tandem still inside. Although I waved my receipt in their faces, the guards insisted, "No, no, go parcel office." Eventually, someone brought the parcel office to us. A little man, equipped with clip board and pen, invited me to sign my name, print it underneath and taking our goods receipt, let us have our bike. I asked him which from which platform departed the train for Negombo. He replied, "Platform 2 at 2:30 but double bike no go!" Each ticket kiosk sold tickets for a different destination. Whilst we looked for the correct one, a man approached us saying: "Train not take bicycle to Negombo, you take taxi." So, we took a taxi but had to cross several railway tracks to reach it. There being no bridges, we had to climb down off the platform and cross the line. The trains do make a lot of noise when they come into the station, so you shouldn't get run down (unless you happen to be struggling with a tandem and panniers.)

For our last night in Sri Lanka, we enjoyed delicious seafood inside a local restaurant. Outside, the heavens opened and we were treated to a wondrous display of sheet and forked lightning that lit up the sky, accompanied by deafening thunderclaps. We thanked Sri Lanka, for a spectacular send-off.

CHAPTER 37

Canada & USA

Alberta, British Columbia, Idaho, Wyoming, Montana

"The great thing about a journey is that you can plan steps along the way but often the greatest times and greatest places are ones you just happen upon by chance."
Colin Stafford-Johnson, Wild Ireland BBC Documentary

<u>Aug-Sept, 2010. 2,105 miles</u>

We planned another little journey with Ed Rodriguez, our fire-fighting buddy from California, this time in the Rocky Mountains. The journey started inauspiciously with three hours parked on a London Heathrow Airport runway waiting for a spare part to arrive for our aeroplane. When we eventually touched down at Calgary good old Ed was waiting patiently to greet us. Travelling north in a bus to Jasper up the Icefields Parkway reminded us why we had wanted to return. This region was without doubt one of the most beautiful bike rides in the world. The Parkway stretched 140 miles into the Canadian Rockies between soaring mountains with tumbling waterfalls, glacier-filled valleys and turquoise lakes, plus the likelihood of seeing a grizzly. We could not wait to start pedalling.

After a day in Jasper, sampling their real ale and nearly getting knocked off the bike by an elk, we set off south along the Icefields Parkway. Being later in the year, we did not get to witness the avalanches which we had experienced in 1994, but even so the scenery was mesmerizing. Just after Athabasca Glacier, which had become a bit dirty and grey under the onslaught of busloads of tourists, a black bear ambled across the road in front of us. Peyto Lake, brilliantly coloured emerald by the ice melt from the Clawfoot Glacier, gave us a boost to tackle the eleven miles climb up the 6,785 feet Bow Pass. At the summit a baby bear sat beside the road. We, rather stupidly, stopped to take a photograph. We did not see Mummy Bear, luckily Mummy Bear did not see us!

Never Say "If Only"

In the Park the campgrounds were rather expensive and provisions hard to get. Most of the stores sold touristy goods rather than a tin of beans. Safety from bears was a major concern. Consequently, in one campsite we were surrounded by an electric fence and most had bear boxes in which we could store our food. Further down the road, an absence of bear boxes meant that we had to hang our food high up in the trees. The weather was variable; one minute it was raining and the next the sun was shining. The rain was a clear winner on points, with low, dark clouds obscuring the surrounding mountains for much of the time. Close to the US border, we rode into the old coal mining town of Frank, with a population of fifty. In 1903 a massive rock slide buried the town killing all the residents apart from the miners working underground, they survived. Boulders, the size of houses, still laid strewn either side of the highway.

Some serious and strenuous riding through the Blood Indian Reservation took us to the US border near Chief Mountain. Young Indian braves used to climb this 10,000-foot monolith to prove their manhood, discover their destiny and find their spirits.

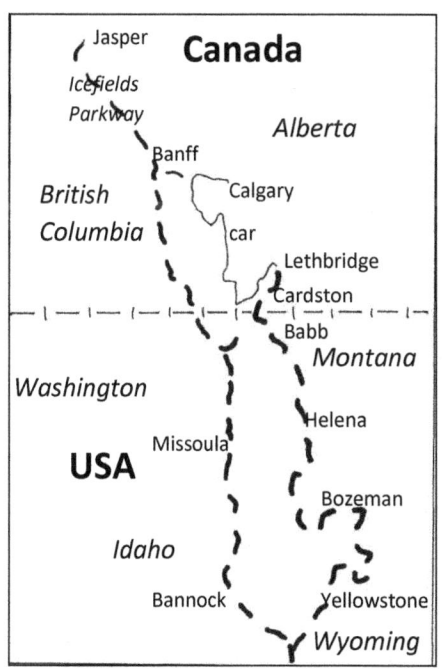

After form-filling at the passport control there was more climbing until we temporarily emerged from the mountains into Big Sky Montana. But it was not long before we were back in the Rockies at the Glacier National Park. Then we had one of those magical cycling days that you wish could be permanently etched into your brain so you could reincarnate the experience at random. Cotton wool clouds floated in a vivid blue sky as we passed a lake surrounded by cliffs and crags and a horizon of saw-like peaks. A six per cent twelve-mile climb up Going to the Sun Road topped out at the Logan Pass visitor centre. Here I chatted with a Blackfoot Indian before enjoying the equally long descent to Lake McDonald, where we enjoyed a refreshing swim in its clear, cold water.

In a restaurant in West Glacier, we got talked at by a Republican redneck who despised Obama and all that he stood for. When he started ranting about immigrants, Mexicans in particular, Ed made tactful withdrawal.

On our way to Missoula through conifer forests into a hot *Chinook* head wind, we were overtaken by a cycling couple carrying *ten* large panniers. David had converted his bike so that he could carry four bags on the back. Even so, he and Martha could still pedal faster than us. After a brief "How ya doin'" they pedalled away. In Missoula we camped in the garden of an old fire-fighter friend of Ed's. Dave and his wife Mara made us very welcome. We had a day looking around the highlights of the city that included the offices of *Adventure Cycling* magazine and the brewery.

We toiled up the Bitterroot Valley where towns conjured up visions of the old Wild West with their log cabins, saloons and casinos. Chief Joseph Pass at 7,241 feet proved to be our biggest climb yet. At the Big Hole Valley we stopped at the site of the massacre, where in August 1877, a band of Nez Perce Indians, mainly women and children, were slaughtered by a force of US soldiers.

We dropped in, literally, at Jackson Hot Springs, luxuriating in the pool while around us, on the horizon, we watched the mountains growing white with snow. The next morning after the sun had melted the ice from our tent, we

Never Say "If Only"

set off up Big Hole Pass at 7,400 ft. A long descent took us to the ghost town of Bannack. In 1862 gold was discovered in Grasshopper Creek, and within a year a township of 3,000 people had sprung up. But the people who rushed to Bannack were not only miners. They included businessmen, outlaws and prostitutes, plus a murderer from California, Henry Plummer. Plummer got himself elected as the town marshal but secretly led a gang of hijackers and robbers who reputedly killed a hundred victims during their acts of highway robbery. A group of vigilantes finally caught up with Plummer and strung him up together with many of his associates.

Leaving Bannack, we took the Great Divide off-road route known as the Big Sheep Creek Back Country Byway. We left our idyllic campground and rode straight on to a gravel road to endure one of our toughest days: how many times have I said that? It was seemingly an endless climb with a few steep descents, mainly on gravel but with a few dirt and rocky trails. The route ran through isolated, treeless cow country with a few lonely livestock ranches. We camped wild beside a small stream, washed and drank water from the creek. It was a cloudless day but as soon as the sun set, the temperature plummeted.

In the morning, we hardly had to turn a pedal for the first six miles as we followed Big Sheep Creek downhill through a beautiful canyon with eagles soaring overhead. At Red Rock Lake, we were lucky to see trumpeter swans. They had an eight-foot wingspan and were once on the verge of extinction. In an increasing wind, we passed over the Great Divide into Idaho, then back into Montana over the Targhee Pass. Black clouds threatened as we entered West Yellowstone, so we found a small bunk cabin for not much more than a camping site fee. This was well timed, for as we moved into the cabin a mini-tornado struck. Later, we walked into town and witnessed the devastation. Trees were uprooted, windows blown in and roofs ripped off, including that belonging to the Best Western Hotel.

On entering Yellowstone National Park, a park ranger instructed us to stay well away from the bison and if we saw one, to remain in our car! The very next morning, however, I had great difficulty exiting our tent as one of the massive brutes lay sleeping on our doorstep. Also, it was bloody freezing with a thick film of ice covering the tent. With an average elevation of 8,000 feet, it could snow at any time throughout the year and this year was no exception.

Allan Pendleton

The next four days were spent shivering the two hundred miles around the Park. We watched the geysers and hot springs bubbling and boiling and cycled over windswept passes with burned out lodgepole pines standing skeletal in fields dusted with snow. We gazed with wonder at the mighty Lower Falls Waterfall that cascaded 308 feet into the Yellowstone River and spotted wolves and a grizzly from afar; bison, deer and elk from a much closer but more intimidating distance. It was indeed, an amazing park and one just as impressive second time round.

Yellowstone was established as a national park in 1872 making it the first national park in the world. It was located over a super volcano known as the Yellowstone Caldera. It is an active volcano and has erupted several times in the last two million years. Its next eruption is likely to cause untold devastation worldwide. It is likely to be one thousand times more powerful than the 1980 Mount St Helens eruption and would create a haze that could cause world temperatures to plunge. Luckily for us there was no eruption while we were there. As if to compensate, we were offered a surreal display of forked lightning. The flashes and accompanying thunder claps were so loud that we actually felt the booms as blows to the chest. I imagined that it was like being in the Somme trenches under artillery fire during World War I. The ensuing rain quickly transformed the campground to a quagmire, further enhancing the comparison with the Great War of 1914-18.

It was time to turn around and head back to Calgary. We rode to Virginia City, an old gold rush town dating back to the 1880s. Evidence of its former glory was the roadside slag heaps left by the prospectors. En route we passed Earthquake Lake that was created when a gigantic landslide sent 80 million tons of earth and rock tumbling into the valley and blocking the Madison River. In the process, a campground was buried along with twenty-eight campers.

Ed needed to go home. His wife, Pat, was not well and needed an operation to deal with her cancer. Our last day together was a tough haul, battling all day into wind and rain. We decided to spoil ourselves by getting a room in a Super 8 Motel at Whitehall. Bliss came in the form of a soft bed with pillows, smooth sheets and a bath with fluffy towels. After breakfast, we relieved Ed of all that might be useful such as a spare tyre, clothes line, plastic wine glass, coffee filter, peanut butter, but declined the offer of his stars and stripes flag.

Ed turned left for Butte, we steered right along the Jefferson River towards Three Forks. Rather than take advantage of a delightful sunny day, we headed underground in the Lewis and Clark Caverns. Upon returning to the surface two hours later, we found that dark, ominous clouds had covered the blue sky. We rode along a busy highway with huge trucks and no hard shoulder. Either side of the road was rolling grassland stretching to the snow-capped hills that fringed every horizon.

We met Louis, a Portuguese cyclist travelling from Alaska to Tierra del Fuego in Chile. "We don't see many cyclists from Portugal!"

"No," Louis replied, "I am he!"

We cycled north after Three Forks, following the Missouri Valley hoping to reach Helena before nightfall. Maggie named this stretch Death Valley because of the great number of crosses that marked fatalities. We counted thirteen in eight miles. We hoped that they were not for cyclists. The traffic was heavy and the shoulder was small. After Townsend we crossed a bleak, wide-open landscape with storm clouds building and thunder booming. Fifteen miles before Helena the heavens opened, lightning and thunder crashed in unison giving us a surge of adrenaline as we raced across the exposed open grasslands. There was no cover, no trees and no buildings. All the traffic had mysteriously disappeared whilst we rode alone across the skyline like a target in a shooting gallery. We wondered if the multitude of crosses were not deaths caused by vehicles but by lightning strikes.

After a day sheltering and drying out in Helena we pedalled out on the interstate, a dual carriageway with a wide hard shoulder. After twenty miles we faced a seemingly impenetrable barrier of hills, but a canyon appeared and, thanks to an ingenious feat of engineering, we slid between vertical rock faces into a beautiful gorge. Even better, the headwind had now funnelled into the gorge and blew from behind. We fairly flew into Wolf Creek for a giant sandwich and fries.

With the wind still on our backs, we sailed out of canyon country into flat pasture land with only the occasional *mesa* disturbing the flat horizon in Big

Sky Country. We followed the Missouri River past the sequence of Great Falls, that powered a hydro-electric plant, to the "Malted Barley Capital of the World", Fairfield, and its giant silos.

Countless warnings had been given about our proposed route through the Blackfeet Indian Reservation and the savages we would encounter there. There were no other campers in the Sleeping Wolf Campground and, apart from some feral dogs and boisterous laughs, shouts and jeers from the nearby bars and casinos in Browning, we were not bothered one iota by the redskins.

The Rocky Mountains, yesterday a mere shaky pencil mark on the horizon, were growing ominously as we pedalled north towards Canada. Our next stop was the federal aided Indian Chewing Bones Campground. The sign at the gate read "open" but the restrooms were locked. There was a lake to wash in so we put up our tent regardless.

It rained all night and cold sleet accompanied us to the small town of Babb, just short of the Canadian border. Yesterday, leaving the Plains, the route was lined with aspens just changing into their autumn colours of red, yellow and gold. Now, in the Rockies, fir trees predominated. At a cafe in Babb, we met a friendly Canadian couple, Willy and Don Peters, who invited us to stay at their place in Beaver Mines, if we were to pass that way.

At the USA-Canada border, Maggie left the queue to find a loo. Moments later, she was frog-marched back by a gun-toting US border guard and received a severe reprimand. Her offence was to wander too close to the Canadian border *before* passing through the customs control. Cold rain and wind tormented us all the way to Cardston. Upon arrival, we spent the rest of the day in the warm library before cooking a meal in the laundrette at Lee Creek Campground. Donning all our clothes we crawled into our sleeping bags and tried to sleep to the pitter-patter of rain drops. In the morning I awoke to the sound of silence. "Maggie, it's stopped raining at last!" Eagerly I unzipped the tent door to be faced with a bank of white snow, several inches deep, covering everything.

Our plan had been to pedal the Kananaskis Valley, the highest paved road in Canada. This was obviously no longer an option but perhaps if we hired a car? Lethbridge was the nearest town with a car hire service. Pushing the bike through the snow out of the campground we found that the roads were wet but amazingly clear of snow. We were told that at this time last year in mid-September, the temperature was 80 degrees Fahrenheit, today it was barely above freezing. The snow had eased but, as we neared the small town of Magrath, we had a tyre blow-out. Ed's spare tyre came into use and we continued over a flat plain to Lethbridge and hired a huge Dodge 5.7 litre pick-up truck.

The World Professional Bull-Riding championships were being held at the Cardston Agridome. It was really entertaining if you enjoyed watching others suffer. Not many riders stayed on board for the full eight seconds, most were promptly unseated and suffered nothing more than a few bruises and damaged pride. Others, not so lucky, were trodden on or gored. It was certainly not for the timid. The craziest part, though, was during the interval. Four men took seats around a card table in the centre of the ring. A bull was then released into the arena. It eyed up the poker players, pawed the ground then charged! The last man sitting was the winner. It was called Mexican Poker.

The snow ceded to rain that continued all the way to Waterton Park. We took an extremely soggy walk before dinner. Our tiny awning was hardly suitable but it was the only shelter in which we could cook. Then our MSR Whisperlite stove broke. We were hungry, cold, wet, and really pissed off. At least we had the truck in which to sit and a bottle of Californian red wine to ease the frustration. It rained throughout the night and only relented in the morning. However, after repairing our faulty stove, we went for a trek. We got very wet feet, cycling shoes were not ideal for hiking. Much of the walk was in the woods which shielded us from the wind and rain but the visibility was almost zero in the dense cloud. Damp and despondent, we drove to Beavers' Mine and the house where Willy and Don Peters, the couple we briefly met at the cafe in Babb, reside. But not permanently, for when we had earlier rung them for confirmation, they told us that they were currently in Edmonton. They insisted, however, that we, strangers, must use their house to shelter from "the horrible weather" and "to make ourselves at home," and told us where they had hidden the key. Later, ensconced in a warm dry environment with beds, bathrooms, kitchen and all mod cons, we thanked Willy and Don, an example of how kind and trusting people can be.

I looked out of our bedroom window in the morning to see a very wintery scene. A heavy snowfall had covered the neighbourhood. Even the tandem, strapped in the back of the pick-up, was coated with snow and looked sled-like and Christmassy. We drove to the Kananaskis Valley, over Highwood Pass at 7,322 feet. We were sad not to be on the tandem but thankful to be in the truck. Continuing onto the Trans Canada Highway we drove back to Calgary. We managed to move our departure date forwards a few days, shook the ice off our tent for the last time and said goodbye to the coldest Alberta summer for sixty years.

CHAPTER 38

Land's End to John o' Groats

*"The real voyage of discovery consists not in seeking
new landscapes, but in having new eyes."*
Marcel Proust

July, 2010. 1,000 miles

I had cycled the End-to-End twice before and there was no way I wanted to do the tedious route again. However, I was very encouraging to my close friends, Martin, Kev and Jason, when they declared that they wished to do it. But, when the driver of their support vehicle dropped out at the eleventh hour, I was the only sucker with no excuses not to step in. Although I hate driving with a vengeance I nobly volunteered. The day before departure we went to collect the back-up vehicle which, I was amazed and terrified to see, was a motor home the size of a fifty-seater coach. It had three double beds, a kitchen, toilet, shower and a storage room big as a garage. Noticing a bald front tyre, I hesitantly climbed up into the cab and turned on the ignition. Immediately a flashing red light lit up on the dashboard indicating that the fuel tank was empty. "Oh, you'll have enough to get to the garage" smiled Steve, the kind owner.

I parked overnight outside our house, filling the spaces usually left free for my neighbours on either side. In the morning, I collected the lads and we drove to Cornwall. The campervan drove sluggishly, even the slightest of inclines threatened to bring the brute to a halt. Somehow we managed to reach Lands End, we unloaded the bikes, took the compulsory photographs and while the lads set off for on their cycles, I drove ahead to a campground in St Agnes. I had only just got there when Martin, Kev and Jason arrived. With a hook-up we were able to microwave a lasagne and have toast for breakfast. As well as driver I was also the cook, so this was probably as good as it was going to get.

Never Say "If Only"

The lads were off by seven the next morning while I chugged along behind. On one particularly narrow section of road with traffic queuing up behind me, the van broke down. After much cussing, I eventually got the bus started and limped to meet the boys in Oakhampton where we rang Steve, who promised to call the AA rescue service and rendezvous in Wellington. However, while hurtling downhill on the A30 at the highest speed yet reached, there was an explosion; fragments of blown tyre showered the windscreen and the vehicle rocked from side to side. Luckily, as I fought to get the beast under control, a lay-by hove into view. "Right, change the wheel." I said to myself. "But where's the bloody spare?" I looked in the owner's manual but the wheel was not where it was supposed to be. Then I realised that the manual was for a lorry. The mobile home had been built onto a truck's chassis! When I finally found the wheel, and attempted to jack-up the monster, the jack collapsed nearly taking my arm off in the process. Repeatedly the jack failed, it just was not man enough for the task. There was an emergency telephone at the lay-by and I tried to call Highways SOS but the noise from the passing juggernauts made it impossible for me to hear anything. I just shouted out my problem and hopefully gave the owner's name and number before retreating to the cab and a book. Just over an hour later, Steve appeared with a colleague and a bigger jack. With the wheel changed and some money for fresh tyres, I drove off to meet the lads in Wellington. They were forlornly waiting at the entrance to the campsite where we had intended to stay but were not allowed in. Either the site owner had a phobia against cyclists or he was just having a bad day: I did not know. Much to his chagrin, I drove through the site and noticed plenty of spare pitches. We spent the night in an industrial park.

Allan Pendleton

Burnham-on-Sea was twenty-seven miles from Wellington and only two miles off our route, therefore, we went to Burnham Pool to meet our families and the local press. "God Allan, you look rough. Are you OK?" asked Maggie as I climbed down from the cab. "Yeah, I'm fine thanks." However, I felt that I had aged twenty years in the past few days.

I had been loaned a satellite navigation system and was getting on fine just following instructions as directed.

"At the roundabout take the first exit" the sat nav voice intoned as I entered Gloucester. I duly turned left at the roundabout and glimpsed, out of the corner of my eye, a sign reading something about *restricted access*. Sure enough I came to a bridge hardly wide enough for a mini car, and with traffic building up behind had to make a 3-point turn, well actually more like a 33-point turn as the road was only inches wider than the van. "Thanks for waiting" I smiled at the drivers who had been patiently queuing behind. "Wanker!" came the collective reply.

The guys had cycled 143 miles to Bromyard and arrived famished. With the smell of burgers and bacon drifting across the campground we decided to have a barbeque. It seemed to take an age for the coals to warm sufficiently, but when I opened the fridge I found a total of six sausages! We all looked accusingly at each other. "Who did the shopping?" Two Welsh families took pity upon us and donated the remains of their barbeque.

After the *grand depart* of our mini peloton, I drove into Bromyard to find a replacement for the bald tyre. No problem, except for leaving £85 poorer. At least now the van was running more smoothly. I think that the earlier lack of power was a result of the near empty tank when we collected the vehicle. Perhaps dirt had filtered into the carburettor.

It seemed a long, long day that day. 14 hours on the road and the section through Runcorn, Widnes and St. Helens was horrible; extremely busy with everyone in a hurry. Kevin received severe gravel rash after crashing into Jason who was forced to brake to avoid an impatient driver. Martin ended up on top of the pile. We went to a pub in a state of shock but after a good meal and a few beers we were laughing again.

In the Lake District I drove to Windermere, then to the top of Kirkstone Pass which at 485 metres was the highest road pass in England. I took my bike out of the boot and whizzed down to the Sun pub in Cross to wait for the team. I waited quite a while as they had got lost. We pedalled back up Kirkstone Pass. The team was trying to make up for lost time, so Martin and Jason were taking it in turns at the front, whilst Kev was tucked in behind. Meanwhile, I was struggling well off the pace at the back. Back at the van it was their turn to wait for me as I arrived puffing and panting. After a quick plate of cold baked beans on bread, it was off again down the mountain to Carlisle. I took the M6 to Gretna where our camp was in a bit of a rough area. We had to leave a deposit for the toilet keys and the grocery store staff were reluctant to let us have a plastic bag for our purchases. Nothing wrong with their fish and chips though!

After Dumfries the route crossed beautiful rolling countryside, part pasture, part moorland. We took a dinner break at Dalmellington where I phoned ahead to book a campground near Loch Lomond. However, the Scottish Open golf tournament was to start the following day and nearly all the campsites were fully booked. Eventually I found a site at Ardlui, which was way further than we had planned. "Hey this is Scotland we can camp wild!" But the gang was adamant and insisted on having a shower. Softies!

So, it was off to Ardlui. I crawled along with hordes of golfing fans, past Loch Lomond and the Open golf course. I pulled into the Loch Lomond Caravan Park. It was only after I had registered and parked up, that I realised that this was not the campground that I had booked. This place was Inverglas. I had to run out to the road to stop the lads before they proceeded to Ardlui.

I cooked pasta and bolognaise and sausages, Kev is a veggie and had tuna, fish aren't meat? I got a bit pissed off, while I'm getting stressed out just getting this bloody great pantechnicon from place to place, then faffing around trying to get them something to eat, they are just sitting around chatting to their families on their mobile phones. But I suppose that if I had travelled when my children were young I'd have done the same, if mobile phones had been invented!

The next day was typically Scottish being wet, cool and windy. But the boys were in high spirits and enjoying the scenery; what they could see of it through the mist and cloud. We met up for lunch, baked beans on bread, under the Commando Monument at Spean Bridge. There were white caps on Loch Ness. I drove through Inverness and the actual street in which I was born. I saw that the house where I lived as a child is now a car sales showroom. If it had been a garage when I was born I might now be a Jag, or even a Rolls Royce; but more probably a rusty Morris Eight or Ford Prefect.

We camped by the Cromarty Firth ready for the final haul to John o' Groats. This last day was cold. The team cycled into a northerly wind in steady rain as folks at home in Burnham-on-Sea were enjoying a heat wave. I gave a Norwegian hitch-hiker a lift to John o' Groats. I then prepared to ride back to meet the lads to be part of their triumphal arrival. Regrettably, by the time I had finished a second coffee with my new Scandinavian friend and donned my pedalling togs, the lads had arrived. After the obligatory photos, in the rain, we loaded up and taking turns at the wheel, we drove home. I insisted on driving the last leg thus completing my role as back-up man. Martin, Kev and Jason had cycled 1,050 miles in 7 days!

Martin, me, Kev and Jason

CHAPTER 39

Costa Rica & Panamá

"It is by riding a bicycle that you learn the contours of a country best, since you have to sweat up the hills and coast down them."
Ernest Hemingway

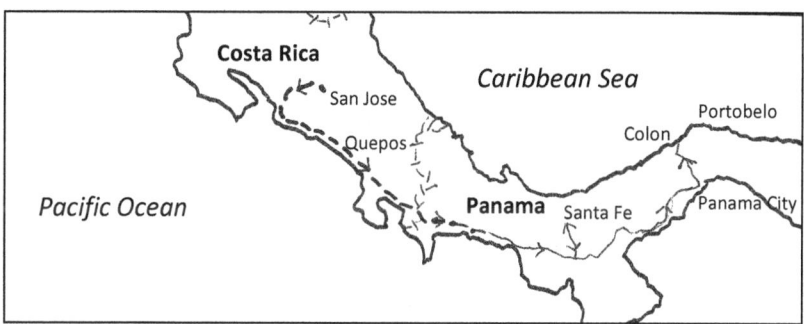

March, 2011. 440 miles

American immigration officials are not renowned for their speediness, consequently we only caught our connection to San José by the skin of our teeth. Our hold luggage, including our tandem, remained in Miami. The bike turned up early the next day and, eager to explore, we set off in the mid-day heat. Not acclimatised to the warm weather, we were soon struggling on a hilly terrain. Near the top of one, particularly steep, hill, Maggie came over dizzy and faint, almost falling off the bike. She lay by the side of the road for some time before feeling strong enough to resume pedalling. Was this an early warning of her forthcoming cardiac arrest? After fifty Kilometres we found a small, simple cabin and decided to call it a day.

We woke early the next day to a dawn chorus from tropical birds and animals, and were on the road by 5:30am. The road became dual-carriageway and sported a sign reading, *"No Ciclistas."* With the encouragement of an elderly local, we pressed on regardless and soon came to a toll booth. *"Biciclistas son prohibido"* said the attendant but with a shrug of his shoulders, he waved us through anyway, free of charge. After a while we branched off the toll road and came to a bridge crossing the *Rio Grande de Tarcoles*. This river is said to have one of the densest populations of crocodiles in the world, 25 crocs per square kilometre and 2,000 in all. They were there in abundance and can grow to seven metres in length. They wallowed in the mud and showed no redeeming features.

When we were in Costa Rica eleven years ago, we saw very little commercial development, but now expensive houses and high-rise hotels were popping up everywhere. American real estate development was seizing the countryside just as the American crocodiles had commandeered the river.

From Tarcoles we followed the Pacific coast, enjoying the surf but not kayaking this time. To the incessant buzzing and clicking of cicadas, we cycled beside the sea, then into pristine rain forest before emerging onto wetland. Scarlet macaws, large parrots with bright red bodies, blue and yellow wings, a long red tail and white faces screeched noisily past. Soaring overhead were frigate birds and vultures. Pelicans were skimming the waves, while egrets, pink spoonbills, storks and herons probed the mud of the salt flats. With such a multitude of feathered life to observe, it was difficult to keep my eyes on the road. Apart from the birds, the stretch before Parrita was a tad boring with miles of African oil palm plantations. The palm oil industry grew after the banana farms were stricken by severe banana blight in 1978.

A guided tour in the *Manuel Antonio Parque Nacional* revealed many of Costa Rica's treasures. If we had not hired a guide we would have failed to see: a toucan, humming birds, a two-toed sloth, iguanas, Jesus Christ lizards, agoutis, white-faced monkeys and many other creatures

We had a pleasant surprise when, just beyond Quepos, the road we remembered as being *ripio,* dirt and gravel, and marked as such on our map, had been resurfaced. To our left was the road to San Isidro de General, the town we had struggled to reach in 2000, and the mountain range that divides Costa Rica. This time we stayed by the coast and continued to a back-packers' *hostál* in the small town of Uvita. There we met Diana and Zilvinas, Lithuanians but residents of Chicago. They were four months into a three-year round-the-world bicycle tour. We rode down to the beach together and enjoyed their enthusiasm. The beach was a long expanse of sand with huge Pacific waves rolling in. Great for surfers but with evil rips for swimming. We sat shaded under a palm tree hoping that a coconut would not fall, listened to the sound of the surf, cicadas and howler monkeys, and watched a never-ending line of leaf-cutter ants carrying their colossal load, miles and miles, in ant terms, to their underground home.

In the morning we said goodbye to Diana and Zil who were working on their web-site, *www.vnextstop.com*. Being computer illiterate has its compensations, writing a log is demanding enough for me. After Palmar Norte we had to ride on the infamous Pan American Highway. Instead of the busy major highway we had expected we found ourselves on a narrow, pot-holed country road. There was the odd bus and truck, but not in the numbers we had feared. But it was hot, over thirty-five degrees Centigrade. At Chacarita the promised hotel did not materialise. A local *hombre* assured us that we would find *cabinas* two kilometres down a side road, a track full of holes like bomb craters. Alas, we could find no cabins. As we sat forlornly pondering our next move, a lady waved and beckoned us across the road. Lloreina offered us use of a room at the back of her house and made us very welcome with cold water, slices of banana, oranges and pineapple. Bingo!

At the border with Panama, the Costa Rican passport control opened at 6am, we got there at 5:30 but already a hundred-metre, five-deep queue had formed. Once the office opened everyone was processed quickly. It is quite easy to get out of a country but not so easy to get in. With our Costa Rican exit stamps we moved on to the Panama Immigration area, only to wait for four hours before we received a *"Bienvenido a Panamá."*

Our fourteen-speed Rohloff gears were not happy. They had been making a grating noise and leaking oil for some time. We thought that perhaps the intense heat was making the oil less viscous. Suddenly, with a resounding 'clunk' the Rohloff 14-speed hub jammed. We could still pedal but riding a loaded tandem without gears was not viable in the long term. Being such a complex piece of kit, repair in Central America was out of the question, so it looked as if we would need to find alternative modes of transport. We crunched along with the Rohloff complaining bitterly whilst it deposited an oily trail to a bus stop on the Pan American Highway. About two hours later, a bus bound for Santiago approached. At first, the driver refused our request to take the tandem but after I had split it in two, we managed to squeeze it into the hold with all the other bags and boxes. It was 130 kilometres to Santiago, through very hilly, rugged and inhospitable countryside with few signs of agriculture or habitation. We would have struggled on a single-speed bike.

In Santiago, we stowed the tandem in a cheap hotel then took an old United States recycled yellow school bus, known as a chicken bus, to the mountain retreat of Santa Fé. Our targeted *hostál* only had dormitory rooms left and we found ourselves billeting with three other English travellers. Claire and Mark from Bristol were riding motor bikes the full length of the American continent: from Prudhoe Bay in Alaska to Tierra del Fuego in Chile. Maurice, a teacher and no less adventurous, was on his way to teach in Japan, in spite of the earthquake and tsunami that had struck the country only four days earlier resulting in 16,000 deaths. We stayed up late drinking beer and swopping tales.

Before returning to Santiago, we took a hike into the surrounding hills and discovered a cock-fighting arena. It had a carpeted floor, padded walls and a raised spectator gallery. A beautiful fighting cock was shackled nearby. It was next to the road and not at all hidden. Is cock-fighting still legal in Panama? We returned to Santiago in another chicken bus. This one had been garishly painted and the silvery parts were polished to a mirrored finish. It was midday and schoolchildren were toing and froing. Like many emerging countries, Panama appeared to run a shift system for school attendance: consequently, the bus was packed.

The 250 km journey between Santiago and Panama City was a mixture of clunking along slowly and painfully on the tandem, hoisting it onto the roof of a chicken bus, into the hold of a bigger bus and, in Panama City, onto the back seat of a taxi with the rear wheel sticking out of an open boot.

The Marparaiso Hotel was happy for us to park it in the foyer while we gallivanted about taking in the sights of the City. We took an evening stroll through Avenida Balboa, along the edge of the bay with a skyline of modern high-rise buildings. Music reverberated while cyclists, joggers and skate-borders whizzed by. Not dissimilar to the Lakeside path in Chicago. The path continued to the old city known as *Casco Viejo*. The buccaneer, Henry Morgan, destroyed the original town in 1671 forcing the Spanish

Conquistadors to move to a rocky outcrop and surround it with a colossal wall. Many of the old colonial buildings were now in a state of ruin or supported with iron props. However, as a UNESCO heritage site much repair work was in progress and, no doubt, much of *Casco Viego* will be restored to its original Colonial splendour, cobbled streets, balconied buildings, plazas and churches. Returning to the hotel we called in at a fish market and tasted *ceviche*, a dish of raw seafood that included fish, squid and octopus and pickled in lime. It was delicious.

After a visit to the Panama Canal we took a short ferry ride to the forested island of Isla Taboga. Here we spent four days walking, getting lost, watching the wildlife and stumbling across points of interest such as the gravestones of British sailors who died of yellow fever early in the 19th- century. We then encountered three crosses of disputed origins: pirates or buccaneers were the most plausible. We also climbed to the high point of the island where the Americans had placed huge guns to defend the Panama Canal. Accompanying us for a couple of days was Pepa, a forty-year-old Belgium who had been travelling the world for twenty years. Pepa was a chef by trade and whenever his resources dwindled, he assured us that he could find a cooking job. Since he was fluent in six languages we thought that he might be a useful companion on our walks: we still got lost!

Leaving the tandem in the Marparaiso Hotel, we caught a bus to Portobelo, translated as Beautiful Port, which it most definitely was not. It was a scruffy small town on the Caribbean coast with water the same brown hue as that in the Severn Estuary at home. Portobelo is a UNESCO world heritage site and has ruins of the old Spanish fortifications which were to protect the conquistadors' spoils from pirates and privateers. At the height of the Spanish Conquest of South America, one third of the world's gold passed through Portobelo. The booty was brought from Peru and Chile to Panama, to be hauled across the Isthmus to Portobelo for shipping to Spain. Many British buccaneers, not least the infamous Captain Henry Morgan, sought a share of the loot and plundered Portobelo on numerous occasions. In the early 20th century the massive fortifications were further diminished as materials to build the Panama Canal were required. Many huge cannons remain and most of the foundations. A half-hearted attempt is being made to restore the fortifications but, when all said and done, Portobelo is a garbage dump, albeit, a historical garbage dump.

The majority of the inhabitants were of African descent and the culture was very different to Panama City on the Pacific Coast. This weekend there was a big festival taking place, *El Dia del Diablo y Congo*. The only half-decent place we could get was a dormitory room at Captain Jack's, with just two bathrooms for twenty plus people. The hostel was full of many nationalities arranging boat passages to and from the San Blas Islands and Colombia. We drank and talked until late. We were woken by the blare of Afro-Caribbean music, *El Día del Diablo y Congo* had begun. A carnival atmosphere had enveloped the town. People were dancing and drinking, revellers were blowing whistles and wearing rags with blacked-up devils and zombies lurking ominously among the crowds, while reggae resonated from banks of loud speakers. The town was packed. Much cleavage was on show with many fat women in tight, clingy clothes. Dozens of armed police patrolled the crowds intimidatingly. Maggie and I, being two of the few Europeans, were targeted, but mainly for photos and all in good fun. It was a memorial of the days of slavery, but everyone was in a carnival mood.

Local revellers with Maggie

Even more guests had been squeezed into Captain Jack's when the water ran out. With no showers, we had to make do with a wet-wipe. The toilets were full to overflowing. We prayed that it would rain overnight but didn't, so we checked out feeling a tad unclean. The town mirrored our feelings. The streets and pavements were strewn with paper, tins, bottles, plastic, discarded garments and disgorged food. Vultures flapped around happily and the town's mongrels fought over the feast.

We took a gaudily painted chicken bus along the coast. At La Guayra, we embarked upon a 400-metre boat ride out to Isla Grande for a few days of blissful luxury. We were ensconced in a beach-side cabin enjoying showers and running water. Then it was back to Panama City where we collected the bike and swopped a yellow US school bus for an air-conditioned coach with comfortable seats. The journey of eighteen hours on the *Ticabus* took us into Costa Rica. We passed through dense cloud forests with enormous trees and ferns, over *Cerro Muerte* at 11,000 feet, to arrive at San José, for our flight home.

Back home, I took the tandem back to St John's Street Cycles in Bridgwater to whinge about the broken gears. A few days later, free of charge, I received a brand new Rohloff cassette direct from Germany.

We received an e-mail from Diana and Zilvinas, the Lithuanians who were pedalling round the world. Well, their adventure came to an early but happy, end. Diana was pregnant.

CHAPTER 40

Musgrave Hospital, Taunton

"Sometimes people are beautiful.
Not in looks.
Not in what they say.
Just in what they are."
Markus Zusak. "'I am the Messenger"

Saturday 30 April, 2011

Maggie had spent the night packed in ice. In the morning, the doctors started to warm her and reduce the sedation. After a while, Maggie's eyes opened, they were blank and unfocused. The ITU Consultant, Helena Lindsay, lifted her hand and said, "Squeeze my hand Maggie, squeeze my hand!" No response. However, as Maggie drifted in and out of consciousness, she became a little more alert each time but also very agitated. She continually tried to sit up before slumping back onto the pillows. Repeatedly, she struggled to raise herself. She was in danger of pulling out some of the leads and tubes and had to be gently sedated again. Much later, during one of her more conscious spells, she looked at me and whispered, "Al." She had recognised me! That short word filled me with emotion and I cried again, but this time with hope and not despair. After a very long day we were offered a room in a hospital bungalow reserved for the families of seriously ill patients. During the night, our daughters, Jo and Julie and I decided to take turns sitting by Maggie's bedside. Jo took the first shift while Julie and I attempted to get a little sleep.

Sunday 1 May

Towards the end of Julie's watch, she called us to let us know that her mum was being moved out of ICU into the neighbouring High Dependency Unit (HDU). This was a good sign! Maggie's condition began to improve at a remarkable rate. She became progressively more lucid. She was very tired and drowsy but restless. It was a battle to keep her connected to the tubes and monitors. There were several wet beds before Julie thought to tape the catheter to the inside of Maggie's thigh.

On one occasion when told that her heart had stopped she replied, "Mm, that sounds serious." To the never ending "Is this a dream?" question, when told that it was real, she sighed "Oh, that's a shame!" On discovering that she had been packed in ice all night, she asked "Does that mean I'm going to live forever?"

Maggie's short-term memory was non-existent! "Where am I? What's happening? Is this real? Is it a dream?" She asked these questions continuously, the answers immediately forgotten. However, this memory loss wasn't important, we were getting our lovely wife and mother back! Perhaps she wouldn't be quite the same wife and mother, but we were not going to lose her; and that's what mattered! Now the tears were replaced by smiles.

And laughs, for Maggie developed a great knack in underplaying things. Throughout Maggie seemed unaware of the seriousness of the situation, and after a couple of hours in HDU she announced "I think I'll go home after I've had a little rest." And to me "You look tired, why don't you get in bed beside me and lie down?"

I had a glance at the consultant's report, which stated "Should the patient survive she is likely to suffer severe organ and/or brain damage". My lover was weak, her voice subdued, she had a bad cough and developed pneumonia. But, most importantly, she **was** recovering from the cardiac arrest.

Monday 2 May

Maggie had a restless night, tossing and turning and getting entangled in the tubes, wires and sensors. I was so grateful for Julie, a trained nurse, who was able to continually untangle her. Consultant Lindsay gave us a summary of Maggie's progress. She was clearly pleased and somewhat surprised by the speed and extent of Maggie's recovery. Ms Lindsay questioned Maggie about past events and received mainly correct replies. "It would appear that short term memory loss may be the extent of the damage. Her physical fitness and well-being had obviously aided her recovery." It was time for another move; this time to Fielding Ward, adjacent to the Cardiac Unit. Here Maggie was free of wires, tubes, probes, sensors and a bank of monitoring screens. This was a release in itself. Few people would be as happy as we were to be in a normal hospital ward, we were elated! Maggie told us that we should not have bothered her sister Ann and interrupted her charity walk in Shropshire, "If anything bad had happened she could have come to the funeral!" Maggie's only complaint was that it hurt her to laugh. Obviously, the paramedic administering chest compressions had done a good job! Today was our granddaughter Abi's eighth birthday. "This is my worst birthday ever." Abi reluctantly complained, with everyone preoccupied and Abi herself terribly worried about her nan. "It could have been worse Abi, much worse!"

Tuesday 3 May

In the morning, I returned to the Fielding Ward to find Maggie's bed empty! My heart plummeted. Had she suffered a relapse? Oh no! The ward sister sensing my anxiety asked, "Can I help you?"

"I'm looking for my wife, Margaret Pendleton. What's happened? Where is she?" "Oh dear." the Sister replied in a rather embarrassed way, "Well you see, umm, Mrs Pendleton has umm, well Mrs Pendleton has, how can I put this? Well I'm afraid that Mrs Pendleton has gone missing!" Gone missing! I almost laughed with relief when, at the ward entrance, a porter appeared leading Maggie by the arm. Apparently, Maggie had gone out into the corridor to make a call on her mobile phone, taken a wrong turn and then got lost. Not knowing which ward she had come from, hospital staff had to scan her wrist band to find out where her bed was located. Also, she was carrying a transmitter in a sporran-like bag, which was connected by electrodes and relayed her heart rhythms to the cardiac unit. On leaving her ward, she had wandered out of range causing panic! But, no worries, our seriously ill patient had not flat-lined, only gone for a walk!

Dr McKenzie, the cardiologist who initially treated Maggie initially, informed us that she would need to have an implantable cardio defibrillator fitted. This device would be placed in her chest and have wires leading from it through a vein into heart chambers. It would monitor the heart's natural rhythms, detect any abnormality, for example arrhythmia, and automatically shock the heart back to normal. Furthermore, a transmitter placed near her bed would monitor her and send signals by satellite that would show her heart's patterns over the previous twenty-four hours. So any unnatural behaviour would be instantly detected. In the afternoon, Ann and Julie joined me by Maggie's bedside. Maggie greeted them with, "Hello you two, have you had a nice weekend?"

Wednesday 4 May

Maggie had a shower, or rather a sponge down, aided by small Irish occupational therapy girl. She was obviously feeling much better and getting stronger by the day, although her chest was still very sore, especially when she laughed. In fact there was a lot of laughing going on round the Pendleton bed, not, perhaps, what one would expect in a cardiac ward. But we all felt so relieved and happy that our lovely wife, mum, nan and friend was still with us. It was impossible not to be happy. The staff did not seem to mind, and the ward sister allowed me in outside official visiting times.

Thursday 5 May

An interesting scan this morning showed images of Maggie's heart. While waiting for the scan she met our friend Andy Blanche, he of John's St Cycles and epic Andean cycle trips. Andy had been having respiratory problems when mountain biking and angina had been diagnosed. He is to have an operation tomorrow, same day as Maggie is having her ICD, an implantable cardio defibrillator, installed. So I had two patients to visit, and shared grapes with Andy's partner, Fiona.

Friday 6 May May

Maggie had an ICD fitted and asked the surgeon for a 'nip and tuck' while he was at it. In the afternoon I wheeled her down to radiology for an x-ray. Later, at about 5 p.m., a young lady doctor, who looked about fifteen, asked Maggie what she would like. "To go home, please" came the reply. "Sorry, but we love you too much to let you go" replied the doctor with a smile, "But if you insist, well OK, but take it easy."

Maggie dressed, packed her stuff into plastic bags scrounged from a nurse, said 'goodbye' and we walked out to our van. Amazing! Just one week after her heart and breathing had stopped for God knows how long, resuscitation, a life-support machine, a ventilator and packed in ice, she walks out of hospital and goes home!!!

At home the whole family were waiting. What joy! Joanne burst into tears, what a week! A few days later it was my birthday – it was my *best* birthday ever. If it had not been for the royal wedding and having responsible people around at the time, well, who knows what might have happened? Ninety-five per cent of people who suffer from sudden cardiac arrest die before they reach hospital. Most of those who survive suffer severe brain and organ damage. Apart from a slightly impaired heart Maggie had recovered completely! All that I can say is "God save the Queen!" and thank our National Health Service. Our Doctors *can* perform miracles.

CHAPTER 41

India

Goa & Karnataka.

"If you reject the food, ignore the customs, fear the religion and avoid the people, you might better stay at home."
James A Michener

Feb, 2012. 365 miles

"What am I able to do?" Maggie asked her consultant, Mr McKenzie at one of her consultations. "Just carry on as normal" came the reply. "But Maggie was not a normal sixty-six-year-old," I responded, "So her normal isn't normal, if you know what I mean?" The consultant shrugged and repeated, "Just carry on as normal." So, we did and barely a month after her cardiac arrest we were back hiking the South West Coast Path. I had prepared myself for a life of spoon-feeding, dribble dabbing and bottom wiping; but instead we could carry on as before, as normal. But what about cycle touring? Maggie's implantable cardio defibrillator and her daily drugs prevented her heart from beating much faster than 130 beats per minute. Even a slow jog made her breathless. Obviously high mountains were out of the question. We set off for India but would remain clear of the Himalayas.

In spite of being assured that the metal-detector in Mumbai Airport was safe for pacemakers and pregnant women, implantable cardio defibrillators were not mentioned, we did not dare risk it. We insisted that Maggie was hand-frisked instead. Mumbai International Airport was a very modern airport. The toilets were clean and well up to the highest Western standards. However, they still had toilet wallahs on duty. On each of my frequent runs to the loo, the attendant welcomed me and held open a cubicle door. When I had finished, he directed me to the hand-washing bowl, turned on the tap, operated the soap dispenser and handed me a wad of paper towels before wishing me a good day. He made me feel important and quite proud of having a poo.

Allan Pendleton

From Dabolim Airport at Goa, we cycled south alongside the Arabian Sea, taking minor roads away from the trucks and buses. We frequently rode on the hard-packed sand of the beaches. This trip was to be more of a holiday than an adventure. We took no tent and cooking stove. We stayed mainly in beach-side bamboo huts and usually ate at stalls. The food was tasty, quite spicy and often fishy; my favourite was seafood sizzler served on a hot skillet. All meals were washed down with a bottle or two of Kingfisher beer. In Karnataka we spent a few days in a hippy yoga farm, where it felt as if we had been transported back to the sixties. We slept in a shack with a plastic roof and were woken early each morning by black-faced monkeys clambering around on the roof wearing hobnail boots.

Occasionally we had to ride on the main NH17. This was the main south to north trunk road and was exceedingly busy. Drivers sped along on either side of the road, overtaking, undertaking – "Blow your horn and may your Gods go with you." Surprisingly, life expectancy in India had risen from thirty-two to sixty-two in the last five decades: but not for the two dead bodies we saw sprawled on a rubbish heap in Karwar.

We returned on much the same route but continued north to Old Goa. From 1510 until the early 19th-century, Old Goa was the principal city of the Portuguese Empire. The city had been decimated several times by disease: cholera, malaria, typhoid, syphilis and with more than a little assistance from the Catholic Inquisition. In the late 16th-century, Goa had over a quarter of a million inhabitants and built vast religious buildings. But disease prevailed and many of the old buildings were destroyed.

It was a short but scary, ride to Panaji. We spent a day wandering around the city and taking in the sights. Slums and new concrete buildings converged and the traffic, as expected, was insane. It was difficult and dangerous to walk around because the pavements were used as parking places for motorbikes. Walking in the dark added an extra challenge; not only did the dark disguise potholes, open drains, dogs and bodies, but some of the cars, many of the motorbikes and *all* the bicycles did not have lights.

It was time to head back to the Airport. After escaping from Panaji we followed the coast road along Miramar Beach, past municipal gardens, a public swimming pool and several new resorts, many being constructed with workers clambering on flimsy bamboo scaffolding. The road was wide and smooth, with no cows, obviously designed to make the area tourist friendly. There were plenty of signs pointing to the Dona Paula Ferry. But at Dona Paula there was no ferry, so we decided to cycle the thirty miles around.

At Dabolim Airport we enjoyed our final Indian experience, queues and bureaucracy. When we finally cleared all the officialdom and passed through the check-in, we looked back to see our boxed tandem alone and ignored. To our relief it caught a later flight.

CHAPTER 42

France

Loire & Brittany

"It does not do to dwell on dreams and forget to live."
J K Rowling. Harry Potter and the Sorcerer's Stone

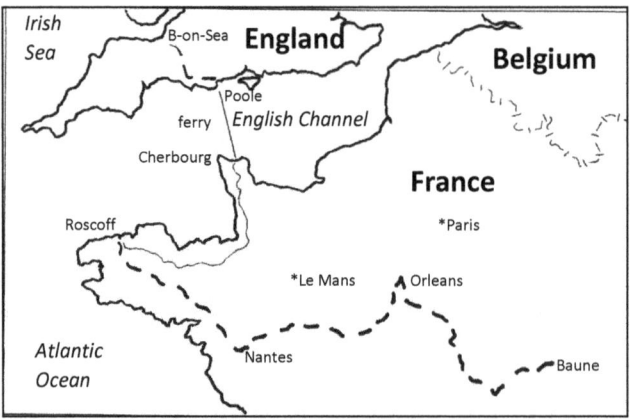

Sept, 2012. 890 miles

Although we had never taken life for granted and realised how privileged we were, Maggie's cardiac arrest really brought home to us how precious life was and how there might not always be a tomorrow. Thus, we celebrated Maggie's narrow escape with a family trip to Disneyworld in Florida.

Later in the year, after a brief skirmish in the Scottish Highlands, we went to France. Richard, our son-in-law, drove us to South Mimms Service Station on the M4 where we boarded the European Bike Express, a luxury coach pulling a large trailer which carried the customers' bicycles. It carried cyclists bound for various parts of Western Europe. Our destination was mid-east France, quite near the Swiss border, at a place called Baune. We arrived at

2:30am. We had to unload in a dark, poorly lit car park in a small industrial site. Eight other cyclists disembarked with us and with great haste, as if this were a timed transition of an Olympic event, they loaded their bikes and, with barely a farewell, pedalled off into the darkness, presumably to pre-booked accommodation. Meanwhile, we straightened our tandem handlebars, strapped on the panniers and wondered: now what?

As the bus had stopped at various service stations in England to pick up passengers, we assumed that the drop-off points would be similar. Somewhere where we could sit inside and drink coffee until daybreak. But no, there was no sign of life, everywhere was closed and shuttered. Even the solitary street light struggled to emit enough illumination to create a dull shadow. Since it was warm and starry, we decided to hit the road.

We pedalled blindly until we came to a junction signposted to Dijon. Not wanting to go to Dijon we turned the other way. We were amazed and felt a tad vulnerable, by the amount of traffic there was at that ridiculous hour on a Sunday morning. We had difficulty in finding a road that led in our general direction but eventually found a beautiful paved track running alongside the Canal du Dheune. I say beautiful, but as we couldn't see it clearly I could only pass judgement on its feel; and it felt beautifully smooth.

As dawn approached, our views were veiled by a thick mist swirling off the canal. It gave the ride a creepy feeling, enhanced by the sound of hidden beasts crashing through the roadside undergrowth and the stroking of our faces by damp spiders' webs. It was not until about 7am that the sun made its red appearance and began to warm our damp and chilled bodies. We found an open *boulangerie*, where we bought buns with currants and *pan de chocolat,* then Maggie's sense of smell led us to a bar serving coffee. This gave us a fuel boost for the final few miles to *Camping du Lac.* As its name suggested, the campground was situated beside a lake with a sandy beach; ideal for swimming and being lazy. We had cycled eighty-five kilometres and had arrived at the lake at 11am, where we would enjoy a lazy day!

The following day, after mending a puncture, we set off at roughly the time we had arrived the previous day. We rode to the medieval spa town of Bourbon-Lancy on the River Loire which we hoped to follow all the way to Nantes. Our next stop was Nevers with narrow, winding streets andhouses dating back to the 14th-century. It once was a Roman city under Julius Ceasar.

We were short of supplies, so set off hungrily the few miles to Cuffy. Ideal for coffee we thought, but, alas, there was no coffee in Cuffy! We continued beside the Loire, mainly cycle paths and easy to follow. Or so we thought, maybe we were too busy watching the herons but we found ourselves circling round a large nuclear power plant with a tall fence topped with razor-wire. Dramatic signs depicting guns, dogs and death to intruders were posted at regular intervals. Then a police car roared up from behind and abruptly stopped in front of us. A young, handsome policeman stepped out of the car; I let Maggie do the talking. We were directed back the way we had come but Maggie was all in a tizzy. "He had such twinkly eyes, oh and an accent that sent my legs all trembly." Judging from her power output, or lack of, Maggie had trembly legs for the rest of the day.

The River Loire levee was linked to minor roads and trails. We passed fields of maize and pastures of grazing cream-coloured cows. Each meadow had a huge bull lying lazily to one side keeping a watchful eye on his harem. There were a few fields of sunflowers, but well past their best. After fifty kilometres, we reached Orleans and had a fruitless search for a campground that was clearly marked on our map. We were told with a Gallic shrug by a beret-wearing local, *"Ferme,"* closed. Never mind, another campground was marked just a few kilometres further on. This turned out to be little more than a concrete parking area for mobile homes, in other words, a dump station. We decided to have a quick look round Orleans before pressing on in the evening. Orleans was another of Julius Ceasar's conquests. In 1429, during the Hundred Years' War, Joan of Arc lifted a siege here against the English. There was a fine statue of the city's heroine near the huge cathedral of Saint Croix. It was a very pleasant city with plenty of cycle paths, bars, restaurants and lingerie shops. We found a municipal campground in the nearby small town of Olivet, where we were able to purchase some wine and a toilet roll, an item seldom found in French campground toilets. Back to the Loire, we pedalled through the narrow-cobbled streets of Beangency, complete with a chateau, a castle, and a church and steeple.

A sunny day saw us stuck in a traffic jam of people and cars attending the Sunday market. Stalls stood all along the river bank making it impossible to ride the bike path. We took to the adjacent road in the shadow of tall cliffs. Burrowed into the limestone were *caves d'vin*, caves used to store barrels of wine, but open for tasting and purchase. The vertical chalk cliffs continued to guard the south bank of the Loire. After a while, as well as the wine cellars, actual houses were built into the rock. Some just used the cliffs as a back wall, but many, often multi-storied, were actually buried into the rock face with only the front wall, windows and doors showing.

Angers was a pretty city; we spent considerable time strolling round the old centre looking in vain for fuel for our stove, although the massive chateau that dominated the town did have the biggest medieval tapestry in the world. We ended up at a Super-U filling station where a kind lady donated a euro's worth of unleaded petrol into our fuel bottle. Another tandem couple joined us later that day from South Africa. We shared tandem tales at our campground and discovered that Rhona and John were lay-preachers, missionaries no less. That evening we enjoyed a meal together and an interesting discussion, but I failed to convert them.

At Mauves, as we said goodbye to the Springboks and the Loire and headed for the Nantes-Brest Canal, it started to rain and hardly let up all day. Consequently, we seldom saw a soul on the canal path. But, we did see kingfishers, herons, a coypu, otters and red squirrels, obviously not adverse to a spot of rain. The rain had left the gravel and sand path very wet and soft, gripping the tyres and making the cycling rather strenuous. There were lots of locks close together and we found ourselves on a canal path but pedalling *uphill*. Then we came to a restricted area where EDF had fenced in a man-made lake used for hydro-electricity. We had to climb a long, steep hill to bypass it, but at the top of the hill there was a campground.

That evening, as we snuggled into our sleeping bags, Maggie remarked, "Isn't it quiet and peaceful here." All we could hear was the minute squeaks from bats as they sought their supper, or would it be breakfast? No traffic noise, no televisions, no radios, no chatter and for once, not even a church bell: it was so relaxing and tranquil. Then, in the distance, a dog began to bark. Moments later, another dog howled a reply, to be quickly followed by shouts from its master. Then we heard the pitter-patter of rain drops on the tent. This shortly became a thunderous beating as a rain storm developed, blowing in great waves with the roar of an express train. Our tent flapped like a cornered chicken and tried equally hard to take off. I frequently had to check our guy ropes, each time getting soaked in the process. Luckily, we were in a well-protected hollow surrounded by tall trees. In the morning the field was covered with debris. Camping remnants, leaves, twigs and even large branches littered the ground, we were very lucky one did not land on us. Most of the other campers had taken refuge in their vehicles, but a large marquee that had stood in the corner of the campground was now nowhere to be seen, swept away by the gale.

After breakfast in the washroom, we set off up the gradual climb of an old railway line. The going was tough because, as well as the glue-like surface, there were lake-size puddles and fallen branches. Plus, the wind and rain blew relentlessly in our faces all day. We were both soaked and there was no way we would camp that night. We found a B&B, still in torrential rain, where our hostess let us park the tandem in her garage and hang up our wet gear. When we had dried out, she loaned Maggie a dry coat and took us in her car to a *creperie*. We had a good meal and tasted the local *cidre,* not dissimilar to our own scrumpy. We walked back and let ourselves in, no key just an unlocked door.

It had been an unpleasant day weather-wise, but a couple of really nice experiences kept us sane, and made us remember what it is we love about cycle touring. As we looked for the route out of Rostrenen, we asked for directions from a lady who was sheltering on the balcony of her house. She told us in French and, thinking that we had understood her, we set off. Five minutes or so later the same lady came up behind us in her car, turned us round and bade us to follow her car until we were on the correct route.

Earlier, in Carhaix, a cheerful young man made a remark about our wet and soggy bread that was strapped to the panniers.

"Would you like a plastic bag for the bread?" he asked, before walking away. He promptly returned with a plastic bag, *plus* a fresh loaf of bread.

"Wet bread not so good." he laughed.

In Rostrenen, a pair of British tourists told us that the Brittany Ferries crews were on strike and that no boats were sailing from Roscoff. We continued to Roscoff anyway, hoping that the dispute would be quickly resolved. It wasn't, and at the port no one had any idea how long the strike would last. We heard that a bus was being provided to take pedestrians and cyclists with reservations to Cherbourg for an alternative ferry to Poole. We had no reservations, but Maggie persuaded the boss to find space for us on the coach. Not only did we get a free 400 km ride to Cherbourg, we also wangled a free night in a hotel; I think they had forgotten that we were ticketless. After a luxurious hot bath and dry fluffy towels, we enjoyed a hotel meal and met a fellow cyclist who had attended college with Maggie in Dudley, 1965-68. What a coincidence!

Due to rough weather, the ferry was late but we still arrived in Poole with enough time to get a few miles under our belt before dark. As Plymouth had been our intended destination, we had no maps or any idea of a route for home. In an Asda supermarket we looked at a road atlas and tried to commit to memory the roads we would need. Initially, we took a paved bike path alongside the A350 towards Dorchester but it did not last long. We were forced to join the traffic on a very busy road. It was rush hour and everyone was in a frantic hurry to get home. Vehicles hurtled along in both directions and most cars shot by missing us by millimetres. Bumper to bumper, they sped as if on a race track. The trucks were particularly scary and to make matters worse, ahead of us the sun was low in the sky making visibility difficult. For the first time on this trip, I was wishing for clouds. Luckily the wind was in our favour and we were able to maintain a good, adrenalin induced, speed. After about twenty miles of terror we reached Puddletown on the River Piddle. The pub had no vacancies but we noticed a group of lads playing football on a recreation ground with acres of grass which was ideal for a little tent, and public toilets. A small grocery shop was still open and had hot pasties, so we spent the last night in Puddletown and enjoyed a beautiful sunset, red sky with mackerel clouds, as if to say "Welcome home."

CHAPTER 43

Thailand

"Don't cry because it's over, smile because it happened."
Dr Seuss

Jan-Feb, 2013. 455 miles

Perhaps it wasn't such a good idea to return to Thailand. Our previous trips had been great, but you never have the same sense of excitement and adventure that you get when seeing and experiencing things for the first time. Our plan had been to island-hop along the Andaman Sea but long-tailed boats, little more than canoes with a long propeller shaft, are not ideal vessels for transporting a tandem bicycle. Plus Maggie got bitten by mosquitoes and developed a dengue-type fever.

Having said that, we still had an interesting trip. On our way to Krabi from Phuket we passed by massive karst stacks, with sheer white limestone walls to which trees somehow manage to cling, and topped with wild jungle, straight from Conan Doyle's 'Lost World'. From Krabi we took a tandem-free trip by long-tailed boat to Raleigh Island, where the towering cliffs are popular for rock climbing. Our boatman promised to return for us at six pm. At dusk a convoy of boats appeared offering trips back to the mainland. But we remained loyal and waited for our man to come. He didn't, and, by the time we had realised that he wasn't coming, we found ourselves alone and abandoned on the island. Resigning ourselves to having to spend a long cold night, and trying not to panic, we spotted a boat just offshore. Waving and shouting we attracted their attention and the vessel, a small fishing skiff with a crew of three, pulled onto the beach. They took us on board and for a fee of 600 bahts (just over £10) agreed to transport us back to Krabi, but with a detour in their pick up truck to their fishing village. Here we guess that they got permission from their wives to have a night out 'on the town' with our unexpected windfall!

Never Say "If Only"

We did a fair bit of cycling at the beginning of the trip, also a little kayaking and some great snorkelling, a spot of beach-bumming and enjoyed many *Chang* beers. However, after two weeks Maggie started complaining about headaches, muscle aches and feeling sick. She had no appetite and shivered in spite of the ninety degree temperature. She spent a couple of days in bed before feeling strong enough to continue. Consequently, we returned to Phuket, mainly by boat, only pedalling between the ports, and flew home.

CHAPTER 44

Cuba

"Never go on trips with anyone you do not love."
Ernest Hemingway

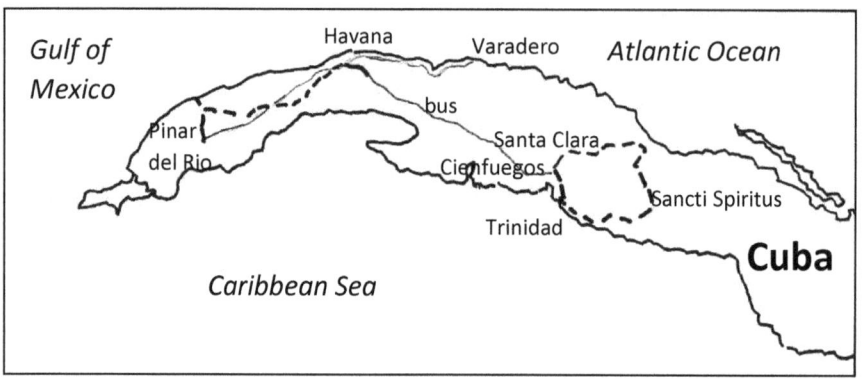

Feb-March, 2014. 550 miles.

We spent an hour queuing to clear immigration, then another hour waiting for our bike to turn up at Havana Airport. We soon realised that patience might be a valuable asset in Cuba. A fairly short taxi ride took us to a *hostál* in central Havana. The building, like its neighbours, dated back to colonial times and like so many of us oldies, was showing its age. There was more queuing at the bank. We learned that once one had secured a place in the line, one could leave and return to the same position later. Now that is what I call civilised. In the bank we changed our pounds for CUC$, convertible pesos, the currency that foreigners used. Cuban citizens were paid in Cuban pesos, which were used for staples and non-luxury items.

Either side of the harbour entrance, we saw the 17th-century forts that the Spaniards had built to protect their Aztec and Mayan booty from English and French privateers. Havana served as a convenient harbour between Mexico and Spain. In Old Havana, *Havana Vieja,* many buildings were in a state of decay, but imposing nonetheless. Havana has scores of museums. One, *el Museo de Navación,* had a model of the largest sailing ship of its era; we, the English, sunk it at the Battle of Trafalgar. That museum, as in all the other museums we visited, was guided and guarded by large women in very short, tight skirts and stockings.

Big waves crashed over the sea wall as we rode along the Malecòn and out of Havana. We took to the *autopista* (motorway) and were soon flagged down by a policeman on a motorbike. He tried to fine us twenty CUC$ for cycling on the *autopista,* but as we wrangled over the fine an old guy pedalled by. Stymied, the cop rode off empty-handed. We soon saw other bicycles on the motorway, plus horses and carts, even an ox pulling a wagon.

We stayed in *casas particulares,* private houses that provide accommodation, basically bed and breakfasts. We found the *casas* a really good way to get a feel of the Cuban way of life. Few of our hosts had a very good command of English so our basic Spanish was useful. The food, without exception, was excellent but often the helpings were far too generous, and we were aware that the Cuban people didn't enjoy that standard of food. Another advantage for us was that there seemed to be a network between the hosts, each would ring ahead and reserve a place for us at our next destination. We pedalled west through small towns and rolling countryside, passing, and being passed, by ponies and traps. Horsemen were common, as were oxen carts. Together, with the veteran cars that spluttered by, we could have been in the 1950s.

In San Diego de los Baños, we were unable to find accommodation. As we stood on a corner wondering what to do next, a man in lycra on a racing bike pedalled up. Enrique was a bicycle tour guide and he offered to try to find us a place to stay. He took us to his house to chat with his wife while he went room searching. He returned – mission accomplished! He escorted us to a nearby property where the residents were busily rearranging their possessions to make space for us. We moved into a room while the previous occupants were going to sleep on the couch. Two Californians, Charles and Morgan, both in their early forties, were also squeezed into the house and later the four of us went to watch Cuban cigars being handmade and of course, sample a few beers. We enjoyed the Cuban *Bucanero* beer but were quickly acquiring a taste for the traditional Cuban highball *mojito,* a cocktail that consisted of rum, sugar, lime, soda water and mint.

The next day we headed for Viñales, through rolling countryside and tobacco plantations, with solitary tower-like limestone stacks known as *mogotes* standing guard in front of a low mountain range. Enrique had arranged for us to stay at his parents, Sonia and Papito.

After a few days exploring the coast, caves and countryside of the Viñales Valley, we caught a *Viazul* bus to Cienfuegos, where we had booked a waterfront *casa particular.* From Ciefuegos we rode along a road with sugar cane and occasional tall chimney stacks marking the sugar factories, to Santa Clara. Santa Clara was liberated by Ché Guevara in 1959, leading to the downfall of the Batista regime. Consequently, Ché is revered more here than elsewhere in Cuba. The mausoleum and museum boasts a very fine sculpture on top of a wall covered with bas relief summarising the Revolution. Suitably impressed and in awe of El Ché and his achievements and aspirations, we left the Plaza de Revolutión and went to find our *casa.*

Vilo and Gilda met us at the door and helped push the tandem through their house to a safe place at the back. Like all the other *casas* we were warmly welcomed and made to feel at home. The rooms were always clean and the food delicious, albeit always one of three choices; chicken, pork or seafood, which was usually lobster. It reminded us of the basic home cooking we had enjoyed as children. The *Parque Vidal* was packed with people in their Sunday best with youngsters strutting their stuff in tight-fitting kit. Outside the column-fronted Palacio Provincial, a band was playing with people dancing in the street. Traffic was banned on two sides of the square and children were given rides around the park in carts pulled by goats. Outside a bar we found a vacant table in the shade of a large tree and as twilight approached, thousands of squawking birds flew in to roost. We soon discovered why our table had been vacant.

Leaving Santa Clara, we passed a life-size bronze statue of Chê holding a child. Many facets of Chê's life were intricately carved on to the monument. Diminutive figures represented his time in the jungle, climbing mountains and even his early experience on a motorbike journey in Latin America. On the buckle of his belt were the faces of the thirty-eight men killed with

Guevara in Bolivia. Further along the road was the memorial, *Tren Blindado,* commemorating the derailing of an armoured train sent by dictator Batista carrying arms, provisions and 373 soldiers in an attempt to defeat Fidel Castro's revolutionaries... However, Guevara and eighteen guerrillas derailed the train using a borrowed bulldozer, captured the weapons and ammunition then forced the soldiers to surrender.

In the central square in Remedios, we had a beer at *El Louvre* which was the oldest permanently open bar in Cuba, dating from the 1800s. Then we wandered across *Parque Martí* to a church to see a unique statue of a pregnant Virgin Mary. Schoolchildren used the public square for lessons in gymnastics and team games and a baseball match was in full flow. Later, in a corner of the Park, some adults had set up sound system with an electric cable trailing through a church window. They had set out some platforms and had a step aerobics class in session. This was typical of the resourceful Cubans.

After a hot, rolling ride through sugar cane and tobacco plantations, we got lost in the labyrinth of narrow, cobbled one-way streets in Sancti Spiritus. We popped into an art gallery to ask for directions from a good-looking young man who spoke excellent English. He tols us that he was an English teacher but he earned more from showing tourists round that small gallery than from teaching in socialist Cuba. It was another hot day as we left Sancti Spiritus. The countryside became more arid, with fields strewn with rocks and good for nothing but grazing. There were more horses on the road than cars. After a long climb, we enjoyed sugar-cane juice from canes being pulped in an old-fashioned mangle. Later, we were almost decapitated by a workman who was unaware of our presence while enthusiastically cutting grass with a two-handed scythe.

Trinidad was another town of narrow, cobbled streets and colonial buildings. Despite being a UNESCO Heritage Site, many buildings were in a state of decay. However, the high ceilings, pillars and classic antique furniture gave the interiors a touch of class and opulence that the exteriors used to have. Some of the larger buildings were under repair and much was being done to restore the city's image. One such building was the *Teatro Brunet,* 180 years-old and devoid of ceilings, roofs and most walls. There was not much more than a large front wall with many stacks and arches. It was no longer a theatre but now *La Casa de Cervezas de Ruinas del Brunet,* a beer emporium. The

Allan Pendleton

Historical Museum did not have a great deal on show except for the building itself. It was built between 1827 and 1830 as a private mansion This opulence was gained from the cruel, slave labour on the sugar plantations!

The Museum *de la Lucha Contra Banditos* (the Fight Against Bandits), on the other hand, presented a different point of view. These bandits were, in fact, the land owners, the educated middle class, the Cubans who didn't want Castro. But Castro won, and the winners write the history. Thus the *Banditos* are depicted as cruel, greedy, torturing assassins.

The *Casa Templo de Santaría* explained the religion that slaves introduced by linking their own beliefs and gods with the Roman Catholic Saints that they were forced to accept. Santaria was still practised by some of African origin. Finally, the *Museo de Arquitectura* gave examples of the design and building of colonial structures but what impressed me the most, was an early flush toilet, courtesy of Mr Thomas Crapper from Yorkshire, England.

Wanting a break from the stresses of intellectual enlightenment, we nosed our way to the south coast, seeking sun, sea and sand. We stayed at a small village called La Boca that was near a fabulous, quiet beach. The snorkelling was excellent with a multitude of brightly coloured fish and pristine coral. I spent too long snorkelling and got a sun-burned back. Maggie spent too long dozing and got a sun-burned stomach. The food reached a new high when we were presented with 'The Trinity'; fish, lobster *and* chicken!

Three days later, with time running out, we had to say a sad farewell to La Boca and headed for Cienfuegos. Cycling happily along with the Caribbean Sea on our left, mountains to our right and the wind in our backs, we suddenly were brought to an abrupt halt. The road ahead was moving! It was totally covered with millions of crabs! Most had black thirty-centimetre shells with red claws but some were a bright orange. It was impossible to avoid them if we were to continue. As we approached, they reared up waving their large red pincers threateningly in the air; as we attempted to pass they would scuttle sideways under our wheels to be squashed. Maggie closed her eyes as I tried to steer a humane path but she could not ignore the teeth-jarring sound of crunch, crunch, crunch. Incredibly we did not get a puncture. Later I discovered that these were Cuban Land Crabs. They lived in the moist forests surrounding Cuba's Bay of Pigs and emerged each year to breed in the sea. Thousands are pulverized by traffic as they cross roads. Their sharp shells cause up to one hundred punctures each day. The smashed crabs provided a feast for vultures but, as they contained harmful toxins, Cubans would never eat them.

One of the survivors

After getting lost in Cienfuegos, again, we took a *Viazul* bus back to Havana. In a famous Hemingway hotel, *Ambos Mundos,* we tried another Cuban cocktail. This was not Hemingway's favourite *mojito* but Graham Greene's "Man in Havana" choice: a *daiquiri*. Actually, I could not tell the difference.

On our way to the airport for our journey home, I received a text informing us that the Virgin Airways crew were sick and our flight had been cancelled. The airline found it difficult to find enough available accommodation for a whole plane load. After four hours cooped up in the bus, we were eventually delivered to the Sol Melia, an expensive all-inclusive resort. Chaos reigned as our bus load checked-in while the sheet lightning that had illuminated our journey delivered the downpour it had promised.

I can't say that we were impressed by our all-inclusive hotel experience. The food was plentiful, but not the quality or as tasty as our *casa* meals. In the morning we walked along a beach which extended for miles, one hotel's patch leading on to another's. Sun beds were parked in rows like a packed car park, each with an over-cooked inhabitant. The only empty beds were marked with towels; the beaches offered little more than sea and sand. Snorkelling, diving and other excursions needed a boat and had to be booked. I think that anyone staying in a Varadero Resort will have seen as much authentic Cuba as we saw of the United Arab Emirates when we once had a brief flight stop-over at Abu Dhabi Airport.

On reflection we realised how much we had learned in our short stay. Now that Fidel has died what will happen to the friendly people of this amazing country?

CHAPTER 45

Norway

"When you are stuck at sea for weeks there is nowhere to escape from people."
C S Woolley, "Thief in Stickleback Hollow"

<u>February, 2013. A Cruise</u>

One item on our bucket list was to see the aurora borealis. The winter of 2013 was reported as being a good year to witness the Northern Lights. A cruise to Norway, that departed from Avonmouth near Bristol, just twenty miles from our home, provided the perfect opportunity. However, the thought of a cruise provoked more than a little doubt and anxiety. The company of old folks, being organised, queues, guides with umbrellas and sitting around for hours did not tick many boxes for us. However, many of our friends who had been cruising lauded the experience. Therefore, with a certain amount of trepidation, we booked our voyage.

We arrived at Avonmouth Passenger Terminal ready for embarkation but saw no ships. Instead, a fleet of coaches were parked on the quayside, waiting to take us to Portland Bill where the cruise ship was docked. We were told that the ship had missed the tide, which seemed to us to be a nebulous excuse. Barely thirty minutes into our bus journey south, the coaches pulled into garden centre less than three miles from our home in Burnham-on-Sea. Here we were left to amuse ourselves for a number of hours because the ship's captain was not ready to receive us! After enduring several hours of piped '50s music, we eventually arrived at Portland, formed orderly queues, were duly processed and allowed on board with the promise of sailing later that evening. The next morning, however, *MV Discovery* was still in the port. Cruise Maritime arranged for another fleet of buses, this time to take us shopping in Weymouth. Among my pet hates are garden centres, bus journeys and shopping. This cruise had not got off to an auspicious start. It got worse!

Dinner that evening was interrupted by an announcement from the captain. He gravely informed us that, due to technical problems, the cruise had to be cancelled. No further explanation was given and the next morning we were all bused back to Bristol. We were never given an official reason for the debacle but rumour had it that the crew, mostly Eastern Europeans, were untrained, inexperienced and unable to adequately launch the life-boats. Thus, the port authorities refused to let the ship sail. We were refunded and given some compensation plus sixty per cent off another cruise. The offer was too good to refuse, so we booked the same cruise in October.

Unbelievably, just two weeks before the sailing date, the voyage was cancelled. We were offered yet another cruise with a cabin upgrade.

<u>February, 2015</u> Two years after our original booking, we once more drove to Avonmouth and again 'saw no ships!' Again a coach trip to Portland, but this time we *did* set sail. Our ship, MV Azores, was almost as old as us. It was first commissioned in 1948 as *MS Stockholm* and was the biggest ship ever built in Sweden and has sailed under ten different names. After three days at sea, we reached the art nouveau port of Ålesund, regarded as one of Norway's most attractive towns. Two days later we were in Narvik, a beautiful harbour backed by snow-clad mountains. Narvik was a town built on processing and exporting iron. The warmth of the gulf-stream ensured that its port remains ice-free. We took a trip on the Ofoten railway, built in 1902 to deliver iron from the Swedish ironworks to Narvik. At the time of construction the Ofoten railway was both the coldest and northern-most railway project in the world. The forty-two-kilometre line was painstakingly carved into the mountainside. This was an incredible engineering project that was largely undertaken by hand. The result was a breath-taking route which took us past deep fjords and through wild, rugged mountains to a ski lodge just over the Swedish border.

Each evening we dined with two other couples, Ken and Cora from the Wirral and Keith and Pam from Manchester. Ken was a union man and held strong left-wing views, while Keith was a Mason and very conservative. I enjoyed playing devil's advocate. We had some heated discussions: not least about religion. Keith and Pam were both born again Christians and both in their third marriages. "Isn't there something in the Bible about 'til death do us part'?" I couldn't help but ask.

After Tromso and another coach trip, the next port of call was Alta, which was located well above the Arctic Circle at seventy degrees north. Here, preparations were being made to celebrate the return of the sun after two months of constant night. An annual fiesta, *Borealis Alta,* that consisted of partying, concerts, culture and Europe's longest dog-sled race, was being held in an attempt to dispel the gloom of winter. In the evening we were taken into the countryside in an attempt to see the Aurora Borealis. The sky was clear and in spite of a full moon, we witnessed a wonderful Northern Lights display. "The best I have seen in five years." said our Norwegian guide. It also lasted longer than usual. I think that we were very lucky.

From Honningsvaag we journeyed to the North Cape, the most northerly part of mainland Europe. On a very windy day this was the most exciting part of the cruise and surprisingly, for one who dislikes bus journeys, it was by bus! The route was over fells with fantastic views of the lakes below and mountains ahead. The wind was blowing snow onto the road and after about twenty kilometres the four coaches formed a convoy behind a snowplough. Another snowplough followed behind. At the North Cape there was a modern tourist centre, but getting there from the bus was a real battle. The wind nearly blew us off our feet. On the headland, 1,000 ft above the sea, was a very photogenic globe but only a few were brave enough to venture outside. It was the strongest wind I had ever experienced.

Back in the buses we returned in the ever-strengthening storm, again chaperoned by two snowploughs. Sheets of snow were blown across the road from the steep hills while the other side of the road fell steeply into the fjord far below. Blasts of wind rocked the coaches as we wound our way down. Each blast threatening to topple us over and send us tumbling down the mountainside. Gone was the laughter and happy chatter heard during the outward journey. It really was a white-knuckle ride with many passengers holding on to their armrests with a vice-like grip; some were murmuring prayers. Our driver wrestled with the steering wheel, fighting against the constant battering from the gale as he negotiated the sharp bends between the snow banks and sheer drops. The bus swayed from side to side, at times, teetering on the edge. It was scary but exciting at the same time. I loved it, an adventure at last.

Allan Pendleton

It was still very windy when we left Honningsvaag. We had a pilot on board to steer us through the passage between the North Cape and the mainland. By afternoon, the wind had increased to gale force and the ship was seriously rocking and rolling. Sick bags were universally issued. The evening show was cancelled, the lifts were out of order and all outside decks and promenades were closed. Many passengers were cabin bound.

Few guests showed for dinner and, with so much ending smashed on the floor, the crockery was replaced by paper plates and wine glasses swopped for plastic cups. Maggie retired halfway through the meal. The weather failed to improve overnight with eighty miles per hour winds and thirty feet swells. Items were crashing and banging, sliding and slamming all night, which made sleeping impossible. Maggie remained in bed all the next day. The captain announced that due to the inclement weather we were now no longer able to berth at Bergen as scheduled; instead we sheltered at Kristiansund.

The following afternoon we ventured out once more but, by the time we reached open water, things got rather wobbly again. Because it was so rough and the forecast was not good, we had to sail more slowly than normal and not have time to berth at some of the promised ports. There was a little disquiet among the passengers, but no sign of mutiny, everyone was too busy clutching handrails or reaching for a sick-bag. Many corridors and even some cabins had been flooded. Staff were sleeping in the restaurants and bars on the upper decks. They were afraid of sleeping below the water-line. Guests had to change cabins due to the instability of beds, cupboards and drawers and in some cases, flooding.

The morning of our fifth consecutive day at sea, brought a much calmer and brighter day. Through our portside porthole I watched the sun rising red over mainland Scotland. '*Red in the morning is shepherd's warning*' and during breakfast more 'white horses' appeared and the boat began swaying once more. By noon, the wind had increased to gale force and the ship was again tossing and pitching. Passengers again retreated to their cabins, staggering along in a drunken manner. Many of the crew were also suffering and complained that this was one of the worst and longest, storms they had ever experienced. The outer decks were once more out of bounds.

Our return to Avonmouth was a bit of an anti-climax. We had woken to the gentle throbbing of the ship's engines with bright sunlight flooding in through the porthole with the sea as calm as a millpond. What a change after a week of gale-force winds and massive waves. Many breathed a sigh of relief, especially those who had fallen or were unable to leave their cabins. I was one of the lucky ones not feeling sick. I must have some of my old man's nautical blood. I don't think that we will take another cruise because the chances of experiencing a similar storm are, regrettably, rather slim.

Towards the end of our cruise we met Liam and his wife from Northern Island. They had also travelled in Patagonia and we spent some time together exchanging traveller's tails. They invited us to a festival called Horizons Unlimited that they were organising in their home town of Enniskillen. It would be a series of presentations from biking adventure travellers. We had planned a trip to Ireland so happily accepted their invitation. When we arrived at the festival site the following June, after cycling in the Wicklow and Mourne Mountains, we were the only pedal cyclists there. Everyone else, hundreds, had motorbikes! Nevertheless, we were made very welcome and thoroughly enjoyed the talks about motor biking travels. Actually, having cycled in some of the countries and routes that they had driven, we were regarded with respect, even if thought to be a little nutty.

CHAPTER 46

A Pain in the Arse

"Getting older – it's crap, deal with it!"
On a birthday card from my daughter

<u>5 May, 2014</u>

"Shit!" I had been stabbed in the back by a red-hot poker. At least that was what it felt like. I gingerly picked myself up off the floor. I had been in the gym performing twisting crunches with a dumbbell, an exercise I had done countless times before. This time, however, something had gone wrong. By the time I had returned home the pain was intense. The only way I could relieve it was to adopt the yoga *child's pose*, kneeling on the floor with my head between my knees. I thought about calling for an ambulance but instead contacted my doctor. Painkillers and an appointment for some time next week was offered. I took the painkillers but made an appointment to see my old friend and physiotherapist Andy Gardner, or his equally talented wife Liz, the very next day. During a sleepless night I experienced shooting electric-like shocks down my right leg. Andy diagnosed a nerve trapped between the vertebrae in my lower back. After an MRI scan and specialist consultations, it was decided that, apart from a rather risky operation that could have dire consequences, it would be best to just grin and bear it!

Over time and copious amounts of painkillers the pain eased but the numbness continued along with a distinct weakness in my right thigh. Apparently some of the nerves that send signals to my quadriceps were blocked. I had previously injured my back doing gymnastics as a teenager at College which, ironically, probably saved me from a different type of drubbing as that very same week I had been selected to box for England. Six months of sleeping on boards and a long forced absence from the ring, coupled with the commencement of a teaching career, stymied any future hopes of wearing an England boxing vest. Now, with my gammy leg and Maggie's half a heart, we would have to choose our cycling routes wisely.

22 August, 2014

"Good morning Mr Pendleton, please sit down." Sister Sharon Tonkin welcomed me into her office and ushered me to a chair. She picked up some papers, paused, then looked me in the eye and said, "We have your results, you have cancer!" I could not believe it. For years I had known that my prostate PSA was high and rising but after five biopsies, two template biopsies and a MRI scan, which had all come back negative, I had become complacent, I had felt indestructible.

Two months later I was in the operating theatre for a radical prostatectomy. I was worried; not so much about the operation but about its consequences. I had a healthy libido and the thought of a sex-free future was terrifying. The consultant, Mr Ed Rowe, was aware of my concerns and promised a nerve-sparing operation, if possible. He achieved it, bless him! *Cancri exitum, libido intactus.* Long live the National Health Service and bless Mr Rowe.

CHAPTER 47

Mark

"You are only ever as happy as your unhappiest child."

September 2015

Julie and Dean wanted a complete family which, for them, was another child, and Ana needed a sibling. Thus, they set out on the adoption path once more. They had now moved to Somerset and to a different local authority. This meant that once again they had to submit to the zealous vetting procedure. However, now that they had Ana from Guatemala, they were regarded as a mixed-race family which considerably improved their chances of finding a relatively young child. Indeed, just a few months after having their adoption application accepted they were put in touch with a two-year-old boy who was currently with a foster family. Mark had been born to a young single girl. The poor little boy had been looked after by his mother's parents, abused and spent an excessive amount of time strapped in a high chair in a closed room. Lack of dental hygiene resulted in the necessary removal of all his front teeth and he was found to be suffering from moderate to severe hearing loss and consequently had no speech.

In a caring and loving foster home, Mark was well on the way to recovering from the nightmare of his first two years when Julie and Dean came along, but his speech was still almost non-existent. With Julie and Dean he recovered from the zombie-like and abusive existence he had endured and was quickly adapting to family life with his new mummy, daddy and sister. Not only did he now have a loving extended family but also became the centre of attention in a group of new friends. By his third birthday he had learned to ride a bike, could swim and enjoyed playschool.

But the legal procedure was still not straight forward as the 'powers that be' always consider the birth mothers rights very seriously. And so it was not until

7 months after Mark had first come to Burnham that a final judgement was made and Mark became a legal member of the family.

Writing this a couple of years later it is great to say that Mark is now a confident, happy five year old, enjoying his first year at school.

CHAPTER 48

USA

A Circuit of Lake Michigan:
Illinois, Wisconsin, Michigan & Indiana

*"Those who can make you believe in absurdities,
can make you commit atrocities."*
Voltaire

May-June, 2016. 1515 miles

I spent my 70th birthday flying to Chicago. My daughters had requested an upgrade but their request was treated with a distinct lack of enthusiasm by Aer Lingus. In Chicago we met up with our old pal from California, Ed Rodriguez, who would accompany us for much of the 1,500-mile circuit of Lake Michigan. This was a ride we had decided to do after reading a book entitled *"50 Bike Rides to do Before You Die"*, which had recommended part of the route.

We enjoyed a reunion and birthday meal with Ed and his wife Pat before she left to fly home to California. The next day we followed the Lakeshore Trail out of Chicago through an area of expensive lakeside residences. At first, I was impressed by the triple-garaged houses surrounded by acres of lawn but after a thousand miles of the same, I began to tire of this display of excess. However, as ever, I did enjoy the big American breakfasts, plus some places of interest such as the museum in Peshtigo, that commemorated the great forest fire of 1871 which caused the deaths of 1,200 people. In another museum in Wisconsin, at Two Rivers, they celebrated the creation of ice-cream sundaes. Dykesville WI was home of the so-called world famous Frosty Tip ice-cream. Escanaba, Michigan, had a church on every block. No cars were allowed on Mackinac Island: only horse-drawn transport. Bay Harbour boasted an abundance of millionaire homes complete with boat house and yachts. However, we anticipated something really special when we arrived at Torch Lake, which was widely advertised as being one of the most beautiful lakes in the world. We cycled its fifty-five miles perimeter but found it short of the promised beauty. Torch Lake was protected by a wall of conifers and maple. Most access points displayed warning signs – Private Property, Keep Out. When we were able to view the lake, we just saw water rimmed by trees. There was nothing to reflect off the lake: no mountains, no volcanoes, no waterfalls, no islands and a lack of discernible wildlife. It was just an expanse of water surrounded by trees. Similarly, disappointing was the Tunnel of Trees through which we had pedalled some days earlier. The area was nowhere near as imposing as many such places in Britain; but then perhaps, being surrounded by outstanding natural beauty at home, albeit on a smaller scale, we are left unimpressed when it came to similar countryside scenery elsewhere. Our route followed many excellent, paved bike paths. Near Sleeping Bear Dunes National Park was one such path that warned cyclists to wear something bright as it was now the shooting season! After Empire, the so-called prettiest village in the world, we rolled into Luddington. Here the final preparations were being made to produce the longest ice-cream sundae in the world for entry into *The Guinness Book of Records*. Main Street was closed to traffic as a half-mile stretch of seamless guttering was set up on hundreds of trestle tables. The gutter was filled with 855 gallons of ice-cream, covered with chocolate and whipped cream, and crowned with over 2,000 cherries. Once the 2,640-foot sundae was filmed, volunteers were requested to eat it up. We duly stepped forward, willing to make our contribution to the record attempt.

After 1,200 miles in less than four weeks, Ed bade us farewell. He had a wedding to attend in California and had to press on. Ed was probably relieved to be able to pedal at his own pace and not be held back by an old couple on a tandem. Sorry Ed, I don't think we were a lot of fun! Now we dawdled along, camping early, chatting to locals and spending time on the beach, including the beach at St. Joseph, voted by Delta Airlines as one of the best ten beaches in the world. Really? No surf, no coral, no fish, no alcohol...but who am I to argue.

The response to our answers to the frequently asked questions "Where are you going?" and "Where you coming from?" was mind-bogglingly repetitive, "Oh my God!" or "Awesome!" Why was I so cynical? It was probably because, throughout this trip, I had felt extremely weary. Trying, on a loaded tandem, to keep up with Ed, who was a very good racing cyclist, had been too hard. Also much of the tiredness was due to lack of visual stimulation. Mile after mile of straight roads lined with trees, trees and yet more trees, does little to lift one's spirits or offer a distraction from the weariness. Overall, it had been a boring ride. However, we did meet some interesting, friendly and generous people. For example, on our second day out, Maggie lost her cycling gloves. When we stopped to purchase a new pair, a complete stranger insisted on paying most of the cost.

"Look on it as a welcome to America gift." Joseph argued against our protestations. On another occasion in a cafe, a gentleman asked if he might join us as at our table. He simply had a coffee while we told him about our journey and scoffed down big breakfasts. He drank his coffee, left and, unknown to us, paid the complete bill as he departed.

As we rounded the south of Lake Michigan, through Gary and into South Chicago, we noticed more poor and black people. Until this point, there had been an excess of excess but now we witnessed poverty, slums, shacks and trailer parks. Back on the Lakeshore Trail, we found our way back to the Getaway Hostel and spent a couple of days sightseeing in the interesting Windy City before returning, exhausted, to England.

While we were in Chicago, the British public had voted to leave the European Economic Community. Teresa May had replaced David Cameron as Prime Minister and Donald Trump was about to be elected as president. When we thought that it could not get any worse, Iceland's part-time football team knocked England out of the European Cup!

CHAPTER 49

Rajasthan, India

*"In a country well governed, poverty is something to be ashamed of.
In a country badly governed, wealth is something to be ashamed of."*
Confucius

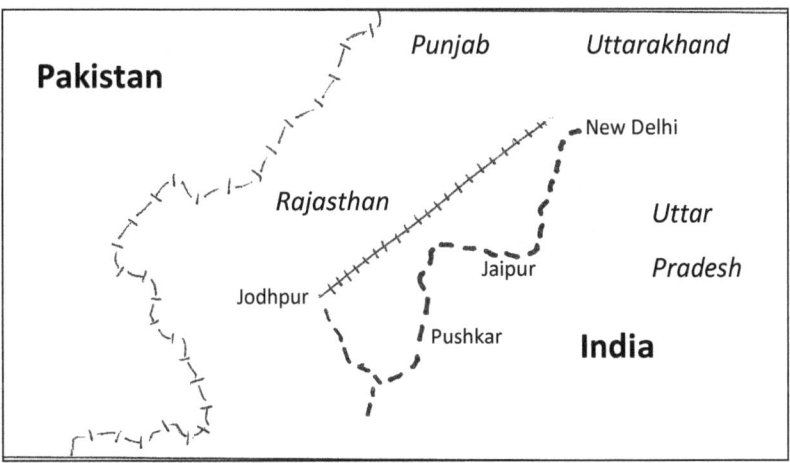

November, 2016. 595 miles

It was Maggie's 70th birthday and we were on a Virgin flight to New Delhi, India. We had joined a cycling group on a trip to Rajasthan, organised by our friends Pat and John Ashwell. In Delhi, we drove to our hotel through a city of seemingly unfinished buildings; many were roofless with piles of bricks and half-built walls as if the contractor had quit halfway through the construction, or more likely, ran out of money. It resembled a war-zone, enhanced by dense smog similar, one would imagine, to the smoke that would hang over a city after a bombing raid. The sun hung in the sky like a huge orange, its rays struggled to penetrate the gloom and emitted relatively little heat.

The tour consisted of a series of coach transfers, our bikes following in a truck emblazoned with the slogan, "Blow Horn". This, we were soon to discover, was India's main, and possibly only, rule of the road. While avoiding main roads and city centres, the routes we followed still provided many challenges. Many were back roads which were little more than pot-holed strips of tarmac and little wider than a bus or truck. Consequently, whenever we heard the blare of a horn we felt extremely vulnerable. Some would teeter dangerously on the edge of the track as the vehicles roared by but for us it meant steering off the road and hitting the dirt, for in India, might is right. In 2013, figures from the World Health Organisation verified this claim because nearly a quarter of a million people were killed in traffic accidents in India. That was 16.6 per 100,000 inhabitants. In Britain the figure was 2.9. We also had to be aware of un-tethered domestic animals that wandered along the roads. Several times, evasive action was called for as cows, goats and even camels, sauntered nonchalantly across our path. In the towns and villages, the animals performed a useful service, especially the pigs, in waste disposal; street cleaning is unheard of in most places, but the livestock does a great job of vacuuming up much of the refuse.

This was so different from our trip to Lake Michigan earlier this year. Instead of the millionaire houses and acres of manicured lawns in the US, there were ramshackle hovels and half-built houses. In place of well-fed, often obese, Americans there were skinny paupers and beggars with hardly a rupee between them. Substitute the pristine forests and clean lakes for sailing and swimming for an arid, sandy desert with the occasional polluted pond. On the other hand, our accommodation was far superior to the tent and motels we had in the USA. Palaces and forts were scattered like jewels across the desert landscape, bearing silent witness to the opulent lifestyle of the ruling classes. Many have been converted into hotels and it we stayed in these grand buildings Although enjoying the luxury we felt a little uncomfortable being ensconced in extravagance while just outside there were emaciated people and beggars with nothing but the rags on their backs.

In Jaipur we took a white-knuckle auto rickshaw ride where the tuk-tuk drivers treated the city streets as a racetrack. We passed vehicles on either side, squeezed through gaps that appeared non-existent, were taken the wrong way down a dual carriage way, weaved, with gay abandon, in and out of oncoming traffic and in the process, took out a motorcycle that had the audacity to try to cross our path. After the collision, our driver paused and looked back as the downed biker struggled to pick himself up. He was still alive, albeit sporting a massive bump on the side of his head. With a shrug of the shoulders, our driver drove on without a backward glance.

Regrettably, one of our group while riding out of the city fell off her bike and broke her arm. After receiving treatment at Jaipur hospital, she and her husband flew back to England for subsequent treatment. On the same day we were informed that all 500 (£6.50) and 1,000 (£13) rupee notes, eighty per cent of the nation's currency, were being taken out of circulation. Apparently, many fraudsters, and those who had never declared their earnings, had been hoarding sacks of loot under the mattress so to speak and thus avoiding paying taxes. Now, when these crooks and tax-avoiders attempted to change their ill-gotten gains into the new currency, they will have to declare the origin of their cash! We honest tourists however, who had recently changed our pounds sterling into 500 and 1,000-rupee notes, were now left with pockets full of worthless money.

The next day we visited the Pushkar Camel Fair. This was fundamentally a religious occasion where Hindu pilgrims would come to bathe in Pushkar's sacred waters. Now it was a huge commercial event where 50,000 camels and horses were traded. A huge area was given over to stalls and vendors of every kind. There were beggars, snake-charmers, magicians, musicians, mystics, performers, best-dressed camel competitions and so on. The streets between the stalls were a heaving mass of humanity. But even there vehicles attempted to push through with continual blasts from their horns.

Udaipur was our next destination, en route we cycled through countryside that could grace the pages of a National Geographic Magazine. Goatherds in loin cloths and turbans tended their flocks, while sari-clad women carried enormous loads on their heads such as urns of water or mountains of wood or hay. Bullocks were used for tilling the land and turning water wheels, with camels being beasts of burden.

The money problem was quickly turning into a crisis. India was fundamentally a cash-economy, the majority of people do not have credit cards or even bank accounts. The Government promised new notes would soon be in the banks and ATM machines, but, not wanting to warn the fraudsters by printing too much new currency, insufficient funds were available. ATMs quickly ran out of cash and the banks remained closed after the weekend. We heard stories of people going hungry, of house and flat evictions, school exclusions, hospital operations being cancelled and a child dying as a result, even suicides.

When the banks finally opened very long queues formed outside. In spite of preferential treatment for foreigners allowing us to jump the queue, we still had an onerous two-hour wait before we were able to change our 500-rupee notes into usable hundreds. Even then, each transaction was restricted to 4,500 rupees (£60).

Our final major destination was Jodphur, a visit to the fort then into the city for a final nerve-tingling tuk-tuk ride to buy spices from the bazaar. We loaded the bikes into our back-up truck then went to the railway station for an overnight journey back to Delhi. Shortly after departing a man came and asked us foreigners if we would like a beer? Great idea we all agreed and readily coughed up 200 rupees each. The man took our money and disappeared – permanently! The next stop was too far away for him to disembark before we had sussed the con and alerted the on-board police. We were reunited with our money but I was disappointed, his ploy deserved success.

Back in the murk of Delhi we had a last supper together then flew home the following day, the day of the Delhi Half Marathon. For competitors it was a sure way to reduce their life-span by a few years I would imagine.

AFTERWORD

Never say "If Only"

"All that is gold does not glitter.
Not all those who wander are lost."
JRR Tolkein, "Fellowship of the Rings"

September 2017

Maggie and I are beginning to feel our years. Hills are getting steeper, miles are growing longer. Getting old is like a toilet roll, the closer you get to the end, the faster it seems to run out. An electric boost on the tandem is a possibility, could put the smile back into cycling. We have a small VW Campervan and have recently spent time in the Pyrenees and Alps, more hiking than biking. We will continue to seek adventures and hopefully with a smile, because there is one thing that we have learned, and that is not to travel with an attitude.

About ten years ago, after a blood test, I was found to have high PSA which often is a sign of prostate cancer. While waiting for the biopsy results, Maggie and I went to Scotland to walk the West Highland Way. We thought that it would be a good way to occupy ourselves and not worry about the future. Walking, however, is a simple activity and leaves one with a lot of time to think. But time in my own head was just what I didn't need.

Although the ninety-five-mile walk was beautiful I didn't find it as enthralling as I had expected. Furthermore, I found the people there dour and unhelpful. In retrospect I realise that **I** was the problem, not the people. I was so wrapped up in my own little world that it was me who was belligerent; and you get what you give! Frown and you receive a frown, smile and you inevitably get one back (apart from US Customs officials). We have subsequently returned to the Highlands of Scotland and found, of course, the people to be both friendly and helpful.

Getting old is a drag, but far better than the alternative.

We must always make and take our opportunities. Never say "If only."

SUMMARY

Walks:

England, North Yorkshire Moors, Lyke Wake Walk, 50 miles
England, West Mendip Way, Somerset, 44 miles
England, Yorkshire Dales, Three Peaks, 40 miles
Wales, Brecon Beacons, Mountain Express, 40 miles
'Tuff Guy' Black Country, England
New Zealand, Lake Waikaremoana, 30 miles
New Zealand, Queen Charlotte Track, 42 miles
New Zealand, Kepler Track, 42 miles
New Zealand, Abel Tasman, 43 miles
New Zealand, Tongariro, includes Mount Ruapehu
Perú, Inca Trail to Machu Picchu
England, Two Moors Way, Devon, 100 miles
England, coast to coast, 200miles
USA, Tetons & Yosemite
Scotland, West Highland Way, 95 miles
England, South West Coast Path, 642 miles
Scotland, Highlands, 50 miles
London, Moonwalk, Maggie, (three times) 26 miles
Wales, Pembrokeshire Coast Path, 186 miles

Bike:

England, Devon, First "100," 4 Jan, 1990
England, Yorkshire Dales, included the hottest day on record – 99°F; Aug, 1990, 100 miles
Ireland, July-Aug, 1991, 620 miles
Germany, Roth, European Ironman Triathlon, July 1992. 10 hours 35 minutes
Northern Spain: Picos de Europa, Aug, 1992, 328 miles
Germany, July-Aug, 1993, 946 miles

North America: New England, Canada to Mexico via West Coast USA. Massachusetts, New Hampshire, Vermont, Washington, British Columbia, Oregon, Idaho, California, Baja California April-Aug, 1994, 5,270 miles
England, Norfolk, April 1995, 187 miles with Julie
England, Devon, June 1995, 200 miles
England, coast-to-coast and back, Aug, 1995, 550 miles
Malaysia, Feb-March, 1996, 950 miles
Wales, July-Aug, 1996, 212 miles,
Wales, Snowden, Rhayader & Taff Trail, May, 1997, 290 miles
France & Spain: Pyrenees, Aug 1997, 573 miles
New Zealand & USA: California, Nov-Mar, 1997-98, 5,540 miles
Netherlands, July, 1998. 704 miles
Romania, Sept-Nov, 1998, Maggie with Julie in Romanian children's hospice
Morocco & Mexico, Oct-Nov, 1998, mountain biking, 484 miles
Spain, Andalucía, Mar-April, 1999, 969 miles
Scotland & England: Land's End to John o' Groats, June, 1999, 931 miles
Thailand, Nov- Dec, 1999, 1200 miles
Bolivia & Peru, April-May, 2000, no bike
England, Lake District, July, 2000, 122 miles
France, Vendee, Sept, 2000, 150 miles
Costa Rica, Nov- Dec, 2000, 885 miles
USA: Arizona to Alaska: Arizona, New Mexico, Utah, Colorado, Wyoming, Idaho, Montana, Washington, Alaska May-Aug, 2001, 4,387 miles
India: Kerala & Tamil Nadu, Feb-March, 2002, 647 miles
France to Spain, Sept, 2002, 955 miles
Australia, Dec, 2002-April 2003, 2,800 miles
France: Normandy, Sept, 2003, 175 miles
England: Isle of Wight, Oct, 2003, 120 miles
Chile & Argentina: Patagonia, Jan-Feb, 2004, 830 miles
Slovenia, Sept, 2004, 465 miles
South East Asia: Vietnam, Cambodia & Thailand, Jan-Feb, 2005, 1,470 miles

Mexico: Yucatán, Jan-Feb, 2006. 620 miles

USA: New Orleans to Washington DC. Louisiana, Mississippi, Alabama, Tennessee, North Carolina, Virginia, West Virginia, Maryland Washington DC, April-May, 2006. 1,685 miles

Tibet & Nepal: Himalaya – Lhasa, Tibet to Kathmandu, Nepal via Everest Base Camp, Oct, 2006, 671 miles
Spain: Mallorca, Feb, 2007, Walking and biking
Thailand & Laos, Nov-Dec, 2007, 676 miles
Scotland, Western Isles, June, 2008, 457 miles
Canada: Quebec, Sept, 2008, 1,121 miles

USA: California, April-May, 2009, 1,591 miles
Scotland & England: Land's End to John O' Groats, July, 2009, 996 miles
Sri Lanka, Feb-March, 2010, 705 miles
Canada & USA: Rocky Mountains – Alberta, British Columbia, Montana, Idaho, Wyoming, Aug-Sept, 2010, 2,105 miles
Costa Rica & Panam*á*: March, 2011, 442 miles
India: Goa & Karnataka, India, Feb, 2012, 365 miles
USA: Florida, March-April 2012, Disneyworld with family
Scotland: North-West Highlands, May, 2012, 326 miles and 50 mile-walk
France: La Loire and Brittany, Sept, 2012, 890 miles
Thailand, Jan-Feb, 2013, 455 miles
Great Britain: Channel Islands, Sept, 2013, 320 miles
Cuba, Feb-Mar, 2014, 550 miles
Turkey: Istanbul, April, 2014, no bike
Norway, Feb-March, 2015, cruise
Ireland, June, 2015, with van, cycled 222 miles
Spain: Pyrenees and Picos de Europa, March-April, 2016, with van, cycled 50 miles
USA: Lake Michigan – Illinois, Wisconsin, Michigan, Indiana, May-June, 2016, 1,515 miles
India: Rajasthan, Nov, 2016, 375 miles
France: Alps, June 2017, with van, cycled 170 miles

"Strangers are friends I haven't met."
Juliette Pendleton

ACKNOWLEDGEMENTS

Initially we would like to thank all the people who encouraged us in so many ways. With friendly banter, hot cups of tea, advice, cold beers and offers of hospitality we were surrounded by human kindness. The other cyclists, camp site owners, bike shop mechanics, complete strangers......you were all wonderful. Travelling with only a bike you are very much at the mercy of humanity, and it never failed us. These days when one is constantly besieged with so much negative hostile news from the media it is reassuring to know that the world is a really big friendly place. To anyone a little hesitant about setting out on an adventure we can only say "Give it a go. People are amazingly good!"

Thanks for the patience and advice from the staff of AuthorHouse UK, especially Dorothy Lee who has helped me take my diary scribblings into a book.

I would also like to thank all my friends and family at home for their love and support. Without the bedrock security that comes from living in a close and caring community like Burnham-on-Sea, surrounded by friends, we both doubt that we would have had the confidence to wander so widely. We always knew that home was just a plane ride, or two, away.

Our friends Pat and John Ashwell have always been there for us, inspirational as fellow marathon runners and cycle tourists of remote and challenging destinations, and especially to Pat for formatting the maps so patiently. Plus a big thank you to fellow author Michael Turner, another traveller of distant lands, for his diligence in editing and typesetting, and to our pal Roger Owen for proofreading.

Special thanks to our daughters who gave us permission to roam. Jo is always dependable and reliable with a lovely family, Rich, Abi and Max, of whom I am so proud. Julie, perhaps not as audacious as she once was, still seeks adventures and is always looking for new challenges. Her husband Dean is a rock and Ana and Mark are very lucky children.

Finally, my wife Maggie is one in a million. Not many women would be happy and able, on their retirement, to pedal over mountains, sleep in a little tent, cook outside on a tiny stove and come back from the dead! I am so lucky we met and that she chose me. My love for her grows stronger with every passing year.

The final word goes to Abi and Max my older grandchildren.

"How come Ana and Mark have a whole chapter each, while we are hardly mentioned?"

"Well, their journeys to be part of our family were a bit more onerous than yours. However, I love you to bits, I think that you both are fantastic and I am very proud of you, but there is nothing more boring than a grandparent boasting about his grandchildren; except, perhaps, someone who goes on endlessly about their holidays."

"Like your book you mean granddad?"

Touché.